DECENTRALIZATION
IN
LATIN AMERICA

DECENTRALIZATION IN LATIN AMERICA

An Evaluation

Edited by ARTHUR MORRIS and STELLA LOWDER

PRAEGER

New York
Westport, Connecticut
London

Library of Congress Cataloging-in-Publication Data

Decentralization in Latin America : an evaluation / edited by Arthur
Morris and Stella Lowder.
  p. cm.
  Includes bibliographical references and index.
  ISBN 0-275-94021-7 (alk. paper)
  1. Decentralization in government—Latin America. 2. Latin
America—Industries—Location. I. Morris, Arthur Stephen.
II. Lowder, Stella.
JL959.5.D42D46 1992
351.007′3′098—dc20   91-17806

British Library Cataloguing in Publication Data is available.

Library of Congress Catalog Card Number: 91-17806
ISBN: 0-275-94021-7

First published in 1992

Praeger Publishers, One Madison Avenue, New York, NY 10010
An imprint of Greenwood Publishing Group, Inc.

Printed in the United States of America

The paper used in this book complies with the
Permanent Paper Standard issued by the National
Information Standards Organization (Z39.48–1984).

10 9 8 7 6 5 4 3 2 1

Copyright Acknowledgments
Figures 9.1 and 9.2 reprinted with permission from R. N. Gwynne,
*New Horizons? Third World Industrialization in an International
Framework*, copyright 1990, published by Longman Group UK Ltd.
Figure 6.1 reprinted with permission from Peter M. Townroe,
"Spatial Policy and Metropolitan Growth in São Paulo, Brazil,"
Geoforum 15, no. 2 (1984), Pergamon Press PLC.

Contents

Part II The Case of Mexico

Tables and Figures

TABLES

FIGURES

Preface

One topic on which there is general agreement between Latin Americans and outsiders is that a high degree of centralization is observable on the subcontinent and that there are various disadvantages to this situation. As a result of the wide interest and range of studies on centralization and decentralization in the area, the topic of decentralization was chosen as the major theme for a conference. The conference was held, perhaps symbolically, in Mexico City— probably the world's largest city and one that has had to face immediate calls for decentralization in the aftermath of earthquake damage.

The Third British-Mexican Geographers Conference was held in September 1989 in Mexico City, co-sponsored by the British Council and the Economic and Social Research Council of the United Kingdom. This volume brings together ideas and observations on decentralization to provide a benchmark study on both the theoretical constructs built about decentralization and the current processes and forms that decentralization is taking within Latin America.

Within the general topic of decentralization itself, a variety of views were presented at the conference on the nature of the phenomenon and its analysis, which cannot be reduced to a single viewpoint. There is no universal process of centralization or decentralization, so there can be no universal set of solutions or policies. This book retains something of the diversity of that viewpoint. It is apparent, however, that there are common subthemes, parallels between countries, sufficiently strong to make general statements so that Latin American decentralization can be identified and compared with processes in other parts of what has been called up to now the Third World.

This treatment does not pretend to be encyclopedic with respect to countries or regions or with respect to processes. The authors have, however, covered among them a good selection of both, and their works cover presently active processes that have been the object of recent field studies. This point is important because decentralization, however defined, is subject to rapid changes in content from one decade to the next in a rapidly evolving continent.

Acknowledgment is made here of the financial support provided by the ESRC and the British Council, which made the conference possible, and of the efforts in local coordination of the conference made by Professor Silvana Levi and her colleagues at UNAM, the National Autonomous University of Mexico. UNAM's Faculty of Arts, together with CONACYT, the National Council on Science and Technology of Mexico, made the necessary financial arrangements for receiving participants at the conference. Thanks are also due to the secretarial and cartographic staff at the Department of Geography and Topographic Science at Glasgow University for the preparation of materials and to the authors themselves for tolerance of editorial interventions.

DECENTRALIZATION IN LATIN AMERICA

1

Decentralization: The Context

Arthur Morris

Decentralization is a topic of great interest today. Over the past forty years the growth of each Latin American country's largest city has continued at a rapid pace in absolute terms (see Table 1.1); however, the proportion of these cities' populations to their countries' total population has declined, perhaps an indicator of new decentralization processes. Centralization in Latin America has generally been of an extreme kind, with one or two metropolitan cities far outstripping the cities of intermediate size. In Mexico, for example, capital-city dwellers were made painfully aware of the need for demographic and economic deconcentration by the powerful effects of the 1985 earthquake, which affected the Valley of Mexico basin and caused massive building damage. Less clearly perceived by local populations, there are diseconomies in the massing of population in one or a few cities at the center of most Latin American countries. These diseconomies result directly from congestion and pollution costs and indirectly from the lack of development of human and physical resources in the peripheral regions and from the negative features that result from a centralized political and administrative system. Such features include the lack of communications between center and periphery; the tendency toward non-democratic government systems because of the lack of communication and poor response to local pressures in the periphery; and the concentration of national investment and expenditure in the center at the expense of peripheries, both on the part of the private sector that seeks association with the politicians and bureaucrats, and on the part of the public sector itself since most power and most decision making are done at the center.

A huge "tragedy of the commons" emerges as private benefits (to migrants moving to the city and to businesspersons setting up or expanding in the city) continue to exceed costs, while costs to society (pollution costs, infrastructural

Table 1.1
Population of Largest City in Some Latin American Countries and Its
Percentage of Total Population

Country / Largest City	Population (in 000's)					Percentage				
	1940	1950	1960	1970	ca 1984	1940	1950	1960	1970	ca 1984
ARGENTINA										
(Buenos Aires)[1]	2410	5213	7000	9400	9928	17.0	30.5	35.1	39.6	32.9
BOLIVIA										
(La Paz)[1]	-	300	400	500	881	8.5	10.0	10.8	10.7	14.6
BRAZIL										
(Rio de Janeiro except São Paulo for 1970 and 1984)[1]	1519	3025	4692	8213	10,099	3.7	5.8	6.7	8.9	7.4
CHILE										
(Santiago)[1]	952	1275	1907	2600	4067	18.8	21.0	25.2	27.7	34.2
COLOMBIA										
(Bogotá)	356	607	1241	2500	4169	4.1	5.4	8.0	12.2	14.8
COSTA RICA										
(San José)[1]	-	140	257	435	395	10.6	17.5	20.6	25.1	19.5
CUBA										
(Havana)[1]	936	1081	1549	1700	1992	19.6	19.6	22.0	19.9	19.9
DOMINICAN REP.										
(Santo Domingo)	71	182	367	650	818	4.8	8.1	12.1	16.0	13.6
ECUADOR										
(Guayaquil)	-	259	450	800	1388	5.2	8.1	10.3	13.7	15.2
EL SALVADOR										
(San Salvador)[1]	103	162	239	375	336	6.3	8.7	9.8	10.9	6.8
GUETEMALA										
(Guatemala City)[1]	186	294	474	770	754	8.5	10.5	12.4	15.8	9.8
HAITI										
(Port-au-Prince)	-	134	240	400	738	4.0	4.0	6.2	9.4	18.0
HONDURAS										
(Tegucigalpa)[1]	56	72	159	281	539	4.4	5.0	8.6	11.2	12.3
MEXICO										
(Mexico City)[2]	1560	2872	4910	8567	14,750	7.9	11.1	14.1	17.8	20.1
NICARAGUA										
(Managua)[1]	63	109	197	350	608	7.6	10.3	14.0	19.1	20.0
PANAMA										
(Panama City)[1]	112	28	273	440	424	18.1	16.0	25.8	30.8	19.9
PARAGUAY										
(Asunción)[1]	-	219	311	445	719	8.7	15.6	17.6	19.3	15.3
PERU										
(Lima-Callao)[1]	-	947	1519	2500	5008	7.4	11.9	15.1	18.6	26.1
URUGUAY										
(Montevideo)	537	609	962	1530	1173	27.3	27.7	37.9	52.9	40.0
VENEZUELA										
(Caracas)[1]	354	694	1280	2147	2944	9.3	14.0	17.4	20.6	18.1

Source: *Statistical Abstract of Latin America*, Vol. 26, Tables 650 and 651. N.B. The figures relate
    to whole urbanized area rather than city proper.
[1]Beginning in 1950, figures are for city proper and adjacent urban area.
[2]All figures are for city proper and adjacent urban area.

costs in transport and power, and regional aid costs) continue to grow and exceed
benefits. This is not to imply that centralization is only a modern phenomenon;
centralization was characteristic of the region when it was part of the European
empires. The region's colonial history was marked by strong bureaucratic rule

with a highly centralized government and public administration in each colony; towns or regions away from the center had no power.

While social scientists have commented on processes such as population concentration and migration, on industrial or other economic centralization, or on the gross inequalities of power and political voice between regions, they have not gained an overview of general trends toward further centralization or decentralization. Instead, the information is dispersed through a mass of literature on public administration, economic policy, regional development, and the like. This text provides the missing overview, first identifying theoretical positions on the subject of decentralization, then describing and analyzing some of the present-day processes.

The term *decentralization* embraces two facets: (1) policies, involving governments and their agents at various levels, that attempt to devolve powers and to subdivide tasks, and (2) an observable process occurring in many areas, whether viewed as a demographic, economic, social, or politico-administrative process, with spatial connotations. Decentralization is commonly understood to be a spatial process—movement out from the center—but it is probably more useful in the Latin American context to regard it primarily as a phenomenon affecting the way functions—economic, social, and so on—are organized with a variable spatial effect. In this social science, rather than territorial definition, decentralization is as relevant to small countries as it is to large ones in the same way that centralization is as powerful in the small countries of Latin America as it is in the large ones.

It is important to differentiate between *deconcentration* and *decentralization* (Jeannetti Davila 1986). Both terms represent processes that fall under the general rubric of decentralization. Deconcentration refers to the simple dilution of centrality by distributing various elements of political and administrative activity to noncentral offices; decentralization implies a transfer of powers and decision-making capacities. For example, deconcentration of a government agency granting credits to industry might involve the opening of regional offices in small cities around the country; these offices would handle the same business as handled by the center, all under central control. Decentralization of this industrial credit function would involve splitting up the central agency into various regional agencies, each with decision-making capacity of their own. Each regional agency would favor its own industries and make its own decisions on granting credit, though each might be financed from central national funds. The extreme version of such decentralization is *devolution*, the wholesale handing over of political powers to a noncentral body. Devolution normally occurs in regions with a history and culture distinct from the center.

The general concept of decentralization is extensible from political and administrative functions to economic and social ones. Deconcentration of industry might occur—for example, with soft drink bottling plants—by setting up identical plants in various new centers around the country while

maintaining central control. Decentralization proper would occur by splitting up the industry into new firms with separate decision centers at individual
headquarters and by producing different types of soft drink for different regional
markets; alternatively, it would occur by creating new firms in peripheral
regions.

The distinction between deconcentration and decentralization proper
demonstrates the complexity of the decentralization process and highlights
the oversimplicity of some governmental decentralization programs.

THEORETICAL CONSIDERATIONS

Where does the set of movements and changes we call decentralization sit
within social science theory? Is it an adventitious set of movements related
primarily to technological change and with no particular significance for the
long-term process of socioeconomic development? Or is it a spatial change
that demands a whole new set of theoretical constructs, an upsetting of the
observed patterns over the whole period since at least the Industrial Revolution? Decentralization is probably neither, but it is a process that requires
more than empirical observation and that may be linked to a number of
theoretical constructs.

Two political-science viewpoints on the subject will be considered first:
a right-wing view and a Marxist view. From a right-wing perspective, decentralization is related to public choice theory, according to which individuals
make their choices of place of residence by comparing the different packages
of services and taxes offered in different towns or areas (Oates 1972). As
a result, according to proponents of the theory, there is a tendency for small
municipalities to emerge, with devolved or decentralized powers and the ability
to respond to community demands. The difficulty of applying such a theory
to Latin America is considerable. Although economic constraints—such as
the greater efficiency of larger units, counteracting any tendency to decentralize, or the fact that many differing elements should be taken into account
before a location decision is made (Smith 1985)—contribute to this difficulty,
more important is the inability of ordinary citizens to choose residences on
the basis of anything other than employment and family needs. Third World
studies of migration always point to the strength of employment attractions
in decision making over the migration target.

From a Marxist view of the decentralization process, in the capitalist state
the elite class interest will favor centralization. Monopoly capitalism is best
aided by a heavily hierarchical and centralized state, within which local government is merely a residual element. Having made major investments in big
cities, monopoly capital will seek to preserve and protect those investments.
Nor will monopoly capital favor power moving from the center even to the
suburbs, where part of the work force is located and where its separate interests may by vocalized (Castells 1978).

There are difficulties in applying a Marxist interpretation to Latin America, partly because such an interpretation admits of no important decentralization moves. In more than one country, both private capital in specific industries and governments within regional development programs, as well as governments, local and national, seeking to overcome physical problems imposed by large cities, have made powerful efforts to decentralize their economies and administrative structures. Were the decentralization efforts aimed merely at relocating industries and economic growth in a few designated growth poles and favoring monopoly capital, then the neo-Marxist critique that the efforts were solely legitimation exercises might be accepted (Johnston 1988). The growth pole type of massive state-led investment is found at Lazaro Cardenas/Las Truchas in Mexico or at Ciudad Guayana in Venezuela, just as it is in Europe at Dunkirk or Fos in France. The state legitimates capital expansion by presenting it as regional development and aid to poorer social groups. In fact, however, decentralization efforts in Mexico, Venezuela, and elsewhere have been varied and continuous and have not consistently favored monopoly capital.

Looking instead at a leading thrust of arts and social science theory, a case can be made for viewing decentralization in relation to postmodernism. A postmodern view has been developed largely in relation to rich countries, and, therefore, in geography and planning has emphasized the "consumer society" aspects of the theory and of the objective landscape. The central features of the theory include the rise of a service economy, growth of new high-technology industries, the consumer society, increased regional inequities, and greater variation in the direction as well as the level of economic and social development (Cooke 1988; Dear 1986). These are features more clearly recognized in rich countries, not in Latin America.

But if we return to what is meant by "modern" for the purposes of the debate, it becomes evident that poor countries too may exhibit the reactions to modern that constitute a postmodern phase. Modern development for a nation involves the imposition of a standard culture over the whole national territory over a long period of time. It involves the heavy centralization of all administrative and political life, with subjugation of provincial government and administration to the central, national institutions. In the economy, it involves the standardization of activities under national or international control; in industry, it involves a Fordist structure of factory production involving assembly-line production systems, large-size firms and large-scale production, concentration of management powers and, frequently, the confrontation of management with massive union power representing the interests of labor; and in agriculture, it involves heavy mechanization and commercialization of farming. Within the cities, there is a standardization of lifestyles and coordination of activities in systems of collective consumption.

At a first, political level, it is possible to see the rejection of centralism and the constant plea for local participation and for the expression of local interests as symptoms of the postmodern era. In Peru, for example, beginning in 1968 a long search was made under the military government for means of generating local autonomous economies and for reviving a strong nativist tradition of local community development. At present, new regions have been formed out of groups of departments and regional councils have been elected in the latest attempt to provide a serious regional government responsive to local concerns and aims. Throughout the Andean countries, the search for local community development has been directed at separate lines of advance for distinctive human groups. This means, in place of a standard form of economic and social development, different kinds of development may endow greater importance to maintenance of community ceremonies and leadership, or to agrarian reform to give farmers their own land, than to the increase of monetary income or public welfare provision. The size of the human groups that seek a distinctive kind of development is itself variable, and could be either a traditional village, or a large ethnic group such as the Shuar Federation of Amerindian peoples in Ecuador, whose aim is not developmental at all but the defense of their own Amerindian culture from the encroachments of modern civilization.

More important, at a level of regional planning, it is possible to identify decentralization as lying within a postmodern set of ideas (Zhukin 1988). In this context, we accept the description of a modern planning philosophy as one that relies on growth at the center, later to be diffused to the periphery through the action of factors such as the relative costs of labor and capital (Friedmann 1966; Richardson 1973). At most, it would be necessary to help this diffusion through the implantation of growth poles as substations transmitting the developmental impulse. The nature of modern development was economic, and it was based on manufacturing industry, to be introduced from abroad or set up behind tariff barriers.

The modern set of ideas was under attack from the outset; however, until recently, it was followed very generally by planners in Latin American countries. A first set of critiques focused on the need to involve the rural as well as the urban in the development process, and in the 1970s rural development became fashionable. Following the admission that purely rural schemes were doomed to fail because not enough attention was paid to the needs for markets for rural produce and for an infrastructure that would ensure rural transformation, the buzz phrase became *integrated rural-urban development*. Such development, however, was still development controlled from the center—progressing along lines controlled and determined at the center. The fate of small rural centers was to be set at distant metropolitan cities.

In the late 1970s, the ideas of "development from below" became currency among development thinkers and prompted a rethinking of not just the target areas (rural versus urban) but also the methods of attack, the actors and decision makers, and even the aims of development. For the first time there was the possibility that regions, or communities, might wish not to travel down the same path but down separate paths, selected by the local inhabitants expressing their own regional preferences (Stöhr and Tödtling 1978). This possibility has not been pursued much further in the planning field because it involves political action rather than theorization, and such action was generally unacceptable to the existing powers. But the ideas have persisted and do form part of the postmodern structure that upholds regionalism and the possibility of expressing regional identity. Such expression may rely on symbols from the region's past, without returning to sentimental traditionalism, and may create a "critical regionalism" (Frampton 1985). This movement sees value in differentiating regions one from another and each from any universal civilization.

Obviously, not all decentralization processes, and certainly not most of those to be described here, fall into the extreme category of regional movements aiming in different directions. Choice of developmental direction involves, for example, allowing regions to restructure their taxes to favor consumption of particular kinds of goods or to restructure their credits to favor specific kinds of economic activity. Such a level of freedom generally is not possible. However, the present processes that reduce central power and state activity and that foster the growth of local initiatives may be the first phase of a long process that eventually will lead to differentiated development. Present observations of the decentralization of industries and of administrative functions may lead to pressure for, and the eventual granting of, some devolution of decision powers and the constitutional structure that gives these powers weight.

A geographer's view of decentralization cannot avoid consideration of what may be termed the spatial theory of decentralization. At its extreme, this view holds that spatial arrangements are fundamental to social, economic, and political structures and that spatial planning is the key to regional development. As applied in the 1960s, this set of ideas embraced the Growth Pole concept, as well as central place theory constructs, for the development of rural regions; its reverberations continue with the kind of rural regional planning advocated by Rondinelli (Rondinelli and Ruddle 1978; Rondinelli 1985).

Decentralization may be regarded as part of spatial planning both in theory and practice. In theory, there exists an optimum size for cities; therefore, the goal of decentralization would be to relocate population from the metropolis, which is too large, to smaller cities, possibly smaller than the optimum. Also in theory, decentralization may fill particular voids in a central place hierarchy by building up a sufficient number of smaller population settlements through in-migration, to the size levels required by hierarchy theory.

Such theories have been heavily criticized for several reasons: there is no real evidence of an optimum size for all the different functions of cities (Richardson 1973; Gilbert 1976), there appears to be a reification of space as an active agent on its own (Gore 1984), and central place theory does not give strong enough grounds to support any given hierarchy of city sizes.

Related to these theories are economic-spatial ideas about balanced development, implying between regions an imbalance that might be rectified by a redistribution of resources and/or population. On this matter Gore (1984) challenges the idea that there can be any spatially optimum pattern or that it is desirable to look for such an optimum.

In fact, it is only in relation to the physical environment that spatial theory on decentralization can be sound. Deconcentration of activities and population may be desirable for countries if a serious ecological problem arises from concentration (air pollution, waste disposal problems) or if the central concentration of population and activities means that the population cannot make good use of known and usable resources. This is of course difficult to demonstrate. For example, Argentina's centralization of population seems excessive, with a third of its population in the Buenos Aires metropolitan area. But the resource base of much of the interior is, as currently known and developed, very slight, with huge regions of desert and semidesert that have no important mineral, water, forest, or soil resources. Brazil's concentration on its coastal regions is similarly difficult to fault given its limited ability to exploit the interior.

Perhaps it is enough to state that some regions, given present technology, are underutilized and should be developed. Such a statement avoids any judgment about whether the opportunity costs of developing a given region make it more sensible to invest human and physical capital elsewhere. Such a statement is also agnostic about the likely future value of different resources and population sizes.

DECENTRALIZATION AS A POLICY AIM

Most of the literature studying decentralization has concentrated on it as an aim or policy of governments. Primary aims of decentralization policies include the achievement of regional development or interregional equity in the case of economic policies (e.g., Aguilar-Barajas and Spence 1988). Decentralization policies to improve efficiency are not common; thus, decentralization may be seen as linked to welfare concerns rather than to concerns of maximum growth or efficiency in production. This is, however, too narrow a view of decentralization aims that may well come within the ambit of right-wing as well as left-wing polities.

Within the economic sphere, manufacturing industry has been the most frequently used tool of decentralization policy, though the case for such policy is not readily made in terms of a single industry. Instead, the spread effect involving several linked industries, within a scheme of, for example, growth poles is emphasized as beneficial, while the costs and benefits to the individual industry are not regarded as important. Complex linkage effects mean that decentralization of an important industry will affect whole regions in their demography, economy, and society. Decentralization benefits are seen as just a small part of the total aim of the program. There is some evidence that decentralization emerges as a first focus of attention in a country's history of regional planning and that it is easier to attract political attention and funds for decentralization than for regional development overall, perhaps because issues such as local nationalism do not appear at an early stage (Morris 1975).

The public voice of pressure for decentralization of the economy may come more forcibly from the center than from the periphery, where many people are unconnected to national political life. Heavy congestion of traffic and high costs of service provision may cause central industries and residents to call for deconcentration measures; the loudest calls may even come from those who do not plan to leave the center. Environmental concerns, such as air, land, and water pollution and the wholesale degradation of the environment, may also be uppermost in the minds of those who live in the center. Fears over resources are also apparent; water supplies to big cities in dry or subhumid regions are an outstanding concern, as in Caracas, Mexico City, and Lima. Power, transport systems, and all public services are increasingly stretched as central population grows. The public also fears certain human groups, especially migrants, who are believed to be responsible for the extra loads on the center and who fail to contribute to any solutions. These concerns may be expressed as economic costs, or they may be voiced as ecological issues. Criticism may also be directed at the town and regional planning that has allowed the situation to arise.

Decentralization aims, apart from economic, are most frequently political or administrative because of the region's colonial and postcolonial history. Today, most Latin American governments have some policy of decentralization or deconcentration to reduce the accumulated effects of hundreds of years of centralism. This centralism was never curbed by the new republics in the nineteenth century, despite federal constitutions modeled after the United States. Most administrative reforms are defeated, it seems, by social class and local power systems that defy any imposed democracy.

Administrative and political aims include providing a more responsive local government, because local politicians are more aware and sensitive to local issues. Concern for greater local participation is also generally regarded as a desirable aim for democratic governments. Of course, to improve local democracy, it is necessary not just to deconcentrate governmental functions (splitting them up and relocating some in the regions) but also to decentralize to some degree the powers of decision making. At the extreme, the decentralization of powers may extend beyond standard decision areas to the formulation of new policies amounting to regional autonomy. Some measure of this autonomy, which constitutes what may be termed devolution, it claimed by many regional movements in Europe, but it is not a common process in Latin America.

In Latin America, there is plenty of room to take measures aimed at decentralizing power before considering total devolution. Many governments own and manage steel mills, hotels, and beauty parlors; privatization could begin in these areas, moving government out of economic sectors where the play of market forces is beneficial. By not supporting such activities, usually run at a loss, the saving of government funds might be invested in the provision of basic welfare. Basic welfare provisions are not made for many regions and social groups; education, health, and basic urban infrastructure are welfare elements that are more acceptable to governments in the region (Urrutia 1990).

DECENTRALIZATION AS AN OBSERVABLE PROCESS

Decentralization does occur as a process in reaction to the pressures of congestion and the loosening of ties between key economic activities and large cities; in the case of political and administrative decentralization, it occurs as a response to a strong regional voice in many parts of the nation-states of Europe. In the advanced countries, decentralization of the economy and population occurred through the effects of recession in the post-1973 crisis, which hit most severely the old centers of production in the major industrial cities. The internationalization and interregionalization of industry have allowed the very largest firms to set up branch plants in outer peripheral regions, leaving only head offices or research and development units in the home cities.

Postindustrialization is also prominent in advanced countries, where there has been a gradual move away from manufacturing industry as the dominant employer and generator of wealth toward service activities of various kinds. The more footloose the nature of these services, the greater is the potential for decentralization, which is realized when there are no strong needs for a central location.

Many workers in modern, high-technology services and in modern manufacturing industries are highly skilled and well paid; their choice of residence is important as a decentralizing force. In some regions, such as the U.S. Southwest, industries have based location decisions on the residential preferences of workers. On a smaller scale, counterurbanization, such as that around London, represents worker choice of residence outside the city while jobs may in many cases remain in the metropolis. Relatively new factors such as the absence of pollution and congestion, differences in social values and cultural norms, access to open countryside, the sense of community, and the previously recognized calculus of space and accommodation in the country versus accessibility in the city are all important in the counterurbanization movements seen everywhere in Western countries.

In the Third World, these factors are scarcely relevant. The value systems found throughout Latin America and among those of high as well as low socioeconomic status place residence in the large city or in its immediate hinterland at a premium. Industrial workers and executives place no premium on country living and, perhaps more surprising, neither do professionals. In Ecuador, for example, doctors are required to serve at least one year in a rural area because the supply of doctors is insufficient in rural areas and well-established doctors prefer to live and work in the city. In rural areas, many doctors visit the village during the week and return to the town every weekend. Also in Ecuador, professionals move to the capital for access to better schools for their children; teachers are unwilling to attempt establishing good schools in the countryside because teachers have no attachment to rural areas and no market exists for such schools.

Evidence, however, does exist of moves toward decentralization in many areas, relating to forces beyond the immediate control of individuals and, in some cases, beyond the control of the state itself. An example is the recession of the post-1973 years, which caused an automatic decentralization. Since the growth segments of the industrial, service, and administrative functions in Latin American countries were all highly centralized in the years of rapid development up to 1973, their collapse or decline in the years since has meant a relative growth of peripheral places less connected to the growth. Unconnected to the main national-provincial urban hierarchy and with a smaller number of bureaucrats in their population, smaller cities with traditional industries and informal economies have come to the fore.

As chapters in this book will show, there have been other factors at work producing decentralization in Latin America. Decline or crisis in the official economy has led to a greater importance for the unofficial, "black" economy, which because of its illegal nature tends to be decentralized. An obvious example is the drug industry, but there are others—for example, a part of the production of precious metals and their ores, notably in the Andean countries. Another decentralizing factor has been the adoption of liberal or neoconservative political systems in a number of countries. A central tenet of such political economies is that the state should be reduced in absolute size and in relation to the private sector. The state should retreat from direct involvement in the economy through the privatization of firms and industries, leaving them to the controls of market forces. Inevitably, a reduction in centralism is necessary since the great public agencies controlling, for example, the petroleum industry are highly centralized themselves, needing close contacts with the government and civil service in the capital cities.

Yet another agent of decentralization is the multinational corporation (MNC), whose choice of plant location may be very different from a national firm's choice. For MNCs, the advantages of receiving grants and credits for locating in the periphery can be far more important than they are for local firms. For global firms, with alternative suppliers in different countries for most inputs and a consequent flexibility of sources for supplies, location relative to world markets is vital; less vital are national markets and the linkage effects possible in big cities.

MNCs and global firms operate a process which may be termed *technical decentralization*, referring to the separation of distinctive stages of production such as research and development, component manufacture and assembly, and their location in different regions. This has long been recognized within the bounds of single nations. The term *branch plant economy* characterizes regions of single nations that receive plants specializing in low-skill jobs like assembly line work, while the central offices of the company retain overall management, design, and research operations. The global firm corresponds to a process of separation, but on a larger scale. Because the number and importance of national firms with a vertical organization of production is small in Third World countries, branch plant economies are not common. Nonetheless, the global firm has made a great impact in industrial location even though it is not always toward decentralization. In many countries, MNCs have chosen only the most important city for their operations; in countries such as Uruguay, for example, it is difficult to see MNCs wishing to establish themselves in any other urban center. Like the old colonial powers, MNCs tend toward hierarchy and central control. It is largely the distortions introduced by particular governments (tariff barriers, regional aids) and by the existence of political frontiers that have led MNCs away from metropolitan cities in some of the countries under discussion here.

SOME PRACTICAL PROBLEMS

For Latin America, decentralization of any form involving government action represents a particularly thorny problem. Most of the literature on the subject describes or analyzes failed attempts at decentralization of one kind or another.

Here, we shall point briefly to some of the methodological problems that are frequently encountered and that relate particularly to theoretical conceptions of what is implied by decentralization and under what banner it can be adopted.

One obvious problem has been the excessively limited scope of decentralization, which has resulted in failure because of the absence of the other required elements. Just as growth pole policies failed for want of infrastructure and related industries and agrarian reform failed for want of any infrastructural improvement or technical assistance to new farmers, so decentralization has failed for want of an appreciation of its complexity and the need for action with respect to many areas.

Some of the most obvious cases of one-sided decentralization, imaginative in their thrust and symbolism but brash in their defiance of ordinary logic, are the removals of capital cities to new locations—Brazil's shift of its federal capital from Rio de Janeiro to Brasília and the similar move from Buenos Aires to Viedma in Patagonia now proposed by the Argentine national government (Gilbert 1989).

A comparable case within the economic field was Chile's decentralization of the car industry from the Santiago region to Arica, located in the Atacama desert 2000 kilometers from its main market. This famous example of decentralization occurred as a consequence of special local privileges on the taxing of imported parts; once these privileges were eliminated, the industry reverted to its original home.

Other examples of the need for a well-rounded decentralization program come from studies of local government reorganizations. In Colombia, for example, attempts to transfer responsibilities from central to local governments, without transferring the relevant financial and decision-making powers and without attempting to build up local skills among government officials, were doomed to failure (Uribe-Echevarria 1986).

The language of decentralization is also often confusingly used when a process of continued centralization is in hand. In Colombia, national convenience and outside support from agencies such as the World Bank allowed the proliferation of over 100 so-called decentralized agencies in the 1960s. They handled such matters as housing, education, electricity, water supplies, and sewage disposal (Collins 1989). These agencies were set up to bypass the inefficiencies and clientelism of existing local governments in the municipalities. However, they came to present a series of inefficiencies of their own and represented a centralizing, rather than decentralizing, influence within local government. Vertical centralization was combined with horizontal disintegration, as the two main political parties were represented at every level of government (Rothenberg 1980). Opposing factions within the municipalities made normal administration of elements—for example, housing policy—almost impossible. Only in the late 1980s did Colombia turn away from this structure to attempt a more territorially or horizontally based set of local government structures whose fate is yet to be seen.

An underlying problem that is not addressed by any of the studies is the irony that governments in the post–World War II years, attempting to present a face of democracy and concern for welfare, have adopted a policy line incompatible with their own tendencies. On the one hand, decentralization, regional development, interregional equity, redistribution, and welfare have been watchwords and symbols of progressiveness. On the other hand, in order to implement such ideas, the state has moved progressively toward intervention involving centralization through the buildup of state welfare programs for health, education, housing, and the like. The state also has invaded the private economy by nationalizing strategic sectors of industry that had been in foreign-dominated hands and by supporting the growth of parastatal agencies for industries such as iron and steel manufacture.

A state-run welfare approach to decentralization would appear to be doomed from the start, representing top-down development with little chance for locally based initiatives. The sole exception is Cuba, where Havana certainly has reduced its centrality and other centers have been created or fortified, but in an environment where most features of modern capitalism have been eliminated.

In Latin America, there is a political and administrative need for the courage to grant some devolution of powers, in a legal and financial sense, to local authorities in order to change the present scene. At the economic and social levels, encouragement is needed for new entrepreneurship to create firms and industries rather than to deconcentrate existing ones. Also needed is support for the local formation of capital through intraregionally selective incentives to savings and investment as well as support for the local formation of capital in land and buildings.

We thus return to the postmodern conception of development. For the central state operating within the framework of modern capitalism, whether of neoliberal or welfare state inclination, the bringing about of appropriate decentralization is beyond its capacity. Decentralization efforts are or should be in the hands of the regions themselves, with appropriate safeguards and stimuli to develop institutions and organizations that suit regional tastes and follow regional differences in history and culture. After several centuries of centralization in Latin America, this sea change will not be accomplished rapidly or with ease.

PART I

DECENTRALIZATION PROCESSES IN LATIN AMERICA

2

Decentralization, Debt, Democracy, and the Amazonian Frontierlands of Bolivia and Brazil

David J. Fox

INTRODUCTION

For a variety of well-known historical, political, and economic reasons, centralization processes favoring the concentration of activities and authority have characterized Latin America. Although political lip service has been paid in many countries to the desirability of reversing the results of these processes, the resources to counter long-ingrained custom rarely have been made available. But centralist tradition is now more strongly challenged: new national and international forces motivated by both political and economic pressures are beginning to change the established position. The demographic forces of high fertility and increasing mobility, which have contributed to both agglomeration and dispersion over the last half century, were strengthened and deflected during the 1980s by some radical changes in the context within which political decisions were taken. First, the international debt crisis forced existing economic orthodoxies to be reviewed and forced many Latin American economies to undergo a fundamental change in direction: in particular, doubt was cast on the compatibility of economic efficiency and centralization. Second, the coincident return of virtually all Latin American countries to constitutional democracy made governments more accountable and responsive to the views of that majority of voters who live outside the traditional national heartlands. These two circumstances have helped enhance the value of the nonmetropolitan areas and have resulted in some significant shifts in the geographic locus of activities guiding change in Latin America.

This chapter will review the ways in which economic and political restructuring has created a climate favoring decentralization in Latin America. It will argue that some frontier regions have enjoyed particular benefits, as recent changes in lowland Bolivia and the western parts of Brazil demonstrate.

Decentralization and Debt

It may be argued that the accumulation of huge debt by Latin American countries was partly a product of the centralist traditions of the continent's *anciens régimes*. The current debt burden is largely the result of credits disbursed under public guarantee to national governments, public authorities, and parastatal enterprises, bodies too frequently and conveniently distanced in time and space to monitor effectively the longer-term value of such hostages to fortune. The ability of many Latin economies to cope with ill-judged liabilities was weakened by a more deliberate aspect of centralization: the manner in which the internal terms of trade had been manipulated to favor the center at the expense of the provinces. Most countries had evolved economies in which metropolitan activities—satisfying some of the requirements of modern industry, servicing government departments, gratifying national pride, or responding to the demands of vocal citizens or organized labor—were effectively subsidized by the provinces. Industrial policies of import substitution produced geographically skewed benefits that heightened the contrasts in well-being between favored areas, notably the center, and disadvantaged areas, notably the periphery. Unrealistic exchange rates helped deny overseas markets to primary producers in the countryside and brought little or no compensating benefits to other segments of the local economy or populace. It seems not inappropriate that the financial crisis that arose from heavy indebtedness should be the main catalyst of the changes that are helping redress what many have come to see as the overcentralization of power and presence within the continent.

The spread of monetarist policies among Latin American countries during the past few years, under the threat of national bankruptcy, has helped diminish the pull of the center and in some respects has actively encouraged a centrifugal process of decentralization. Some countries are further along the stages of the so-called adjustment process than are others (Selowsky 1990). The architects of the new economic policies have, of necessity, relied heavily on guidance from the International Monetary Fund (IMF); this reliance has resulted in a degree of similarity among the economic prescriptions adopted by individual countries and a shared experience of the consequences that follow their implementation. It is thus possible to generalize about the nature of a typical IMF-inspired restructuring program and note some of the implications for decentralization.

A prime objective of all adjustment policies has been the establishment of a more open economy through the removal of internal and overseas trading barriers—for example, import dues and quotas, export tariffs and prohibitions, domestic subsidies, monopolies, and price controls on basic consumer goods. This can and has provided a stimulus to the more dispersed primary activities of agriculture and mining, especially where production is destined for overseas markets in the developed world. In contrast, most domestic manufacturing has been twice hit as competition in price and quality from imported goods has become stronger and as the disposable income of the local customers has declined. In almost all Latin American countries both the major manufacturing region and the main market for manufacturers is the capital city; as a result, the center has been especially hard hit.

A second characteristic of restructuring has been a reduction in government expenditure, both in absolute and relative terms. Since a disproportionate share of the direct and indirect benefits of such expenditure was concentrated at the center, it is the center that has been most exposed to exchequer cutbacks. Scaling down state expenditure has been part of a wider objective of reducing the involvement of the state in national life. In economic terms this has meant the streamlining of state bureaucracies, the dismemberment of state monopolies, and the privatization of erstwhile state institutions and activities.

A further way in which the privileged position of the center has been attacked has been through fiscal reforms designed to increase government income. There has been a switch away from taxing production and toward taxing consumption. Taxes on income, profits, and property, including productive land, have fallen more heavily on the center than on the periphery; value-added tax has been widely imposed and has also increased the contribution made by the center. In contrast, royalties, customs dues, and levies on particular commodities generally have been cut—to the greater benefit of the provinces than of the metropolis.

Decentralization and Democracy

The remarkable return to democracy in most of Latin America during the 1980s has also played a part in encouraging decentralization. In the 1980s, autocratic regimes with a vested interest in tight central control were replaced by elected governments. The power of oligarchies accustomed to ruling from the center was reduced and the regions were given a larger voice in the affairs of state; the regions have since made increasing demands for a more equable distribution of the benefits of citizenship. The decline of patronage and the rise of an increasingly technocratic approach to government have made it more difficult to square the circle between the rhetoric of populism and the realities of life for large sections of the electorate: it is harder to ignore the impoverishments of history and the glaring disparities between center and periphery. The new politicians of Latin America have to reconcile a growing democratic accountability with economic strategies designed to exploit inequalities in comparative advantages. Nevertheless, it seems clear at the beginning of the 1990s that the moves toward administrative decentralization and greater popular participation in decision making will continue, in spite of economic austerity and thanks in no small respect to the support offered by the multilateral lending agencies.

Decentralization and the Role of Frontiers

In the nature of their origins, frontier regions have long been peripheral to the economic and social life of most Latin American states. Many still retain their traditional distance from central control; where that control is exercised, it may be different from the control exercised elsewhere in the country. Their position and status often have meant that the full contribution of frontier areas to national wealth has been unrecorded; by default, indexes measuring degrees of national centralization have been exaggerated.

In recent years, however, frontier zones have become more significant contributors to national life as *de jure* ownership has been reinforced by *de facto* occupation. Increased population pressures in traditional core areas, a lessening of the perceived attractiveness of metropolitan life, improved physical access, a reduction in the friction of distance on the transmission of ideas and materials, the removal of legalistic barriers to settlement, and the growing permeability of international and provincial barriers have helped draw migrants to settle previously empty lands and have given value to the varied resources of many frontier reaches. Some such resources are natural and their discovery and subsequent exploitation have yielded a net gain to the national endowment; others are man-made and their value has grown with the increased importance of frontiers to the economic life of Latin America.

The growing incorporation of frontier areas into national life has given them more of the characteristics of their respective heartlands. While protectionist policies were in fashion, the extension of central attributes to the periphery steepened the institutionalized escarpment that many international boundaries presented to their next-door neighbors; the height of such escarpments grew and *contrabandistas* and legitimate traders took advantage of the economic and political discontinuities. Since the second half of the 1980s, however, fiscal hurdles have been lowered, cross-border traffic has increased, and legitimate entrepreneurs have been encouraged to look beyond national borders when expanding their interests. The political initiatives for closer economic integration and cooperation associated with the 1960s and 1970s have been reinforced in recent years by a number of border integration projects, substantial and credible binational projects, and various private sector developments; international official lending agencies have smiled on such proposals and have added impetus to changes already in hand (IDB 1989a, 79–89; IDB 1989b, 13–15, 97–101). In general, the comparative advantages offered by borders—in the past, the private preserve of favored groups or individuals—are now more widely available and may even have been co-opted by the state. This has heightened their appeal and reinforced those more general processes currently encouraging decentralization.

This chapter examines the frontier zones on either side of the Bolivian-Brazilian border to see to what degree they provide evidence of decentralization and a strengthening of the periphery. Here, change is extensive, rapid, and largely unregulated and its impact on the geographic balances within the parent countries is significant and growing. They provide interesting contrast with, for example, the Mexican border zone adjoining the United States (examined elsewhere in this book).

The Amazonian Frontierlands

The taming of Amazonia over the past decade or so is a topic of genuine popular interest, and there is no need to generalize about its nature. This account will confine itself to detailing some of the recent developments in the part of Amazonia that lies across the Bolivian-Brazilian border and to charting some of the more easily measurable changes (see Figure 2.1).

One in every four Bolivians—over a million and a half people—now live in the departments of the Oriente; in 1980 they were home to only one in every five and in 1970 only one in every six Bolivians. The population of the city of Santa Cruz tripled between 1950 and 1969 (to about 109,000); it doubled (1978, 279,000) and redoubled to an estimated 442,000 in 1987. Santa Cruz became the second largest Bolivian city in the early 1970s; between 1978 and 1987 it grew more rapidly than any other departmental capital. In 1970 fewer than two million Brazilians lived in Acre, Rondônia, and Mato Grosso (excluding Mato Grosso do Sul); by 1985 the number had more than doubled. Rondônia's population grew from 111,000 in 1970, to 491,000 in 1980, to about 1,150,000 in 1987 (Goodman and Hall 1990, 25). Admittedly, these states account for only one in every thirty Brazilians, but their share has risen from one in fifty in the past two decades. Much of the recent immigration to the area has yet to be recorded; it is clear that census figures are inaccurate and underestimate the scale of the demographic changes. It is easier to enumerate townspeople and settled country folk than frontier pioneers. Unfortunately, published official population figures are not only unreliable and geographically biased but are out of date; they offer only a tenuous basis on which to extrapolate into the future.

Official information on economic changes is even less reliable. It is probable that the majority of the production in these frontier reaches goes unrecorded since it accrues to the criminal and informal sectors that flourish there, remote from central control, and since it may not enter the official economy. Available evidence suggests that this frontier area is strengthening its contribution to the national lives of both Bolivia and Brazil and is assisting, albeit spontaneously and largely unwittingly, the deliberate policies of decentralization recently adopted in La Paz and Brasília. Although the two sides of the frontier share many similar qualities, the national heartlands where policies are made are very different. Brazil for a long time has been more active than

Figure 2.1
The Bolivian and Brazilian Frontierlands

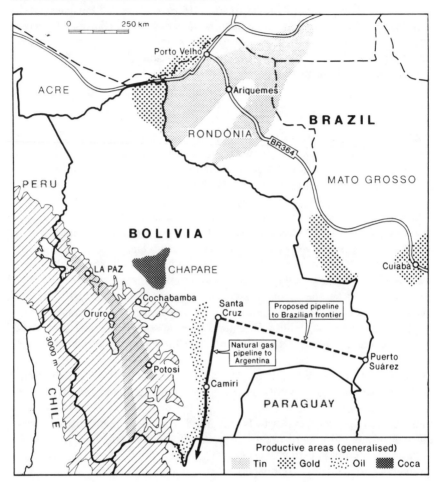

Bolivia in promoting decentralization in Amazonia. In neither country, however, has the state been as important an agent of change as either the combined efforts of individual citizens or the constraints of exogenous demand.

RECENT CHANGES IN THE BOLIVIAN ORIENTE

The first half of the 1980s saw the balance of both political power and economic activity in Bolivia shift toward the Oriente; that shift has since been accentuated; due in part to the economic volte-face the country has undergone since mid-1985 following the election of President Paz Estenssoro. The previous government had lost all authority and, as in Argentina in 1989, the new president's predecessor stepped down before his elected term of office expired. The new president inherited an economy burdened by huge debt, the highest inflation rate in the world, a parallel dollar exchange rate fourteen times the official rate, falling industrial output, a declining income from exports, and the weekly depreciation of the purchasing power of wages. His New Economic Policy (NEP)—promulgated as Supreme Decree 21,060 in August 1985 within a month of being elected to office—transformed the structure of both the formal and, more important, the informal economy. The policy was a dramatic move designed to bring order out of chaos and to return Bolivia to the path of economic orthodoxy. The hope was that Bolivia would cease to be seen from the outside as "a hopeless case" and become eligible for the external help needed in order to emerge from the economic catastrophe engulfing it. The NEP was a neo-liberal, monetarist policy designed to win the support of the IMF: the peso was floated, the money supply strictly controlled, public sector salaries frozen, almost all price controls and subsidies removed, taxation increased and redirected, all areas of public expenditure reviewed, and almost all expenditures sharply cut. It was a policy that explicitly rejected most of the values that Paz Estenssoro had espoused and it deliberately undermined many of the fundamental economic structures he had put in place following the 1952 Revolution a third of a century earlier.

Remarkably, the NEP remained intact four years after it was introduced and many of its original aims had been achieved: when Paz Estenssoro left the Palacio Quemada for the final time in 1989 he had steered his country safely through a second revolution and Bolivia was being held up in the international fraternity as an example for others to emulate.[1] Equally noteworthy is the fact that he was able to pass the mantle of responsibility to a duly elected successor—albeit his nephew—in a country previously plagued by coups and a flagrant disrespect for constitutional government. Furthermore, although President Paz Zamora was not the candidate of Paz Estenssoro's Movimiento Nacionalista Revolucionario (MNR) party and was critical of the NEP during his election campaign, once in office he pledged his government to continue the austere policies initiated by his predecessor. Although the new president is from Tarija and his electoral support was strongest in the southern Altiplano, it was the political weight of the Oriente that swung the presidential election his way. The support of the kingmaker Hugo Bánzer—whose Acción Democrática Nacionalista (ADN) party did particularly well in Santa Cruz (Bánzer's home department), Beni, and Pando—ultimately gave Paz Zamora the prize. The price paid was an equal share of cabinet seats and national policy-making for the *banzeristas*: a boost for the Oriente.

The Decentralization of Mining

The NEP encouraged the decentralization of the country's economic life. Its effects were first felt on the mining industry, incontrovertibly Bolivia's most important industry.[2] In 1985, the state mining sector, organized within the Corporación Minera de Bolivia (Comibol), was responsible for two-thirds of the country's metallic mineral production, for three-quarters of the formal employment in mining, and—according to unfriendly interpretations—for losses to the public purse of US$720 million between 1981 and 1985. With the NEP came the promise of administrative decentralization, the reality of wage constraint, and the threat of mine closures implicit in a policy prohibiting deficit financing. The collapse of the tin price following the effective bankruptcy of the International Tin Council rendered all Bolivia's tin mines—and tin had been the staple of the country throughout the twentieth century—demonstrably uneconomic, many irredeemably so. The state mining sector—created from the nationalization of the mining empires of Bolivia's erstwhile tin "barons"— was in the nature of its history more dependent upon tin than the smaller, residual, private mining sector (the so-called medium mines, which from 1952, had also been less sheltered from commercial considerations). The resolve of the government to implement its policy was demonstrated in 1986 when Comibol declared redundant two-thirds of its labor force (of 27,500—the most sizable body of organized labor in the country). At the same time employment in the medium mines was halved (to 4,000). Most Comibol mines were placed on standby while overseas mining experts analyzed whether and under what conditions the mines could be run profitably and therefore be worth reopening; they concluded that only two tin mines (Huanuni and Colquiri) were worth further investment. The emasculated work force is now only a quarter of what it was in 1985; this, combined with a 50 percent reduction in the real value of wages paid (in cash and kind) has transformed the cost structure of Comibol.

The restructuring of Comibol has exacted a substantial social toll (UNITAS 1987). Since the average miner's family numbers between six and seven members, some 125,000 people have been directly affected by the redundancies; add to these those indirectly dependent on the mines and the figure doubles to a quarter of a million people, or 5 percent of the national population. The bleak Andean setting of most mines means that alternative employment is not available locally. The loss goes beyond employment because Comibol, like many of the private mining companies, has traditionally (though since 1986 no longer by mandate) provided much of the public infrastructure— schools, health centers, transport—which elsewhere would be the responsibility of the state.

Mines deemed to have no commercial future in both the state and private sector have been turned over to mining cooperatives and memberships offered to ex-employees. Those who accept join the growing army of peasant miners that now form the majority of Bolivia's miners. Catavi, during the twentieth century the greatest tin mine in Bolivia (and, indeed, the world), closed in 1986 and was turned over to 4,000 members of four newly created mining cooperatives. Such cooperatives impose virtually no cost on the state; in practice, membership removes any residual responsibility the state may feel for its former servants. Redundant Comibol miners were given severance payments, but most of the old mining areas had little beyond their minerals to sustain the miners and their families. Many of those made redundant took up the offer of free transport to leave the mining camps—home perhaps for several generations—and look for a new life elsewhere. Some made their way to the nearer towns and joined the oversubscribed ranks of those barely subsisting in the informal economy; a few were helped with temporary "makework" employment provided by the undersubscribed Emergency Social Fund. Many, however, headed east, crossed the continental divide and wound their way down through the dank cloud forests to enter the frontier world of the Amazon lowlands: a more dramatic change of milieu is hard to imagine.

The Green Gold of the Oriente

There have been two powerful lures in the east (see Figure 2.2). The first is the green gold of the coca plant and, in particular, that variety (of Erythroxylon coca) from which cocaine can be derived.[3] This grows most satisfactorily in the Chaparé lowlands east of Cochabamba accessible by road from the west since the early 1970s and currently the source of over 80 percent of Bolivian leaf. The growing of coca for the international drug trade has been the economic success story of Bolivia during the 1980s. But by being outside the orbit of legitimate control, its very success has further emphasized the part played by decentralization in the real life of the country.

The growth of the coca economy has been dramatic. In 1972 there were an estimated 3,000 hectares of coca plantations (producing 2,500 tons of leaf) in the Chaparé; a 1991 estimate, which is probably on the low side, is over 40,000 hectares producing over 100,000 tons of leaf, more than double that in 1982. Estimates of the number of families currently supported by growing coca for cocaine range from 40,000 to 100,000. The leaves are treated locally and transformed into a coca paste (a ton of leaves yields up to 5 kilograms of paste): expenditures on chemicals, kerosene, transport, labor, protection, and bribery all feed back into the local economy. Coca brought between $200 million and $400 million into the economy of the Chaparé in 1988 when the price paid to cultivators for their leaves was about $2 per kilogram. One estimate of the total income generated by coca in 1988 was $750 million of which half stayed in Bolivia; in early 1990 President Paz Zamora reported that Bolivia's cocaine trade had an annual turnover of $1.5 billion in 1989 of which some $600 million (equivalent to Bolivia's entire earnings from legitimate exports) remained in the country. Whatever the true figure, it is

Figure 2.2
Growth Rates of Bolivian and Brazilian Commodities

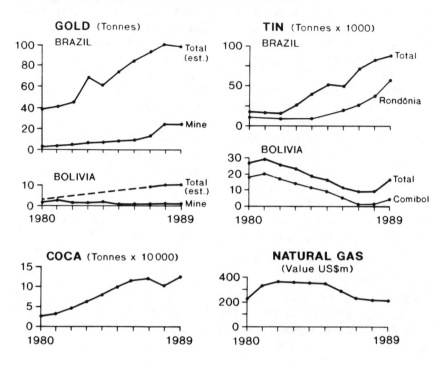

clear that a large part of the success of the official restructuring program has, paradoxically, depended upon the unofficial income from drugs. The Oriente has been crucial in allowing Bolivia to return to economic stability.

But Bolivia's economy is under threat. Trafficking in drugs has long been illegal in Bolivia, but it is difficult to combat, even if the will to do so is there; it is widely believed that senior members of the military government of the early 1980s enriched themselves hugely from the trade. It has been only since 1986—after the implementation of the NEP and since Bolivia was deemed eligible once again for external assistance—that Bolivia has begun to succumb to overseas pressure to take measures to curb the drug trade. Several Vietnam-style, U.S.-Bolivian military attacks have been launched against the infrastructure of the trade, legislation was enacted in 1988 making the growing of coca for paste illegal (the growing of coca used for traditional purposes was not outlawed), and since 1987 growers have been offered incentives to switch to alternative crops. But until 1990 none of these moves made much of an impact in the frontier region of the Chaparé. The dilemma the government has had to face is a real one: failure to cooperate in the global antidrug campaign will undermine relations with the United States, yet any success will undermine the economy and might disrupt the social quiescence that has been a necessary concomitant of economic stabilization. Indeed, the growers, including new growers from the "relocalized" miners—naturally antagonistic toward a state that in their eyes has served them badly and quite used to organizing resistance to central authority—have mobilized forces on occasions.

In 1990, however, a new situation emerged in the Chaparé; for tin, it was a market-led transformation. The attack on the drug cartels in Colombia led to a collapse in the price of coca leaf: a carga (300 pounds) of leaves that fetched $200 in early 1989 was worth less than the $30 break-even price in 1990. The changed economics of the coca market offered a window of opportunity to official attempts to promote crop substitutions. Suddenly, lines of destitute planters began to form outside the offices of the eradication program offices to collect $2,000 for every hectare of coca uprooted; by the end of 1990 over 20 percent of the acreage under coca twelve months earlier had been set aside. The United States agreed to give additional economic and military aid to Bolivia and has given some impetus to the government's $3.5 billion Plan Coca por Desarrollo published in early 1990; in 1991 Bolivia agreed to the deployment of U.S. military to assist local forces. However, there remains the distinct possibility that harassed processors of cocaine will move out of Colombia and into eastern Bolivia and reestablish the local market for coca; Bolivia exported an estimated 30-55 tons of cocaine in 1990. Whatever happens, it would seem that the impetus to regional economic decentralization, which the Chaparé has given the country in the past decade, will be extended in the future.

The Allure of Real Gold

Official prospecting for alluvial tin and gold in the Oriente began in the late 1960s. Concessions in the frontier zones had long been reserved to the state (and many of these so-called fiscal reserves had been set aside for the Corporación de Desarrollo de las Fuerzas Armadas to benefit the armed forces and were seemingly sacrosanct). It was Comibol and the United Nations–sponsored Instituto de Investigaciones Minero-Metalúrgico that first sent parties into the forests of the Pando in the far north of the country looking, unsuccessfully, for workable deposits. Between 1976 and 1986 the British Geological Survey, in cooperation with its Bolivian counterpart Geobol, mounted an intensive investigation of the mineral resources of 200,000 square kilometers of eastern Santa Cruz and the northern Oriente. The work drew attention to a number of promising secondary gold deposits as well as to hard rock deposits requiring substantial capital investment before yielding a return. In October 1985 a new division of Comibol—the Empresa del Oro del Noreste—was created to prospect for gold in the Pando and the *marcha del oro al norte* had begun. Twelve months later, Comibol had identified seventeen sectors and planned to sublicense fifteen of these to ex-employees from its traditional area of operation. By 1987, a large number of new mining cooperative members and many independent groups were attacking an ever-increasing number of alluvial and eluvial deposits. In addition, experienced gold miners from the Tipuani cooperatives at the foot of the Andes and migrant Brazilians from across the Abuna and Mamoré rivers joined the veritable gold rush, which continues today. In 1990 some 300 Brazilian dredgers were working Bolivian waters, with the connivance of the local Bolivian civil and military authorities.

Very little of the gold produced in the Oriente directly enters the formal economy of the country. Although all gold produced in the country was required to be sold to the Banco Minero, its branches in the Beni closed in the mid-1980s because of lack of business. Only in 1988 when the Banco Central made a pragmatic decision to pay 5 percent above the going London price for gold sold to the Banco Minero did official production figures begin to suggest the scale of operations. There was an eightfold increase in official gold production in Bolivia between 1986 and 1988, and it is estimated that about half the gold produced in Bolivia is now legitimated by being sold to the state. The overall level of gold production in 1990 was almost certainly at least twice the official figure of 5,180 kilograms, worth $64 million; even within the official total, half was credited to ''other sources,'' defined as ''minerals of unknown provenance sold by middle men'' (ANMM 1991, 47).

Gold, including that from heap leaching operations in the Altiplano, has probably been the most valuable metal mined in Bolivia since 1987. Perhaps the majority of Bolivia's most attractive mineral prospects lie in the largely unexploited periphery of the country.

This view is likely to be tested during the next few years. A new mining code was presented to Congress in late 1990 and adopted in 1991 which had the effect of removing the long-standing restrictions on most mineral exploitation within 50 kilometers of the country's borders. Protagonists of the changes claim that some 30 percent of the country's accessible mineral reserves are there. Further, in September 1990 a new investment law was enacted that removed legal discriminations imposed on foreign investors, including mining companies, working in Bolivia; it gave specific permission for Comibol to enter into joint ventures to exploit its concessions. Comibol has taken on some of the characteristics of a holding company with individual mines seemingly being fattened up until they are sufficiently attractive to find new owners. The withdrawal of the state from direct involvement with mining seems some time away, but the prospects of privatization must be in the minds of many. Certainly the antagonism of those in the traditional mining areas to the disposal of mining rights to foreign capital remains strong and opposition has been locally effective. But that opposition is weaker in the periphery, and already a number of the world's mining multinationals have staked claims in the Oriente, adding to the centripetal forces mounting elsewhere in the economy.

Conclusions

The frontier offers other opportunities to entrepreneurs that are being more fully exploited than in the past. For example, as Amazonia becomes more populated, as access to the frontier regions becomes easier, as unmanned border crossing points proliferate, and as cross-border transactions continue to generate windfall profits, smuggling increases. Estimates of the value of contraband entering Bolivia (thus avoiding customs dues and value-added tax, although possibly incurring backhanders at the frontier) suggest it is equivalent to over a third of the value of legitimate imports. This, like many of the other growth sectors of Bolivia's Amazonian economy, is largely outside the official economy (as is an estimated 62 percent of the country's economic life) and makes it difficult to measure the full impact of recent economic decentralization in Bolivia.

The agribusinesses of soybean farmers, cattle ranchers, and timber fellers are all making substantial profits from the taming of the eastern frontier and some profits will be declared; profits will increase as a result of a new policy favoring exporters. New roads and rural development schemes promoted since 1985 by international development agencies have also helped in the process of decentralization. The continued exploitation of state-owned oil and natural gas fields east of the Andes is making a significant contribution to the legitimate economy of the state. Current negotiations to pipe Bolivian natural gas to the border town of Puerto Suárez and to build a generating plant to transform the gas into thermoelectricity for the Brazilian market are making progress; the building of a fertilizer factory and a polymer plant in the Cachuela Esperanza region are longer-term projects. All are predicated on raising credits from multinational official lending agencies, anxious to promote examples of transborder cooperation and to weaken the traditions of national centralization. There has been a fundamental shift in economic, demographic, and political balance away from the old centralized Andean state toward that half of Bolivia that lies east of the Andes, a change likely to be reinforced during the last decade of the twentieth century.

BRAZIL'S NORTHWEST FRONTIER: THE VIEW FROM THE CENTER

The momentum of decentralization in recent years on Brazil's northwest frontier has drawn on a blend of public policy inputs, the actions of individuals, and the play of external forces. The relative importance of these elements has varied over time, as events in Rondônia well illustrate.

The first serious attempt to formulate a development policy for Amazonia was made under the 1964 military government.[4] It decided, for largely geopolitical reasons, to try to integrate Amazonia into national life and in 1966 published decrees and acts that provided the legal framework for

Operation Amazonia. Operation Amazonia, through the Superintendency for the Development of Amazonia (SUDAM), created incentives designed to attract large investments of domestic and foreign private capital and credits from multilateral aid bodies. Its goal was to turn enclaves of Amazonia into productive elements of the national economy; development initiatives were undertaken mainly by the private sector but with limited state backing (Hall 1989, 7–8). There were exceptions: SUDAM's first regional plan (1968) called for Acre and Rondônia to be given preferential treatment in the allocation of public investments, but this was not implemented.

The 1970 Program of National Integration (PIN) changed official development strategies. The key to PIN was the construction of a coarse network of all-weather highways designed, as it is popularly claimed, "to unite men without land to land without men"; drought in the northeast and agricultural modernization elsewhere had provided a reservoir of potential travelers. The roads were built, beginning with the Transamazonica, and today there are very few areas of Amazonia further than 500 air-kilometers from the nearest highway. Unfortunately, because most of the roads cost much more to build than their budgets allowed, many of the other planned improvements in the public infrastructure were not completed. This did not discourage prospective migrants, but the absence of infrastructure combined with a general ignorance of environmental conditions claimed a heavy toll from those who took the new roads to a new life and did not deter others from following them.

The onset of the 1973 oil crisis led to a revision of the aims of Amazonian development policies; attention became focused on the urgent need to promote exports to meet the increased cost of imported energy. The revised policies were given form under the Programa de Polos Agropecuários e Agrominerais da Amazonia (Polamazonia). Polamazonia identified fifteen regions or growth poles within Amazonia, each thought capable of supporting at least one export-oriented activity—such as plantation agriculture, large-scale livestock ranching, commercial lumbering, or mining. The agents chosen to create those exports were not the poverty-stricken sodbusters arriving in parts of Amazonia in large numbers but capital-rich corporations and entrepreneurs seeking to take advantage of a favorable investment climate: tax liabilities in the Brazilian heartland could become profitable investments on the periphery thanks to the fiscal policies of the state and its help in the provision of physical infrastructure.

A substantial part of Brazil's publicly guaranteed overseas debt was acquired to exploit the supposed resources of Amazonia; historically, of course, the Brazilian outback is no stranger to debt bondage. In 1981 a new development strategy (Polonoroeste) was declared for Rondônia and the western part of Mato Grosso. Polonoroeste eschewed the capital-intensive, export-orientated philosophy of Polamazonia and substituted one in which environmental conservation (through restricted deforestation and sustainable agriculture based on the cultivation of cocoa, coffee, and rubber) and an improved social infrastructure were the basic aims (Mahar 1983, 322). Unfortunately, the program coincided with a decline in the government's disposable income. Economic concentration in 1981, the global debt crisis in 1982, the failure of voluntary austerity programs and their substitution by those in line with the IMF, and the withdrawal by the new government in 1985 from its agreements with the IMF all contributed to the government's failure to meet its share of the cost of Polonoroeste. The World Bank, which agreed to contribute one-third of the $1.5 billion capital needed to carry the project, withdrew its support in 1985 following a critical report on the scheme by the U.S. Congress in 1984.

Military rule came to an end in 1985, although vestiges remained in the border regions. Democracy, in 1986, did not bring with it any genuine change in development policy; other problems loomed larger. President José Sarney's term of office was marked by spiraling inflation—briefly checked under the short-lived Cruzado Plan of 1986 and the tougher Summer Plan of 1989—a rapprochement with the IMF in 1988, increased expenditures on servicing the public debt, and uncertainty in other areas of public expenditure: the public sector deficit in 1989 was 12 percent of gross domestic product (GDP). The reduced ability to fund longer-term development plans led to widespread disillusionment over the public sector's ability to promote growth and development. The 1989 Program for the Development of the Frontier Fringe of Western Amazonia (Proffao), which gave the military wider powers in those areas (such as Acre) where the "problems of isolation are most grave" (Allen 1990, 16), largely confirmed that view. In addition, increased international concern with the environmental damage being done by developments within Amazonia called a halt to some of Amazonia's externally financed projects.

The election of President Fernando Collor de Mello in March 1990 (when inflation was running 6 percent per day) brought immediate monetary reform and the promise of the same kind of neoliberal, market-orientated economic policy that Bolivia initiated five years earlier: strict control over the money supply, a floating exchange rate, the removal of subsidies, a balanced budget, a reduction in public expenditure, tax reform, the privatization of state-owned companies, and the removal of trade barriers. To some extent, western Amazonia had been pursuing its own informal monetarist policies before Collor's dramatic decree. Public expenditure had been reduced, the involvement of the state in the local economy had not reached the levels elsewhere in the country, taxes were lower, many of the services provided by the state elsewhere were met by the informal or private sector, and free market exchange rates were widely employed. Accordingly, the difficulties of adjustment, which will face all parts of Brazil should economic reform be sustained (and in late 1990 the IMF seemed reasonably satisfied with progress), will be less severe in Rondônia and adjoining frontier territories than in the "industrial triangle" of São Paulo–Rio de Janeiro–Belo Horizonte; this will help maintain the slight movement in the direction of decentralization in the immediate future.

The Yellow-Brick Road

The importance of the state in promoting decentralization can be illustrated by the impact of the national road-building program on Rondônia. The opening of the 1,500 kilometer long road (BR-364) from Cuiabá to Porto Velho in 1970 has been the most important catalyst of change in Amazonia; it genuinely linked a frontier area with settled Brazil. Tens of thousands of spontaneous immigrants from Paraná and Rio Grande do Sul have streamed into Rondônia along the road. Seventy percent of those from Paraná interviewed in 1980 were landless agricultural laborers, victims of a policy of agricultural modernization, made redundant as mechanized soy cultivation replaced hand tillage and the demand for labor in coffee plantations fell.

The early migrants benefited from the possibly fortuitous fact that the road cut through a zone of relatively fertile red clay soils subsequently discovered to cover no more than 10 percent of Rondônia (a proportion high by Amazonian standards); these soils gave the (then) territory a misleadingly favorable reputation among later migrants. The flow of immigrants continued at an accelerating rate: from about 60,000 a year in the 1970s, to 100,000 a year between 1980 and 1983, to 160,000 between 1984 and 1987. Some migrants have moved on as part of a continuing frontier process: feeder roads were built and the extension of the Transamazonica westward from Porto Velho into Acre acted as a valve during the second half of the 1980s. Nevertheless, the population of Rondônia was growing by 14 percent per year in the late 1980s.

Life for the recent settlers is more difficult than for the earlier pioneers. A poorly educated migrant with few resources save his muscles finds himself at the bottom of an existing social and economic structure. The general infertility of the soils, the inequalities of land tenure, the exacting impact of cattle raising, and the longer-term environmental costs of tax-offset schemes have all helped dampen initial enthusiasm and confidence in the long-term agricultural potential of much of the area. By mid-1989 a quarter of the forests of Rondônia had been cleared and much of the land left unusable. The damage done to the traditional forest-gathering economies was seemingly irremediable. Increasing international concern about the direct and indirect effects of the reduction of the Amazonian forests froze international funding of the extension of the road into Acre and forced the government to review its policies.

Much of the new agricultural production of Rondônia and Acre is for subsistence, and its economic contribution can only be estimated. It clearly contributes to supporting some of the one in ten Brazilian migrants who prefer to move to Amazonia rather than to the towns and cities of the center. But even on Brazil's northwest frontier, urban life has a stronger draw than rural life. Indeed, fewer than half of today's migrants intend to work on the land.

Mining and the Role of the *Garimpeiros*

The remarkable contribution that minerals have made to the regional economy during the past decade is more readily measurable. Mining in Amazonia has been favored by government economic policies, and parastatal companies have been heavily involved in the new developments; mining projects have attracted substantial external investment and overseas credits and have drawn directly or indirectly upon the expertise of the world's multinational mining houses. In general, geographic dispersion of activity has been balanced by strong central control. Although benefits have accrued to Amazonia, the interests of national and international bodies have been paramount. Although mining still contributes a relatively small proportion of the national GDP, the mines of Amazonia make a larger contribution to export earnings. Indeed, whatever their contribution to the decentralization of economic activity within Brazil, new mining ventures have given Amazonia a position of central importance in several international metal markets and positions far from the periphery in a number of others.

Rondônia has shared in the remarkable development of mining during the past quarter of a century.[5] But mining in Rondônia has followed a different pattern than elsewhere. It has not come about through the mechanisms of deliberate planning and heavy capital investment in modern techniques of bulk mineral extraction and expensive transport infrastructure. Rather, it has grown through the efforts and hardships of large numbers of independent prospectors, the *garimpeiros*, with the minimum participation of the state and only a modest contribution from national mining companies. In twenty years the *garimpeiros* have turned Rondônia into a producer of minerals on a par with Bolivia. As in Bolivia, tin and gold have been the key elements.

Alluvial and eluvial cassiterite, the oxide of tin, was discovered in Rondônia in the 1960s (hence the subsequent Bolivian interest in the Bolivian side of the border), and in 1970 an estimated 40,000 *garimpeiros* and would-be *garimpeiros* poured into the territory as the new road helped make it accessible. In 1971, 2,250 tons of tin concentrate (the production of a single medium-sized Bolivian mine at the time and virtually all of Brazil's output) emerged from remote Rondônia. With new discoveries, production tripled by 1980. It increased a further fourfold during the decade; in 1989 production was perhaps 30,000 tons. Much of that production came from the Bom Futuro deposits near Ariquemas. These were discovered as recently as September 1987. Within weeks of the discovery, 10,000 freelance miners made a huge clearing in the forest, which became studded with open pits and craters; two years later, 45,000 men were at work. In 1989 only Malaysia and Indonesia produced more tin than Rondônia; in the short spell of ten years Brazil has become the world's leading tin producer. Today it effectively controls the world tin market.

The majority of Rondônia's production comes from the *garimpeiros*. Favored subsidiaries of some of the multinational mining companies were granted concessions over the heads of the *garimpeiros* "for public order reasons" but found, even with the support of the army, their rights were unenforceable. The mining companies in Rondônia, unable by force of numbers to assert their rights over their concessions, satisfied themselves by becoming, in effect, purchasing agents of the Bom Futuro concentrates. Paranapanema, Brazil's largest privately owned company built upon the wealth generated by ownership of the Pitinga tin deposit in Roraima (discovered in 1982 and now the most important single source of tin in the world), has been the main official purchaser. It had the most to lose from a flooded market and, *pace* the International Tin Council, has had sufficient funds to meet the cost of a large stockpile. By mid-1990 new legislation had been introduced to strengthen the position of the companies, limit the traditional rights of *garimpeiros*, and reinforce attempts to underpin the world's tin market. The government agreed to the formation of the Empresa Brasileira de Estanho (Ebesa) which would buy up and market some 80 percent of the tin production of the *garimpeiros*. Perhaps more significant was the unrelated decline, to some 20,000, in the volatile population of Bom Futuro: a particularly wet season, the replacement of manpower by bulldozers and dredges, and the discovery of gold at Surucucus in Roraima had turned many of those seeking their fortunes toward another frontier.

It is difficult to value precisely the income generated by the tin fields in recent years. This is partly because for much of the 1980s there were alternatives to the official markets for tin and government policies often made these more attractive—the frontier situation of Rondônia facilitated this. In March 1990 an interministerial commission of the Brazilian government reported that an estimated 20 percent of Brazil's tin production (some 50,200 tons, or 30 percent of the noncommunist world's output) was smuggled out of the country in 1989; it claimed that about 4,000 tons of *garimpeiros'* tin had been smuggled by road into Bolivia. Although tin purchased from *garimpeiros* was subject to a state tax, a major financial incentive to smuggling existed in the big discrepancy, which existed before the Collor reforms, between the official and the "parallel" exchange rates between the *novo cruzado* and the dollar. The domestic price of tin offered by Cacex (the federal import/export agency for cassiterite which banned exports for "strategic purposes" in 1988) was measured in *novo cruzados* at the official, lower, dollar exchange rate; foreign traders (or Brazilians with hard currency) exchanged money for *cruzados* at the parallel rate and then bought tin in Brazil with "cheap" *cruzados*, later selling it abroad at its international value. The discrepancy between the rates made Brazil's centralized bureaucracy vulnerable to a variety of other scams, to the disadvantage of the state and to the enrichment of others (including, indirectly, the decentralized informal economy of Rondônia). Cash-flow problems following the Collor reforms in March 1990 cut the dollar price of tin concentrates in Rondônia by a third; subsequent moves toward a free market exchange rate may legitimize more of Rondônia's production.

A Golden Decade

In recent years Rondônia also has become a major source of gold. This is part of a wider surge in gold production in Brazil over the past ten years: today there are some 16 major gold workings and 2,000 individual operations in Amazonia. National mine production has increased fivefold since 1981 (to 22.8 tons in 1989, a trend to be continued in the 1990s), thanks partly to heavy investments of capital and expertise by South African companies reviving old mines and developing new ones while hedging against political and reserve uncertainties at home. But the major increase has been from *garimpeiros*: they raised their output by over 50 tons in the same period (to about 80 tons in 1989, although only 25 tons were registered with the Departamento Nacional da Produção Mineral). Together their production has made Brazil the world's fifth largest producer of gold.

During the 1980s, Rondônia became one of the major areas of *garimpeiro* gold working in the country. The gold lies in the beds of the rivers' tributary to the Madeira, as in Bolivia, and working conditions are similar. Much of the gold is recovered from many hundreds of primitive dredges: some of the gold is collected by divers working from barges and rafts, clenching air lines between their teeth. It is a dangerous job because air lines can be snagged by floating logs or cut by rival gangs; many divers are hit by the "bends" and find themselves disabled. The death toll among divers is high: since 1980 an estimated 2,000 have lost their lives. There is a more widespread lethal danger from the mercury used to recover the gold; much of if has entered the local environment and many *garimpeiros* and their families are exposing themselves to slow mercury poisoning.

The local price of gold is now pegged to the parallel dollar rate in an attempt by the Collor government to bring more of the production into the open. But the official local price is only about half that of the free market due to the narrowing of the difference between the free market rate and the official rate, the cutting of inflation, and the imposition of an increased revenue-raising 35 percent gold sales tax. These considerations and the cost (although still not heavy as yet) of obeying new environmental laws make it likely that a substantial proportion of the production will continue to be deflected into the shadowy black economy for some time to come. An educated guess of the annual value of the *garimpeiros'* input to the informal economy of tin and gold production in 1989 and 1990 is about $300 million. This gives an indication of the deficiencies inherent in using official data to calculate, for example, national indexes of decentralization.

Tens of thousands work in the gold *garimpo*, and the total number of those in Rondônia dependent upon the incomes of the *garimpeiros* must be about a quarter of a million people. Although mining economists and civil servants may dislike the lack of accountability of the *garimpeiro*, few would minimize his importance as an informal agent of decentralization on the cutting edge of the frontier. The *garimpeiro* system is one that has stood the test of time in pioneer Amazonia. It provides employment and thus a degree of temporary security in an otherwise precarious existence. The system normally requires the *garimpeiro* to supply his labor and equipment and the so-called *fornecedores*—most of them businessmen from outside the region—to stake in advance the capital costs (food and sometimes other supplies) of a prospecting venture; both parties share equally the proceeds of a successful exploration and accept their share of the risks of failure. Such security is rarely more than a fleeting experience and, as in farming, is vulnerable to the vagaries of adverse weather. What the system does offer is the freedom to work without supervision and some vestige of hope for a better future. A very large number of very poor people benefit from the system: there are probably 500,000 *garimpeiros* at work in Amazonia (estimates vary between 300,000 and one million), ten times the number formally employed in mining. Although short-term gains to those in the system are apparent, long-term benefits are uncertain: robber economies leave little in the bank for the future. With time it seems likely that the interests of the *garimpeiro* will be sacrificed to those of organized capital, and the authority of the state will play a larger part in the development of the region. This may move the balance of advantage away from the periphery and toward the center once again.

CONCLUSIONS

The examples used in this chapter show how the particular attributes of frontier regions may be harnessed, wittingly or unwittingly, to counter the tendency toward centralization that has for long been a characteristic of Latin American countries. The peopling of previously empty lands has brought new resources into play; the opening up of national economies to international forces has helped give added value to places previously marginal to the concern of the state (Figure 2.2); the interest of supranational development agencies in fostering cross-border cooperation has helped draw attention to opportunities previously ignored or unknown.

Some frontiers are regions where the major forces at work are those that drive the individual entrepreneur to exploit them for his own ends; questions of the legality or illegality of his actions and of the long-term impact of his activities on the environment or on society are small matters compared with the imperative of making a living and caring for his family. The tangible benefits from what history may later recognize as a parasitic economy may have more immediate appeal than the longer-term returns of sustainable development. This gives some frontiers a dynamism and a character missing elsewhere. Other frontier regions have been co-opted into the conventional life of the state, and the state has recognized some of the benefits that can accrue from exploiting their peculiar spatial properties.

The decentralizing role of frontier areas in Latin America is likely to persist. In the nature of things there are more untapped natural resources to be discovered there than in the old core areas; new colonists tackling new problems may lead to desirable innovations; and the rigidities imposed by an existing social structure are likely to be lessened. Frontier regions have ceased to be national cul-de-sacs and are increasingly viewed as international crossroads. The political and economic policies of almost all the Latin American countries as well as pressures from outside may be expected to further decentralization at the national scale and bring benefits to the continent. Whether the same claim can be made on an intercontinental scale seems less certain. The whole of Latin America is peripheral to the global core of the industrialized countries. Many of the changes that have been described or implied in the frontier regions have been stimulated by the demands of the First World; in satisfying these demands, the gross economic, political, and social disparities between the North and the South are made more apparent.

NOTES

1. See, for example, *The Economist*, 7628, 11 November 1989, 16; "From basket case to test case," *The IDB*, August 1989, 7. Contextual material on Bolivia may be found in *Bolivia: Quarterly Analysis of Economic and Political Trends* (written since 1985 for the Economist Intelligence Unit by David Fox).

2. For fuller accounts of changes in the Bolivian mining industry, see the annual summaries in the *Mining Annual Review* (Fox 1979–); for a fuller review of the impact of government policies on the mining industry since 1985, see Fox (1990). UNITAS (1987) documents some of the effects of the crisis on the miners and their families.

3. For an early account of coca growing in the Chaparé, see South (1977); for more recent accounts, see Eastwood and Pollard (1986) and, for example, "The cocaine economies," *The Economist*, 8 October 1988, 25–28. Colin Sage (Wye College, University of London) is preparing a report on the substitution program following field work in 1990.

4. For recent reviews of Brazilian policies toward Amazonia, see Mahar (1989), who argues for a new agroecological zoning approach to development policies; Hall (1989), who offers a critique of the lessons to be learned from the Greater Carajás Program; Treece (1987), who details the deleterious impact of the same program on the indigenous Indians; Bunker (1985), who reviews the underdevelopment of Amazonia and explores the incompatibility between centralized objectives and sustainable development; Moran (1983), who has edited a series of research findings emphasizing the need for new policies; and Baer (1989), whose review of the Brazilian economy includes, in the latest edition, chapters on regional imbalances and the economic performance of the country up to 1987. Baer (1989, 336) comments that in no year has federal expenditure on explicit regional programs exceeded 10 percent of government investment.

5. For a brief survey of current mining developments in Amazonia, see Fox (1989). Cleary (1990) offers a graphic account of the lives and rewards of the modern Brazilian argonauts. The technical press (for example, *The Mining Journal, The Metal Bulletin, Latin American Commodities Report*) carries occasional reports on contemporary mining matters in Amazonia.

3

Spontaneous Population Decentralization in Peru

Sarah A. Radcliffe

As in other Latin American states, Peru's spatial economy is characterized by a high degree of regional inequalities and the concentration of power, population, and privilege in its capital, Lima. Regional income differentials are highlighted by profound sociocultural and geographic distinctions among the narrow coastal belt, the highland sierra, and the eastern Amazon jungle basin. The Peruvian state is historically weak, divided by regional rivalries and an unconsolidated bourgeoisie and unable to undertake substantial or sustained policies on decentralization. Despite the emergence of development planning in the 1950s, decentralization policies had more notable political than economic impacts and represented intricate attempts at placating regional bourgeoisies and encouraging foreign investment (Slater 1989; Fitzgerald 1979).

Complex structural changes took place in 1968–1980 under the radical military government of General Juan Velasco and to a lesser extent General Francisco Morales Bermudez, who attempted a "Third Path" of development between capitalism and socialism. The Agrarian Reform law of 1969, minimum wage laws in the late 1970s, and state patterns of investment all contributed to the redistribution of population and development around the country, although the major aim of industrial decentralization remained unrealized (Jameson 1979). However, beyond the state's attempts at decentralization, movements such as the spontaneous jungle colonization highlight processes that, in conjunction with the spatial context created by government practice and international factors, influenced decentralizing spatial patterns. These processes arose under conditions of worsening structural economic crisis in Peru's development and have continued since the early 1980s.

It is these processes that are the focus of this chapter. Decentralization is defined here as the reduced control of the center (Lima); the indicators used to highlight the decentralization process include demographic changes and migration flows and the continued buoyancy of the informal sector, all of which occur outside state control. The spatial adjustments arising from these factors are greatly complicated by the existence of gender-differentiated patterns.

From the 1940s, the migration streams to Lima (the primary destination for most internal migrants) slowed progressively; in-migration rates to the capital began to drop while those of emigration rose. Despite continued regional inequalities between the more urbanized and industrialized coast and the largely rural, agricultural Andean sierra, population movements responded to factors above and beyond government regional planning control and the concentration of private investment in Lima. In the 1970s over 26 percent of internal emigrants in the past decade left Lima, the second highest percentage of migrants after the sierra (Aramburu 1983, 70). Between 1972 and 1981, population growth in Lima stagnated due to declining immigration. Other centers of Peru have increased their relative share of population flows (Table 3.1). Although Lima is the center of investment and public employment, other regions have experienced a great expansion in job opportunities. The geographic spread of employment and its increasing diversity transformed the labor markets throughout Peru, thereby initiating an effect on migration flows. As noted by one writer, "Since the 1960s in Peru there has been a reorientation of the migration flows such that now they are directed towards

Table 3.1
Peru: Economically Active Population over Six Years by Sex and Branch of Activity, 1972–1981

Activity	Economically - Active Population (%)			
	1972		1981	
	M	F	M	F
(Population)	(3,071,400)	(800,200)	(3,978,400)	(1,335,500)
Primary a	46.7	18.7	41.3	21.8
Mining	1.7	0.2	2.3	0.4
Manufacturing	11.6	16.1	10.6	10.3
Utilities	0.2	-	0.4	0.1
Construction	5.5	0.2	4.9	0.3
Commerce	9.0	15.8	10.4	16.6
Transport	5.2	0.8	4.9	1.1
Finance	1.2	1.0	2.3	2.2
Services	12.5	37.7	16.7	31.8
Not specified b	6.4	9.5	6.2	15.4
Total	100.0	100.0	100.0	100.0

Source: Census 1972, 1981 (INE 1974, 1983).
[a]Includes agriculture, fishing, and hunting.
[b]Includes those seeking work for the first time.

the intermediate-sized cities, prompting a process of secondary urbanization''
(Aramburu 1983, 67).

This chapter focuses on how population movements responded to changes in
the spatial economy of development in Peru; it does not focus on the policies
of regionalism and development, discussed by others (Slater 1989; Portocarrero 1982; Wilson and Wise 1986; Fitzgerald 1979; Thorp and Bertram 1978;
Stepan 1978; Alarco 1985; Lowenthal 1975; Jameson 1979). What processes
shape population flows and lead to the restructuring of employment around the
country? This chapter suggests that in the 1972–1981 intercensal period decentralization trends arose from the restructuring of labor opportunities that took
place in the 1970s. State planning, while significant in creating the context for
population mobility, was not the sole agent in decentralizing population flows
away from Lima. The dynamic organization of production, reproduction, and
populations in Peru also played a role in decentralizing population flows.

An important distinction needs to be made at this juncture between formal
and informal activities. Formal activities (such as state policies and national
and international development and investment [Fitzgerald 1979]) develop a
particular spatial configuration (Slater 1989), while informal activities (such
as unregulated commerce and spontaneous colonization, drug production, and
smuggling) give rise to alternative labor markets and spatial patterns of production. Formal and informal activities interact to inform population relocation decisions over time and to direct migration flows.[1]

Peripheral in the world economic system, Peru is the site for distinct processes (which reorganize those spatial divisions of labor) occurring in the
developed world (cf. Massey 1984). In First World countries, the relationship between policies and regional economies can be seen as the process of
achieving a spatial configuration beneficial to the capitalist mode of production which subsequently creates a socioeconomic infrastructure limiting further capital accumulation (Massey 1984; Gregory and Urry 1985). Such a
process entails conflict between classes and the simultaneous destruction and
creation of economic relations and class alliances, yet it assumes a degree
of integration among regions of the country.

The contrasts with Third World countries such as Peru are great. First,
in Peru the formal capitalist sector does not provide the major motor for the
transformation of the spatial economy. Beginning in the 1970s, the fastest
population increases and job expansion occurred in regions and sectors
dominated by the ''underbelly'' of the capitalist world economy, especially
informal sector activities and, later, drug production (cocaine). Second, formal planning takes place within an international context of unequal exchange
which channels development and policy in specific directions. In Peru, state
and private priority is for export production with specific spatial implications.
Moreover, state infrastructure is both limited and concentrated in certain urban
centers. Welfare and collective consumption concerns influence labor
redistribution, work opportunities, and hence migration.

PROCESSES WITH UNDERLYING IMPLICATIONS FOR DECENTRALIZATION

Apart from the Agrarian Reform and minimum wage legislation, all the factors analyzed below have influenced labor market structures, demographic processes, and the degree of population decentralization experienced by Peru in the postwar period. Clearly their relative importance varied with the type of government in power, the international context for foreign investment, and the political processes occurring in Peruvian society (Thorp and Bertram 1978; Fitzgerald 1979; Slater 1989). The Agrarian Reform and minimum wage legislation receive more attention here as they were introduced in the 1972–1981 period and are widely regarded as having influenced population decentralization, although this was not the policy intention of either measure.

Changing Production Context

Throughout Peru's history, considerable regional differentiation has persisted, developing inside and between regional class alliances each with their own labor processes and capitals to defend (Wilson and Wise 1986, 107; Slater 1985). Overall, the geographic configuration of labor markets and their structure influence the pattern of population redistribution, as regional demand and redundancy shape the spatial demand for labor.

After the economic crisis of the mid-1970s, Peru's regional divisions of labor became set in the context of a high-inflation, stagnant economy in which manufacturing collapsed. The production context was influenced in these years by state investment that grew significantly (Portocarrero 1982; Wilson and Wise 1986). Government-funded projects in irrigation and capital-intensive development created few jobs and benefited around 100,000 families (Slater 1989, 188; Maos 1985). In the highlands, regional state development projects had a restricted spatial impact due to the concentration on mining enclaves and on energy and transport, while a lack of interregional cohesion over projects enhanced Lima's position. Private investment was encouraged to go into marginal areas, receiving incentives and bank assistance (Wilson and Wise 1986, 99; Jameson 1979).

Labor markets had their own dynamics during the 1970s which held implications for patterns of decentralization. While continuing to be highly gender differentiated, labor markets (particularly urban ones) experienced rapid growth in the female economically active population (EAP), which outpaced increases in male EAP. Between 1972 and 1981, female EAP rose at 3.4 percent annually compared with a 3 percent rise in the male rate, and in urban areas female employment rose at 5.5 percent per annum (Gonzalez Vigil 1983, 115; INE 1983, 27; INE 1984; 34).

Government Policy

With the growth of a formal planning infrastructure in Peru beginning in
the 1960s, regional development and planned decentralization became integral
parts of government rhetoric, espoused by both neoliberal conservatives (Fernando Belaúnde) and military radicals (Fitzgerald 1979, 244–54; Wilson and
Wise 1986). Government policy from the late 1960s to the mid-1980s was
informed by an attempt to reduce regional inequalities and promote development through the exploitation of previously remote or underutilized resources
(Slater 1985, 1989). In practice, however, investment, credit, and facilities
were concentrated on the coast and in export-oriented production with easy
access to the coast (Portocarrero 1982).

The military government's pattern of expenditure had a specific effect on
decentralization. In the 1968–1975 period, four coastal departments received
55 percent of total public investment, while the coast as a whole received
three times the amount given to other regions (Wilson and Wise 1986, 96).
Important too in influencing migration to the coast were state investments
in irrigation projects (Chira-Piura in the north; Majes in Arequipa) and the
subsequent growth in demand for temporary labor (Wilson and Wise 1986,
101; Maos 1985).

While the 1968–1980 period saw policies that exacerbated uneven regional
development by favoring the coast, a slight shift toward the jungle occurred in
1975–1980 when agricultural credit and capital investment in transport and
petroleum grew to account for a greater proportional share of government monies
(Slater 1989, 166). Integrated regional development projects in the jungle (Alto
Huallaga–Bajo Mayo, Pichis-Palcazu) were a belated response to spontaneous
migration from the sierra and were oriented toward extractive industries (Wilson
and Wise 1986, 109). In the 1970s, the jungle departments of Loreto, Madre
de Dios, and San Martín received a high share of state investment for petroleum
extraction and road construction (Slater 1989, 170–74).

More generally, state tourist and social infrastructure investment occurred
during the 1970s and early 1980s, benefiting urban middle classes outside
the capital (Martínez 1983, 232; Wilson and Wise 1986, 106). As the government invested money in departmental capitals for the provision of services
(such as education and health), opportunities for professional employment
rose in tandem and a skilled work force moved to urban areas. In Cuzco,
for example, increases of nonnative female employees in 1972–1981 far outpaced increases of nonnative male employees, responding to rising female
employment opportunities in state education and health departments. In
numerous cities, tourism developed with state initiative; in Cuzco and Puno,
the tourism sector received both state and private investment. By 1983, the
three departments of Cuzco, Puno, and Arequipa received some 16 percent
of the grants to departmental development corporations (Organismo Regional
de Desarrollo, or ORDES).

Overall, however, in the 1970s, "many apparently decentralized projects tend[ed] to reinforce the prevailing concentration of economic activity in the most developed zones" (Portocarrero 1982, 452). Lima and the coast continued to receive high priority, despite government rhetoric espousing industrial decentralization.

Private Initiative

Private initiative must be considered in both its economic and political aspects, as Peru has experienced the rise of independent economic sectors (often with low capital inputs) as well as the rise of a politically significant regionalism. Beginning in the 1930s, governments had to consider regionally based political powers in Arequipa and the southern highlands which had autonomous economic bases. By the 1970s, regional movements and economies had shifted spatially to emphasize the northern coastal areas economically and the jungle departments politically.

During the 1970s in the formal sector, private industry tended to form centralized spatial economies by locating on the coast. The state left decentralizing locational decisions to the private sector, a policy that effectively reinforced centralization. Benefiting from preexisting infrastructure and government concessions, international investment concentrated its activities on the coastal region, especially in Lima-Callao with its easy access to port facilities and bureaucracy. This process was confirmed when, with the introduction of IMF policies in the late 1970s, a number of state-owned industries were privatized.

Nevertheless, economic infrastructure development, although minimal, underpinned the growth of provincial economies and the emergence of regional middle classes (Guillen 1983; Slater 1985). In turn, these classes created demand for services, with effects on population distribution. It is these regional classes, comprising small and medium farmers, manufacturers,and organized labor, that pressured the state during the late 1970s to reactivate regional development ORDES, which provided political loci but few economic benefits (Wilson and Wise 1986, 106; Fitzgerald 1979; Slater 1985).

Significantly, it was non-state-directed rural development that led to the expansion of the agricultural frontier and its associated labor markets independently of the Agrarian Reform. With the agricultural frontier's extension into the selva, maize and rice production expanded at this time, creating demand for labor on medium-sized farms (Verdera 1986, 36–38; Figueroa 1985; Caballero and Alvarez 1980).

Segregated Labor Markets

Between 1940 and 1981, Peruvian labor markets retained their historical gender-segregated structure, with profound implications for the nature of population flows and the impact of decentralizing factors on male and female workers (see Table 3.1). In the 1972–1981 period, however, the spatial configuration of these labor markets had distinct effects for decentralization by gender.

During the 1970s, female employment underwent considerable changes in terms of size and sectorial activity: a massive incorporation of women into the labor market took place, canceling out their specialization in manufacturing employment (Yáñez 1985, 164). Increasing female economic participation arose from women's urbanward migration and the incorporation of previously "inactive" women into the labor market. As the economic crisis developed in the mid- to late 1970s, families were forced to diversify their sources of income, and older women entered the labor market in force. Throughout the 1970s, female employment remained segregated in certain sectors that often lay outside government regulation. In 1974, 85 percent of economically active women were employed in predominantly female occupational categories (excluding agriculture). Out of a total of 107 occupational categories, just 12 accounted for two-thirds of working women (Scott 1984, 169).[2] Women's work was found particularly in the informal sector, usually filled by migrant women or older women, themselves often ex-migrants. Nevertheless, a concentration of female workers in informal activities continued alongside formal sector participation, where they were found in a limited number of industries (Scott 1984, 45). Within manufacturing, nine-tenths of women were found in consumer goods production (Yáñez 1985, 147).

In terms of national labor markets, male manufacturing employment in Lima increased in total numbers between 1972 and 1981, although its percentage share declined. Writers have noted that this change determined a shift in population distribution away from Lima (Verdera 1986). The fastest-growing employment sectors for men in Lima were commerce and sales, which jumped by 62 and 66 percent, respectively, and between them accounted for 51 percent of male jobs in the capital (Scott 1988). Minimum wages had only a tangential impact on these sectors of male employment. While the factors listed above tended toward male population decentralization, job opportunities for women continued to be located in urban areas, particularly on the coast. The regional implications of this pattern for decentralizing population are examined below.

Agrarian Reform

Designed to develop agriculture and indirectly slow the pace of rural-urban migration, the Agrarian Reform of 1969 was introduced by the progressive government of General Velasco. To develop the rural sector, a class of large dominant landowners was removed from their rural power base, thereby transforming social structures and breaking up large estates, although the reform's land-distributive effects were relatively minor. In place of hacienda estates, cooperative-type agrarian ventures were introduced on the coast and in the highlands, former hacienda workers received land and work in the new enterprises (Caballero and Alvarez 1980).

Within the context of the Agrarian Reform, two factors particularly influenced the nature of population decentralization. First, the population-retention effects of the Agrarian Reform were highly unequal geographically and had a decentralizing effect largely on the coast (in the sense of retaining population in the coastal countryside and regional capitals). Second, the reform had distinct effects on men and women, due to the state definitions of beneficiary status.

The reform's impact was greatest on the coast: census data show that urbanization was relatively unimportant in this region, despite high population increases. On the coast, permanent workers received the most land per family (3.8 standardized hectares) and represented the largest share of beneficiaries (25 percent) (Caballero and Alvarez 1980, 45). By contrast, the Andean villages, historically those providing a large share of rural-urban migrants, received the smallest average amount of land. Peasant villagers comprised about half of the sierra beneficiaries, although the actual amounts of land redistributed to this group were tiny (0.4 standardized hectares, mostly poor quality pasture land). The ability of the Agrarian Reform provisions to slow migration, by turning potential migrants into landowners and small farmers, was thus unequal geographically. In the highlands, the reform did not provide adequate means of sustained peasant livelihood, and migration on a permanent and temporary basis continued. In highland departments where peasant communities comprised the majority of the rural population, urbanization quickened in 1972–1981.

Moreover, the ability of the reform to create employment was limited, even directly after its implementation. According to one analyst, the reform's capacity to generate employment affected 16.6 percent of the agricultural work force and 25 percent of the rural population in need of work (Caballero and Alvarez 1980, 53). Both on the coast and in the sierra, beneficiaries of the reform were forced to maintain diverse income-generating activities including seasonal or permanent migration. Members of coastal cooperatives continued to work outside the enterprise: one study found that around 70 percent of household heads had at least one other employment (Figueroa 1985, 14). Similarly, members of highland SAIS (cattle ranches with peasant villages) combined work on private plots and other activities to supplement work in communal enterprises. In terms of expressed policy, the Agrarian Reform was unsuccessful, unable to provide employment, land, and adequate living standards to a large percentage of rural dwellers.

Furthermore, the gender-differentiated impact of the reform released women from rural areas, as they were excluded from beneficiary status (except as widows and single mothers with young children [Deere and León de Leal 1982]). However, although changes in the census definition of female agricultural work render estimates difficult and preliminary,[3] it is clear that in certain jungle and highland areas female agricultural labor increased (INE 1983; Scott 1988). In other areas, women were excluded from participation in rural development and migrated to nearby and distant cities (Wilson 1985; Radcliffe 1986).

Minimum Wage Legislation

The differential effect of the Agrarian Reform was followed by national minimum wage legislation, introduced in 1978. Minimum wage laws attempted to guarantee subsistence income levels for large sectors of the population. The influence of these laws on migration flows remains to be put in context, because Peruvian labor markets in 1972–1981 expanded in sectors, such as the informal sector, where wage security does not apply. While the government effectively applied minimum wage legislation to certain occupations (in petrochemical industries and on the coast [Slater 1989]), it did not (and could not) cover an increasing share of the working population in the unregulated informal economy. During the late 1970s, moreover, the minimum wage lost value consistently (Slater 1985, 155).

Gender differences in the nature of labor markets were significant in determining the impact of minimum wages on labor markets at a regional level, although the pattern in both male and female labor markets was for increased reliance on informal sector employment. While male employment declined in manufacturing and rose markedly in the commercial sector, unregulated domestic service remained a significant female work option as did informal commerce.

SHIFTS IN MIGRATION FLOWS, 1972-1981

The decades between 1940 and 1981 saw many changes in the population geography of Peru: as in other Latin American and Third World countries, Peru underwent a rapid process of urbanization and internal migration, which resulted in the increase of urban population from 47.4 percent in 1961 to 65.2 percent in 1981.[4] As noted above, Lima was the first city to attract the increasingly mobile population (1940–1950), followed by other coastal cities, such as Arequipa (1950–1960), and then Trujillo and Chimbote (1960–1970) (see Figure 3.1; Yacher 1987).[5]

In 1972–1981, the direction and pace of migration around Peru changed significantly. The extent and reasons for this shift are the focus of the rest of this chapter. From receiving 56 percent of internal migrants recorded in 1972, Lima's share declined to 45 percent in 1981 (Aramburu 1983)—Lima still received some half a million people, a larger number than other cities. Lima also contained approximately 28 percent of the population and a third of its labor force, with its population of 4.6 million (Aramburu 1983). Between 1972 and 1981, Lima grew at 3.9 percent per annum, well above the

Figure 3.1
Population Changes in Peru, 1972–1981

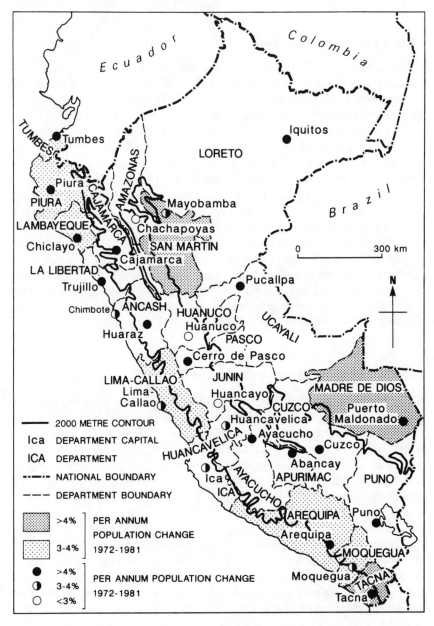

national average of 2.6 percent; it thus continued to grow, although at a slower pace than previously. In this capacity, the metropolitan area remained the center of government, administration, and industry.

Urbanization of the population remained an important trend throughout the country in this period: overall, urban populations grew at 3.9 percent per annum, compared with a rural average of 0.8 percent per annum. In 1972–1981, the fastest urban growth rates were recorded for cities of the jungle and frontier departments and to a lesser extent for highland departmental capitals (see Table 3.2). Sierra cities such as Cuzco, Puno, Ayacucho, Abancay, and Cajamarca grew rapidly, as did smaller towns (Verdera 1986, 30). The entire departments of Arequipa and Huánuco gained population with general development and mining, respectively (Aramburu 1983, 70). How do these population and migration trends relate to the processes affecting

Table 3.2
Peru: Population Growth by Department and Departmental Capitals, 1972–1981

Department	Popn. (1981)	% p.a. change (1972 - 1981)	Departmental capital (% p.a. change 1972 - 1981)	
Amazonas	268,121	2.59	Chachapoyas	(1.7)
Ancash	853,896	1.31	Huaraz	(4.1)
Apurimac	342,964	0.68	Abancay	(4.9)
Arequipa	738,482	3.16	Arequipa	(4.4)
Ayacucho	523,821	0.93	Ayacucho	(5.2)
Cajamarca	1,083,267	1.32	Cajamarca	(4.7)
Cuzco	874,463	1.64	Cuzco	(4.5)
Huancavelica	361,548	0.42	Huancavelica	(3.2)
Huanuco	505,653	1.71	Huanuco	(2.6)
Ica	446,902	1.97	Ica	(3.0)
Junin	896,962	2.45	Huancayo	(2.9)
La Libertad	991,913	2.27	Trujillo	(4.4)
Lambayeque	708,820	3.29	Chiclayo	(4.5)
Lima-Callao	5,447,345	3.87	Lima-Callao	(3.8)
Loreto	474,973	-1.21	Iquitos	(5.1)
Madre de Dios	35,788	4.23	Pto. Maldonado	(10)
Moquegua	103,283	3.24	Moquegua	(3.5)
Pasco	230,989	2.49	Cerro de Pasco	(4.9)
Piura	1,155,682	3.01	Piura	(4.4)
Puno	910,377	1.20	Puno	(5.6)
San Martín	331,692	4.18	Mayobamba	(3.9)
Tacna	147,693	4.84	Tacna	(5.6)
Tumbes	108,064	3.62	Tumbes	(4.2)
Ucayali [a]	219,533	-	Pucallpa	(5.1)
Peru	17,762,231	2.58		

Source: Elaborated from census statistics by the Instituto Nacional de Estadística (1983) and Yacher (1987).

[a]Ucayali was created in 1980 from Loreto Department.

decentralization discussed above? We now turn to analyze the specific regional trends in the 1972–1981 period that indicate some degree of population decentralization.

POPULATION DECENTRALIZATION, 1972–1981

During the 1970s, diverse regional developments led to the redistribution of distinct labor types and the reorientation of migration flows. By focusing on labor market structure and segregation within the context of socioeconomic changes and state policies, a regionally specific picture of population decentralization can be gained (see Figure 3.1; Table 3.3). Three types of nonmetropolitan growth areas for 1972–1981 are the focus of this analysis: jungle departments, frontier coastal departments, and sierra cities.

Table 3.3
Peru: Departments Ranked by Population Growth, with Economic Specializations[a]

Department	% pa growth (1972-1981)	Regional Economies (coefficient of specialization)	
Tacna	4.84	Diverse industries	(3.2)
Madre de Dios	4.23	Foodstuffs	(6.8)
San Martín	4.18	Tobacco	(24.6)
Lima-Callao	3.89	Mixed industries	
Tumbes	3.62	Wood & cork	(85.2)
Lambayeque	3.29	Petrol & derivatives	(8.6)
Moquegua	3.24	Chemicals	(18.7)
Arequipa	3.16	Mixed processing industries	
Piura	3.01	Petrol	(28.2)
Amazonas	2.59	Foodstuffs	(5.9)
Pasco	2.49	Wood & cork	(84.0)
Junin	2.45	Nonferrous metals	(13.1)
La Libertad	2.27	Foodstuffs	(3.9)
Ica	1.97	Diverse metals	(6.5)
Huanuco	1.71	Wood	(78.0)
Cuzco	1.64	Beverages	(6.7)
Cajamarca	1.32	Foodstuffs	(4.9)
Ancash	1.31	Iron & steel	(33.8)
Puno	1.20	Non-metal mining	(16.8)
Ayacucho	1.93	Diverse processing	(17.8)
Apurimac	0.68	Beverages	(10.4)
Huancavelica	0.42	Drinks	(11.4)
Loreto [b]	-1.21	Wood	(54.3)
Peru	2.58		

Source: Growth rates from Yacher (1987); economic data from Henríquez et al. (1979).
[a]Only formal sector economic data are included in these calculations, therefore excluding drug production, smuggling, and informal sector activities.
[b]Ucayali was separated from Loreto in 1980.

The fastest-growing cities, and several of the fastest-expanding departmental populations, were located in tropical jungle areas east of the Andes. Departmental growth rates in Madre de Dios, San Martín, and Loreto reached between 4.23 percent and 4.18 percent per annum in 1972–1981. Rates of urbanization in these areas varied but were notable in Iquítos (capital of Loreto) and Puerto Maldonado (Madre de Dios): the latter was the fastest-growing city in Peru at 10 percent per annum (from a base of 5,309). By comparison, urban growth in San Martín was negligible.

During the 1970s, as a result of previous state investment, male employment opportunities expanded rapidly in these departments with the development of diverse petrochemical industries in Loreto and with the extraction of primary materials elsewhere (foodstuffs, tobacco, wood and cork, gold). The opening up of agricultural frontiers in the jungle, independent of the Agrarian Reform, offered opportunities to male farmers, who continued to comprise the majority of agricultural labor. Colonization appeared to arise from spontaneous moves by sierra peasants.[6] Employment in both formal and informal sectors favored men in jungle departments, particularly in resource extraction (rubber, nuts, gold—for example, male migrants from Cuzco, Puno, and Arequipa moved to Madre de Dios in considerable numbers (Martínez 1983, 226). Similarly, the area around Pucallpa, Loreto, underwent rapid expansion in the 1970s, based on forestry and wood extraction, with a 25.4 percent rise in industrial activity in the 1974–1979 period (Slater 1985, 162).

There were many fewer economic opportunities for women, who comprised a small share of the EAP (14–16 percent compared to the national average of 24.6 percent). Nevertheless, a relatively large share of working women were found in domestic service, ranging by department from 13 to 16 percent of female EAP over fifteen years (11.5 percent national average). With the influx of middle-class employers connected with state-run petroleum projects, domestic service was given a boost, no doubt underpinned by drug money[7] (*Quehacer* 1989, 58). Whatever the cause of rising numbers of domestics in the jungle, it is correlated with the explosion of urbanization: Iquítos grew at 5.1 percent while the number of women in domestic service jumped to 10.2 percent. Given the limited female work opportunities, however, it is not surprising that female migrants from all jungle departments outnumbered male migrants (INE 1983). The jungle can thus be characterized as an area of attraction for male migration flows, with growth in economic sectors outside state-controlled developments. This compares with the formal economy-led growth of the frontier coastal departments.

Overall, urban growth on coastal frontiers was higher than departmental growth rates, although the differential was not large (see Table 3.2). The coastal frontier departments were characterized distinctly in terms of economic structure and socioeconomic opportunities for migrants. At opposite ends of the country, Tacna and Tumbes saw rapid demographic growth during the 1970s, while secondary growth occurred in Moquegua, Piura, and Lambayeque (see Figure 3.1). Many of these developments were initiated by state investments in industry and economic infrastructure which continued to be concentrated on the coast. Chimbote (Anchash) grew initially on the basis of the nationalized iron and steel industries and fishmeal production at 3.3 percent per annum, while Piura, Lambayeque, and Moquegua expanded with petrochemical processing. Agricultural investment in large-scale irrigation projects affected Piura and Arequipa.

State investment and policies guaranteed certain job standards and numbers, encouraging migration flows. Minimum wage legislation was applied in state sectors, although pressures on the political economy meant that many work conditions went unregulated. However, expansion of state welfare services effectively increased employment in coastal towns, drawing in a skilled female and male work force. Tumbes was predominantly a male migration center, experiencing a rise in state agricultural investment in the late 1970s, particularly in cattle ranching, while road construction, prompted by geopolitical concerns over Ecuador's border, drew in male laborers (Slater 1989, 175). Tacna, Moquegua, and Lambayeque's diversified economies drew in male and female migrants. Under military rule, Moquegua and Tacna received large-scale investments in the mining sector, boosting employment (Slater 1985, 159), and Tacna provided work for male labor in private and state mines. Moquegua registered the highest state investment share in 1969–1975 for its energy and mining industries, particularly the copper refinery in Ilo near the coast (Slater 1989, 170; Wilson and Wise 1986). By contrast, female migrants found employment in domestic service and in textile manufacture. Female economic participation was relatively high at 21.4 percent with a concentration in the foodstuffs, chemicals, and beverages sectors. In fish canning and processing, nine-tenths of employees were women, highlighting the regional- and gender-segregated labor market structure (Yáñez 1985, 150).

Overall, migration to the coast, especially at the frontiers, involved both men and women. Industrialization has occurred in sectors that employ men and women, while the relative expansion of upper-income groups may have stimulated demand for domestic and other services. The effect of minimum wage legislation cannot be discounted in making these cities relatively more attractive vis-à-vis Lima (Verdera 1986).

The pattern of decentralizing population in the sierra was distinct. The classic view of demographic patterns and migration in Peru has always identified the Andes as the source of peasant migrants to the coast. During the 1970s, however, while it remained true that the sierra provided the largest share of migrants, the latter were increasingly directed internally toward highland cities, rather than outside the region. The percentage of regional emigrants fell by a surprising 9.4 percent between 1967 and 1981, while immigrants rose in the same period (Verdera 1986, 14). In the southern Andes (except Arequipa and Apurimac), intradepartmental moves became the most important by 1972, drawing in population to cities and large towns (Martínez 1983, 218).

Such decentralization entailed the retention of population in local towns, which consolidated their position as central points for underdeveloped rural hinterlands. Departmental growth rates fell below national averages, yet the capitals of Cuzco, Puno, Ayacucho, Abancay, and Cajamarca all saw significant increases over the decade (5.6 percent in Puno; 4.5 percent in Cuzco). Rural stagnation and the expulsion of peasant labor from small plots of land contributed to this regional pattern of development. Puno, Cajamarca, Ayacucho, and Apurimac received insignificant amounts of state investment in 1969–1980, although certain highland departments benefited from private and government investment in tourism, as noted above.

Peasant areas around the highland cities historically supplied a stream of young female domestics. Due to the relatively slower growth of middle classes in these regions, however, female urban employment did not increase proportionately. Much female work in the sierra remained in agriculture[8] and craftwork, both customary sectors of women's employment. By contrast, male migration was oriented toward the cities, especially the southern Andes where expansion in tourism entailed a boom in construction and demand for cheap peasant labor. The expansion of tourism was critical, as it provided the region with a great number of clerical, hotel, and service jobs (Tamayo 1981, 274). In the sierra overall, male opportunities developed in commerce and to a lesser extent in mining. Urbanization in Andean departments appears due to the retention of local male populations and a relative increase in state welfare, which necessitated the immigration of service and professional workers.

During the 1970s then, Peru's spontaneous decentralization process gained certain clear features. Male migration appeared to be decentralizing as it was directed toward rural areas and small provincial towns, as well as nonmetropolitan cities, while female migration continued to be directed urbanward, as female labor markets expanded largely in cities. However, female migration flows to secondary coastal cities outpaced those to Lima, such that a decentering of the female population did occur to some degree.

APPROACHES TO DECENTRALIZATION IN PERU

In the 1972–1981 intercensal years, economic and demographic decentralization shifted in a geographically uneven way, reorienting the spatial relationships between regions while destroying neither the fundamental unevenness of Peru's spatial economy nor the concentration of political power and resources in Lima (Wilson and Wise 1986). Peru remained a highly geographically diverse and unequal country: "Peru is not a national space but a group of regional spaces articulated with Lima" (Gonzalez de Olarte 1982, 218).

If this is true, then to what factors may we attribute shifting population flows around the country in the last intercensal period? The reasons suggested by other writers tend to focus on economic restructuring as a principal factor. The economic crisis of the mid-1970s, it is argued, caused a major reduction in the rate of absorption of migrants into the cities (particularly Lima), while rural stagnation resulted in the growth of highland cities. Verdera (1986) suggests that changes in agrarian structure and a minimum wage policy in the 1970s led to the restructuring of the labor force and a decentralizing income distribution. According to Verdera, minimum wage guarantees made secondary cities relatively more attractive, while the Agrarian Reform resulted in greater labor opportunities in rural areas (with a concomitant rise in the male agricultural labor force). The economic crisis exacerbated these trends, and a decline in manufacturing in Lima led to lower absorption of industrial laborers and a subsequent decline in internal migration toward the metropolitan area (Verdera 1986, 46).

Verdera shows how departmental increases in male agricultural labor, associated with the Agrarian Reform, correlate broadly with lower rates of urbanization. Where male agricultural labor markets expanded quickly (in Junín, Arequipa, Cajamarca, Pasco, and Huánuco) due to the development of agriculture for urban consumption, rates of urbanization slowed. In departments where expansion of agricultural jobs was lower than the national average, such as in the southern Andes, urbanization advanced rapidly, particularly in these regions' capitals.

Although data on minimum wages are relatively weak, Verdera suggests that minimum wages must be taken into account, as there is an inverse relationship between decreasing migration flows to Lima and a certain equalization of income between Lima and the rest of the country. Secondary cities become relatively more attractive to migrants, who are concentrated in low-wage sectors covered by the legislative provision. While this analysis provides a broad picture of factors behind Peru's decentralization, three criticisms can be noted and are related to the nature of the Peruvian state, to regional diversity, and to gender-segregated labor markets.

First, previous analyses of population redistribution grant a central role to the state and its interventions, which have, it is argued, determined the shift in population flows.[9] But despite consolidating an infrastructure and administration for regional planning during the 1970s, the state never fundamentally challenged unequal development (Fitzgerald 1979, 254). In other words, the processes by which regional divisions of labor were created and reproduced over time, through the spatial organization of capital, were only partially state-directed. Such reorganizations of labor take place in both informal and formal economies, upon which state policies have differential and only occasionally decentralizing effects.

Legislation such as Agrarian Reform and minimum wage laws had specific regional implications and gender effects. Rural reform had a geographically skewed impact on job creation and rural security, whereby male coastal workers were affected more than *serranos* (people from the highlands) and female peasants. Similarly, minimum wage legislation affected certain sectors of the labor force and played a spatially differentiated role in the retention of population outside Lima. For example, the rapid expansion of female domestic service employment outside Lima suggests that female migration flows were indeed reorienting away from the capital (Verdera 1986, 50). But the reasons for this decentralizing trend are not the existence of state-guaranteed wages security but rather the changing geography of middle-class employers as the hirers of domestics. Growth rates in numbers of non-Limeña domestics were nearly five times that in the capital, and in 1981 the total numbers of provincial servants outnumbered those in Lima, a reversal of the situation in the 1960s (Verdera 1986, 48–50).[10]

Second, the political economy of the state's priorities underlies a marked regional diversity in levels of development. The degree of regional diversity is underplayed in previous analyses, which tend to ignore the differences in regional resources, culture, income levels, and histories of development. These models have not deepened our understanding of geographic development processes in Peru, despite suggesting a series of important economic factors that have spatial effects (Slater 1989). A detailing of regional economic-demographic processes is thus required to understand tendencies of decentralization.

A final point that needs to be made concerns gender differentiated migration flows. The uneven development of regional economies has gender-differentiated effects. Past models of Peru's decentralization tend to treat migrants as a homogeneous population (Verdera 1986; Slater 1989). However, data on Peruvian migration and circulation patterns reveal the fallacy of this assumption (Escobar and Beall 1982; Martínez 1983; Radcliffe 1986; Laite 1985; Collins 1988), thereby limiting the applicability of such models. Gender differences affect the impact of socioeconomic change in rural areas and explain the continuing movement of female migrants into urban centers, with the simultaneous retention of male populations in rural areas.

Such an approach changes the relative weight placed on Agrarian Reform and minimum wage legislation as factors explaining the reorientation of migration in Peru. Decentralizing processes took place at different rates and directions for the sexes, reinforcing the point that state policies on regional development had an uneven impact on the sexes.

CONCLUSIONS

Between 1972 and 1981, decentralization processes in Peru could not challenge the primacy of Lima: demographic growth in jungle areas, sierra cities, and coastal frontier departments, while rapid and sustained, left Lima as the metropolitan area of the country. Nevertheless, in the 1972–1981 intercensal period, processes leading to demographic decentralization were consolidated, as migration flows and population growth rates outside Lima gained pace. The reorientation of migration flows resulted from several overlapping and interrelated factors. Restructuring of the agricultural sector, especially on the coast, and increased stability in landownership underpinned the development of new employment opportunities for male (and female) agricultural laborers. On the coast, and to a lesser extent in the jungle, agricultural populations were retained in rural areas thereby reducing out-migration to a certain extent and attracting previously urbanward migration. Another crucial factor was provided by the restructuring of nonagricultural sectors, shifting from the relative preponderance of manufacturing to the prevalence of service and commercial jobs among male and female labor forces. While minimum wage legislation necessarily provided for some leveling of income sources between Lima and the provinces, the most notable change in employment was its "informalization," which by definition tends not to gain from government legislation concerning wage levels and work conditions.

While jungle and frontier coastal departments attracted male labor for industry, agriculture, and raw materials extraction, other destinations attracted female labor. Female employment expanded in informal sector jobs and in provincial domestic service, both predominantly urban occupations (Radcliffe 1990). The highest rates of domestic service employment were found in departments with a middle class and fast urbanization rates and in those with long-term departmental capital growth rates (Tacna, Arequipa) (Verdera 1986, 49).

This chapter has concentrated on decentralization in the period from 1972 to 1981, yet many of the same factors mentioned above continued to apply in the late 1980s and early 1990s. President Fernando Belaúnde (1980–1985) responded to sustained pressure from provincial middle classes with populist projects in the regions without increasing regional autonomy or incomes. President Alan García started his term in 1985 with commitments to increase investment in agriculture and to develop the southern sierra, policies that, although not aimed at decentralization per se, held the promise of regional development. Despite introducing a law for the creation of autonomous regions (*Sur* 1989a, 2), García's government was hampered by international debt and an increasingly destructive and costly guerrilla-military war. In the face of these severe limitations on planned decentralization, Lima remains the center of administration, government, industry, education, and investment. The economic crisis worsened in the 1980s: average household incomes fell from a factor of 100 in 1980 to 76.1 in 1983; by 1984 only a third of workers were adequately employed (Slater 1989, 191). After 1987, deepening economic instability was clear: inflation reached some 2,300 percent per annum in April 1990, living standards fell constantly for the majority, and political violence became generalized throughout the country, causing international emigration and the movement of refugees to Lima (Bourque and Warren 1989).

The context of the growing informalization of the economy and the relative collapse of formal sector activities in the 1980s would appear to have highlighted certain trends toward decentralization, especially in relation to frontier and jungle areas. Since the 1981 census, the relative attractiveness of frontier regions has been enhanced. With food subsidies in Peru and high inflation in neighboring countries, profits were made by smuggling goods for sale abroad. Beginning in the early 1980s, significant expansion occurred in opportunities for smuggling across international boundaries, and it is likely that these opportunities drew in population (*Sur* 1989b, 4). Coca production for the international drug trade since 1975 transformed the jungle economy of San Martín and Loreto. During the 1980s, coca production for cocaine processing grew rapidly and extensively in this region: the Huallaga valley in San Martín became the largest coca-producing area in the world. Coca production was largely a male sector in terms of employment (*Quehacer* 1989, 55). Although coca had been grown for thousands of years by Andean peasants, the internationalization of cocaine processing increased demand and encouraged small farmers to colonize high jungle on the eastern Andean slopes (Morales 1986). While the illegality of this production restricts data availability, ethnographic sources suggest that peasants who previously moved to Lima may prefer now to migrate to the jungle.

Decentralization processes thus occurred within a worsening economic, political, and social crisis from which Peru was unable to recover (Amat y León and Monroy 1988). Overall, contemporary decentralizing processes were occurring within a "crisis economy." The restructuring of employment was based not on productive growth (although there were exceptions) but more characteristically on sectors such as informal commerce, drug growing in San Martín and Loreto, and smuggling. Such a crisis economy could not provide the basis for sustained redistributive development; it exacerbated a haphazard, uneven, and largely unregulated response to the situation of regional development.

The experiences of the past twenty years, however, demonstrate how the state and mobilized regional groups can have an impact on regional development and decentralization (Ballon 1986). In the future, it can only be hoped that constructive and sustained political and economic decentralization regain their importance and that Peru balances out the regional and social inequalities that characterized it in the early 1990s.

NOTES

1. A focus on both factors is justified by the partial role played by the state in directing decentralization and development (Portocarrero 1982; Wilson and Wise 1986; Slater 1989). Changes in population flows arise through the growth of the informal sector, through gender divisions of labor, through the transformation of production, and through state action.

2. They included nurses, teachers, midwives, secretaries, social workers, librarians, domestic servants, washerwomen, cooks, seamstresses, hairdressers, and dietitians (Scott 1984, 34).

3. Verdera (1986) discounts data on female participation in agriculture, due to a "disproportionate" rise in female EAP arising from the definitional changes.

4. Peruvian census data defines "urban" as including all towns over 2,000 inhabitants plus district and provincial capitals, regardless of size. Census data are limited in overall validity, due to underrepresentation and/or inaccuracy in rural and remote areas.

5. See Slater (1989), Fitzgerald (1979), and Thorp and Bertram (1978) for details of earlier periods.

6. Government action came later when Belaúnde's government in the early 1980s attempted to create local development projects (Wilson and Wise 1986, 109).

7. Migrant women may also enter prostitution, although information on this occupation is lacking.

8. Census data underestimate female participation in agriculture in the Andes (Deere and León 1982), while cultural norms undervalue women's contributions (Radcliffe 1986).

9. Writing about regional changes undergone by Peru during recent years has a similar tendency to emphasize official state interventions, which admittedly benefit from more complete data sets (Wilson and Wise 1986; Slater 1989; Fitzgerald 1979; Jameson 1979).

10. Domestic service employment may be underestimated in official figures, due to legislation that denies employment.

4

The Role of Intermediate Cities in Decentralization: Observations from Ecuador

Stella Lowder

Decentralization is often interpreted as a desirable developmental process without much consideration as to what it entails or what it can be expected to achieve. In Ecuador, government administrative agencies have treated decentralization as no more than a classificatory device to distribute state infrastructure equitably across the territory, while planners associate the process with regional development projects. Neither of these interpretations challenges existing highly centralized decision-making structures or takes into account the impact of private-sector processes. Moreover, they both ignore the possibility that state action may exacerbate spatial unevenness in well-being. Ecuador's overt efforts, since the early 1960s, to stimulate economic development often rebounded in unexpected ways on particular sectors and regions, just as measures to promote social well-being exaggerated spatial differences once filtered by class and occupational groups. The rigidly hierarchical administrative system based on provinces, cantons, and parishes tended to benefit capitals of the provinces regardless of economic dynamism or of need; the activities that generated the most positive regional overspill were seldom those promoted at great expense by the state, many of whose organizations strengthened centralization.

This chapter considers the case for decentralization in one of the smallest Latin American countries, whose fortunes have been closely tied to export earnings. As the analysis of the impact of state policies reveals, development usually has been interpreted in terms of the national economy rather than in terms of the prosperity of individual regions and social groups, whose comparative standard of living often has been affected adversely. The repercussions of general economic policies are also revealed in the patterning of the demographic and employment structures of individual towns and cities.

These variations reflect less the type of activity in a settlement's hinterland and more the organizational structure of that activity. Moreover, a detailed examination of five cities reveals how the association of highly centralized and hierarchical administrative systems with fragmented localized power groups contributes to the very different fortunes of particular regions.

THE CASE FOR DECENTRALIZATION

Ecuador is a small country in terms of population (9.5 million, 1985 estimate). Its present levels of gross domestic product (GDP) have been attained relatively recently and on the back of oil revenues. The country has two primary cities—the hubs of land and air transport systems—which house the greatest concentrations of educated labor, higher salaries, and high-level services. They monopolize commerce and industry: in 1974–1979 only just over a quarter of manufacturing jobs and a mere 15 percent of investment was located outside capital-city provinces. Entrepreneurs seem unwilling to consider any other locations; recently, the capital high in the Andes acquired plants that refine palm oil and make wood veneers, even though the inputs for palm oil and wood veneers are produced on the coast and in Amazonia, respectively. Given that most new industries produce consumer nondurables, the wisdom of decentralizing this production is questionable. The lack of substantial locational change arising from the few statutory measures formulated reflects these realities.[1]

Has development been constrained by the concentration and centralization of resources in the primary cities? Few would deny that the present levels of concentration of both public and private financial and executive structures are inefficient and disadvantage those residing elsewhere. In 1974, the political capital, Quito, and the commercial capital, Guayaquil, had by far the highest per capita fiscal incomes; Quito accounted for the highest per capita public investment, while Guayaquil benefited from the highest per capita fiscal expenditure (JUNAPLA 1977). Quito accounted for nearly a third of public employees in 1982; all employment contracts of civil servants, regardless of where they served, were validated there, as were their prospects for promotion and nearly all of their monthly salaries. Every loan and patient treated by the social security agency was registered in Quito.

The private sector was equally concentrated and centralized; over 40 percent of all private employees worked in Guayaquil. In 1987 the primary cities absorbed 86 percent of the credit extended by private banks; few branches existed in towns of under 15,000 people (Portais 1987). Every senior line officer of any government agency or private firm spent much time in either Quito or Guayaquil seeking permission to proceed with quite minor matters. Every entrepreneur is forced to do likewise when dealing with the paperwork attached to imports and exports, credit, insurance, and sundry permits. Such a degree of centralization in a country where transport is unreliable and time consuming is clearly disadvantageous to those located outside the favored centers, while increasing the congestion for those within.

Ecuadorian governments have defined decentralization in practice as the greater spatial distribution of production and greater equity in regions' urban infrastructure. Highly centralized administrative structures have been utilized to achieve those ends. The first was approached through infrastructural investments planned at the national level and through three regional development agencies concentrating on developing hydraulic resources funded and controlled by the central government. Only one such agency concerned itself with a poverty-stricken area; it was comparatively underfunded and operated under local direction (Lowder 1990a). Efforts to achieve greater urban equity were also highly centralized: in 1981, only 19 percent of municipal income stemmed from the taxes and service charges generated locally (CONADE 1981, 9–12). The rest was made up of grants and loans doled out by central institutions funded from national taxes and oil revenues, such as the National Participation Fund (FONAPAR) or the National Municipal Development Fund (FODEM). While the grants from the former were supposed to redress economic imbalances, the loans were directed at locations where infrastructural investments were most likely recuperable through commercial charges. In both cases, the volume of funds allocated to any municipality depended on yet another tier of central agencies, the Fund for National Development (FONADE) and the Consortium for National Development (CONADE), respectively.

Representatives from other provinces argue that a greater distribution of resources is unlikely while political and economic power and decision-making is centralized and concentrated in space. At present there is a vicious circle of self-fulfilling prophecies; low municipal power and resources result in low pay and poorly trained and motivated staff, whose shortcomings are used by the central government to justify restricting their role. The fact that city mayors cut their political teeth by demonstrating their ability to extract resources from the central government encourages the state to guard jealously its image as the magnanimous dispenser of funds.

The ambiguity between avowed goal and the means of achieving it is explained by political realities. Ecuadorian governments since the 1950s, whether military or civilian, were heavily influenced by American views regarding the threat of communism and the proper (dominant) role of the private sector in development. Military regimes (1963–1966 and 1972–1979) upheld the power of traditional elites most associated with land, while civilian regimes tended to forget the populist stances adopted when in opposition to placate modern commercial elites when in power (Corkhill and Cubitt 1988). The fact that few civilian regimes completed their terms reflected their political instability, being based on groupings around charismatic leaders rather than on policy-based parties. Rivalries in Ecuadorian politics are complicated further by the mutual antagonism between coastal exporter and highland bureaucrat, which even the Jaime Roldós-Osvaldo Hurtado team (1979–1984) was unable to overcome. The survival of constitutional government from the mid-1970s can be attributed to copious oil money, for Roldós, Hurtado, and their successor, León Febres Cordero (1984–1988), governed despite the stalling tactics of parliaments dominated by oppositions.

Given this fragility of government, it is not surprising that, although decentralist mantles were assumed, devolution of power has not been on the agenda. It would seem that fear of populist uprisings of the very poor—ever more of whom were resident in the primary cities and who, from the mid-1970s, might be swayed by increasing union activity—played a role in keeping decentralization out of focus. It was not the size of the primary cities per se that caused concern but the association of migrants in them with unemployment, or at least underemployment, with economic and social marginality, and with unrest fostered by the inability of the metropolitan authorities to supply them with essential infrastructure and services. This fear was exacerbated by the removal of the literacy bar to voter registration in 1978.

General investment policies to boost the economy could be sold to the masses as a means of creating opportunities for displaced populations and seemed politically innocuous. Unfortunately, the promotion of particular forms and types of production exacerbated regional disparities, partly because the measures were directed purely at economic growth and ignored the need for any structural changes in society. This attitude colors the way Ecuadorian governments of all political hues have linked the causes of migration and uneven spatial development to circumstances beyond state control, such as the natural environment, colonial legacies, or the workings of the international economy.

UNEVEN DEVELOPMENT AND STATE POLICIES

No politician can be blamed for, or be expected to transform, altitude, rainfall, and soils. Yet, although few would disagree that physical endowment is a primary cause of Ecuadorian uneven development, regimes have been unwilling to accept the logical consequences—that emigration should be encouraged from the most disadvantaged regions on grounds of efficiency and humanity. On the contrary, the state frequently encouraged its most deprived citizens to take on marginal and hostile environments, such as the coastal forests and Amazonia, rather than support demands for less discriminatory treatment in more favorable ecological zones (Barsky et al. 1982; Black 1985).

Successive governments' uneven promotion of agrarian technology rebounded in the spatial pattern of the costs of production and profitability: state credit schemes have benefited the larger commercial producer and processor, while the smallholder, sharecropper, and peasant producer of food crops were shunned (Middleton 1981). In the 1970s, the state's monopoly over the marketing of selective crops and its imposition of purchase prices for them and of ceiling retail prices on a range of basic foods led to gluts, wastage, the loss of some harvests, and shortages in others, owing to inadequate storage and handling facilities (Lawson 1984). The inflexibility of the pricing systems contributed to the suppression of these measures in the 1980s in the face of decreasing production, abandoned land, and food shortages. Government policies created artificial conditions, which favored some types of production and consumers at the expense of others, so that certain sectors withered and impoverished the locations involved.

Ecuador's colonial heritage was often blamed for discrimination against the indigenous population and the very inequitable distribution of all forms of wealth, especially land. Seemingly, more egalitarian structures have not emerged, despite agrarian reform, increased educational facilities, legislation introducing minimum living wages, and the state's increasing direct participation in the economy. Governments bypassed the problem, for example, by giving colonization precedence over agrarian reform in 1972 and by passing measures relevant only to specific groups. For instance, minimum living wages and social benefits are usually irrelevant to the 44 percent of the economically active population (EAP) working in small-scale production, commerce, and services and to the self-employed. These measures benefit the types of employee concentrated in the primary and the larger intermediate cities. Education is also a prime urbanizing agent; it seldom results in greater incomes for agricultural workers. Thus even welfare measures often reinforced discriminatory structures and exacerbated spatial differences.

Exogenous factors, in the form of global commodity markets and transnational corporations (TNCs), have been identified as agents of uneven development. Ecuador's vulnerability as a supplier of world markets is undeniable, although few complaints were uttered when it benefited substantially from the inflated oil prices in 1976 or from previous booms centered on cacao, coffee, and bananas. Exogenous factors may have determined the extent of the bonanzas, but they did not determine who gained or how and where the profits were invested, as profits were filtered through resource control structures that did not necessarily return them to the producer region. In the case of the nationalized petroleum industry, revenues were used to stimulate the economy.

The state chose to maintain stable exchange rates that grossly overvalued the currency and to promote private enterprise via such generous financial and fiscal incentives that capital became cheaper than its opportunity cost (World Bank 1979, 1984). Fiscal and financial policies promoted capital at the expense of labor, industry at the expense of agriculture, and, unwittingly, dependency on imported inputs and technology (Sepúlveda 1983). The public and private bureaucracy organizing and servicing these activities mushroomed. Petroleum products and certain imports, such as wheat, were heavily subsidized (PREALC 1982). These actions not only contributed to uneven development but enhanced primacy, given the type of production promoted and the concentration of the domestic market.

THE VIEW FROM THE PERIPHERY

The state administrative system, based on provinces, cantons, and parishes, proved too static and inflexible to cope with major changes in production and its associated spatial demography. The complacency of the social groups and places benefiting from resources awarded on the basis of tradition, rather than to further economic growth or support greater social needs, bred increasing frustration from settlements in areas meritorious on both accounts but without sufficient clout to penetrate established networks of interest. All too often they became the pawn of the dominant regional interests during elections.

Changes in Production and Population Distribution

The Ecuadorian system concentrates power in the provinces and in particular their capital cities (see Figure 4.1). These capitals were designated a long time ago when communications were exceedingly poor. Their spatial distribution reflected the isolation of densely populated Andean basins and coastal bridgeheads. This pattern survived, as capitals, dynamic or stagnant, represent the province. As political representation and the magnitude of state grants are weighted by population, there is active resistance to the secession of territory to create new units. Thus, recently founded coastal settlements have had great difficulty acquiring even cantonal capital status, regardless of their population size. Although nearly 60 percent of the national population lived in the sierra up to 1950, continual migration resulted in the coast being the most populous region since 1974. All the sierra provinces, except Pichincha containing the capital city, had negative net migration rates in the 1960s and 1970s, while all the coastal ones, except drought-torn Manabí, had positive ones. The explanation lies in the indirect impact of agrarian reform and agricultural policies and the introduction in the sierra provinces and the introduction in the late 1950s of bananas, which affected far greater territory than their predecessors, in the coastal provinces.

The hurricanes and disease that decimated Central American banana plantations in the late 1950s caused Standard Fruit and United Fruit to seek an alternative source of supply; Ecuador's coastal plain provided an attractive combination of a sparsely populated, suitable environment accessible to male migrants accustomed to hard conditions and very poor standards of living. Banana cultivation spread from the export ports of Guayaquil and Manta northward to gateway towns on inland routes, such as Quevedo and Santo Domingo, finally reaching the port of Esmeraldas. Bananas replaced the former mixed production of cacao, rice, and coffee. Over a decade later, the need to substitute a more disease-resistant variety of banana encouraged the introduction of palm oil and henequen, while ranching became a dominant activity. The dominant area of banana cultivation shifted to the southern coast and the hinterland of Machala.

Figure 4.1
Ecuadorian Cities and Towns

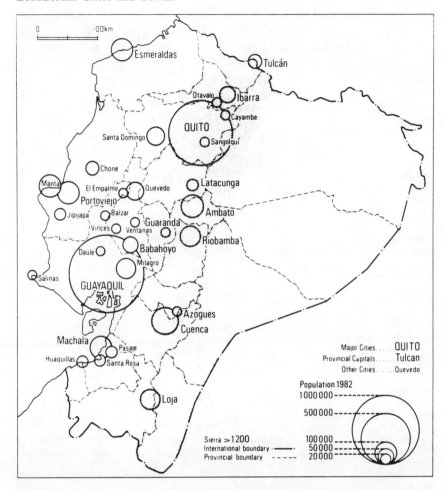

These developments had no counterpart in the sierra, where urban populations reflected city roles as administrative and market centers and grew in
proportion to the outreach permitted by gradually improving road networks.
Azogues and Guaranda, capitals situated in small, high-altitude basins populated
by very poor peasants, failed to thrive. Tulcán and Latacunga, hemmed in
by the Colombian border and sandwiched between the capital and Ambato,
respectively, grew slowly. A degree of autonomy was guaranteed the other
five capitals by the distance and topography separating them, but these also
constrained their markets.

These changes in the spatial pattern of production are reflected in settlement growth rates by size and region (see Table 4.1, column 2). Nationally,

Table 4.1
Characteristics of Ecuadorian Cities and Towns

	1 provincial capitals 1982	2 popn. inc. 1950 - 1982 % p.a.	3 popn. 1982 '000s	4 men per 100 women 1982	5 popn. rank 1982	6 function rank 1982
Sierra Cities:						
Quito	*	4.5	866.5	89	2	1
Cuenca	*	4.3	152.4	85	3	3
Ambato	*	3.7	100.5	87	6	7
Riobamba	*	2.9	75.5	90	10	8
Loja	*	4.9	71.7	89	11	6
Ibarra	*	4.3	53.4	88	14	13
Tulcán	*	3.4	31.0	94	17	18
Latacunga	*	3.2	28.8	92	18	15
Otavalo		2.3	17.5	82	26	29
Sangolqui		5.0	15.0	104	29	24
Azogues	*	2.5	14.5	82	31	17
Cayambe		2.1	14.2	87	32	24
Guaranda	*	2.0	13.6	81	33	18
Coastal Cities:						
Guayaquil	*	4.9	1199.3	90	1	2
Machala	*	8.6	105.5	99	4	5
Portoviejo	*	5.9	102.6	87	5	4
Manta		5.3	100.3	92	7	8
Esmeraldas	*	6.2	90.4	88	8	10
Milagro		5.5	77.0	96	9	16
Santo Domingo		12.7	69.2	96	12	11
Quevedo		9.1	67.0	94	13	12
Babahoyo	*	4.9	42.3	93	15	14
Chone		4.6	33.8	84	16	20
Jipijapa		4.0	27.1	91	19	20
Santa Rosa		5.5	26.7	109	20	23
Pasaje		5.3	26.2	99	21	24
Huaquillas +		9.6	20.3	102	22	49
Daule		4.6	18.9	95	23	29
Salinas		6.1	17.7	124	24	29
Balzar		5.9	17.6	97	25	33
El Empalme +		4.7	17.0	95	27	24
Ventanas		7.5	15.9	100	28	42
Vinces		4.3	14.6	92	30	43

Source: Columns 1, 2, and 4: Delaunay, D., et al. (1985); Column 3: Carrión, F. (ed.) (1986), p. 106; Column 6: Portais, M., and Rodríguez, J. (1987), in Allou et al. (1987), pp. 64-65.
+ No data available prior to 1974.

the most rapid per annum growth over 1950–1982 (5.47 percent) was ex-perienced by towns that had attained a population of 50,000 to 100,000 by the end of the period. Cities between 100,000 and 200,000 had also grown at over 5 percent per annum, while the metropolises and towns of 20,000 to 50,000 experienced average annual rates of 4.74 and 4.46 percent respectively (Larrea 1986, 111). This profile mirrored the explosive growth of towns such as Santo Domingo and Quevedo on the coast; sierra growth rates declined progressively across the size categories, ranging from 4.53 percent for Quito down to 3.32 percent for the smaller towns.

The comparatively slow growth of sierra provincial capitals has been attributed to their inability to absorb labor, which accounted for their high female sex ratios (see Table 4.1, column 4). Average urban sex ratios were progressively more skewed toward women the larger the settlement. Seven of the twelve with ratios of less than 90 corresponded to sierra provincial capitals, including the national capital. Two more were coastal provincial capitals, and even Guayaquil only had a ratio of 90. Coastal ratios were more balanced, with towns under 20,000 displaying a slight male bias. The most extreme female bias corresponded to stagnant Azogues and Guaranda, while the only male-dominated ratio in the sierra corresponded to a rapidly growing dormitory for Quito.

State Allocation Systems

There is no doubt that the larger provincial capitals possess a greater range of economic infrastructure accruing from state and private investment (see Table 4.1, column 6).[2] The hierarchical administrative system has been concentrating resources in provincial capitals over a long period. This explains why the accumulated investment in the built fabric and infrastructure of provincial capitals in Andean backwaters often surpasses that of far more dynamic coastal cities of much greater population today. Political status also causes inequity in treatment within the coast—for example, Machala and Esmeraldas, as capital cities, received much more prompt and generous funding in response to their rapid growth than Santo Domingo and Quevedo. Consequently, about 70 percent of the homes in Andean cities of over 50,000 people had running water in 1982, compared to less than one-fifth of the residents in their coastal counterparts. But perhaps an even greater source of inequity stems from the impact of state administrative systems, directly and indirectly, on employment structure in terms of the "formality" of employment in cities, the wages associated with it, and the multiplier effects of both.

Rapid development in the 1970s left an indelible imprint on urban employment structure. The impact of the state's financial approach was evident in increasing industrial activity. This led to greater urbanization and centralization of industrial production in the primary cities, although a few provincial capitals also benefited; it also led to a general contraction of artisanal activity, especially in smaller towns and the countryside. Furthermore, urban-based white-collar employment grew more rapidly than blue-collar employment in the transport sector anchored in cities expanded, as did the urban construction sector. Civil servants made up a substantial proportion of the labor forces of provincial capitals; the average for cities of more than 50,000 inhabitants in 1982 was 20 percent. It exceeded 30 percent in the smaller sierran capitals and accounted for half that proportion in lower-status coastal cities with substantial growth where the private sector evolved independently. Thus, provincial capitals, especially in the sierra, had larger nuclei of their labor force in stable "formal" occupations than their coastal counterparts and, especially, smaller coastal towns. This regional discrepancy was compounded by the linkage of rural and urban labor markets on the coast.

Production structures in the vicinity of cities also had an impact on employment structure. Most coastal export crop booms stimulated massive land clearance followed by intensive planting, nearly all of which was done by hand. Thereafter much of the demand for labor was for specific tasks. Modern entrepreneurs had no interest in retaining labor beyond the essential, nor did monoculture allow seasonal complementarity. Unfortunately, the same was true for ranching, once the pastures had been established, and for shrimp farming, once the tanks had been excavated. The choice faced by redundant wage labor was between the hazards of the fast-declining colonization frontier and the nearest city from which the casual rural and urban labor markets was articulated; men waited at designated crossroads in the early hours for proprietors' trucks in search of laborers. Demographic evidence of this trend takes the form of high male ratios at coastal settlement peripheries. Rural sex ratios were universally male biased, but in 1982 ratios exceeding 120 were found on the peripheries of Machala, Santo Domingo, Quevedo, Santa Rosa, and Balzar; seven other towns scored 110 or more. Such "labor rings" are a sure sign of unintegrated sex-selective migration; on average, migrants contributed 64 percent of the growth since 1950 of cities with sex ratios above 120 at their peripheries.

Employment structure is inextricably bound to wage structure. In 1975, occupational wage differentials highly rewarded occupations concentrated in cities (INEC no date). Education differentials supported this structure, with university graduates earning over five times the illiterate, while a white-collar job generally paid double that of a blue-collar one. Doctors, lawyers, and engineers—professions found only in cities—topped the earnings ladder, followed by directors and managers who achieved only 75 percent of professionals' average earnings. Although executive administrators earned just over a third of that of a professional and routine office staff, increasingly women, were only marginally better off than the servants accommodated by their employer; both earned far more than tailors and shoemakers, the occupations most associated with artisans and more common in smaller settlements. Government increased the statutory minimum wage several times so that these differentials decreased slightly in the period up to 1980, but this only affected those employed in the formal sector, which was also concentrated in cities.

Variations in intercity wages reflected the primacy and the shortages of particular skills in specific cities. Pay differentials between primary and intermediate cities were not very great for comparable educational and occupational levels. However, the difference in concentration of professionals, middle-class occupations, and even servants at city level was very marked. Generally, wage levels in the capital were 20 percent higher than any other city. The exceptions were the blue-collar workers in Machala's factories, who earned on average more than those in Quito, and the staff in Cuenca's finance sector, who were paid nearly a third more than those in Quito and 13 percent more than those in Guayaquil. Higher average wages were reported for primary and intermediate cities with the greatest investment in modern capital-intensive industry; of the intermediate cities, only Cuenca and Ambato had significant proportions employed in manufacturing. Taking all sectors into account, Portoviejo and Ambato emerge as generally low-wage cities, while Cuenca, Machala, and Manta were comparatively high-wage cities, offering rates only 10 percent lower than primary cities (Berry 1984).

Wages and the stability of employment are only partial indicators of effective demand. The skew of income distribution in Ecuadorian cities ensures that the population thresholds required to support production other than of basic goods and petty services are generally high. Moreover, the multipliers of a formal job in public services have been estimated as 1:3 as opposed to the 1:5 or more of an employee in the private sector. In addition, variations in purchasing power have a regional dimension: on the whole, sierra residents spent significantly more than coastal ones, although households were smaller and dependency rates lower. Residents of Quito spent more than anyone else, twice as much per month as residents of Latacunga, Machala, or Manta and over two-thirds more than a resident of Guayaquil or Esmeraldas, whose comparatively high average expenditure can be attributed to the staff employed in the state oil refinery.

The employment structures of intermediate cities have significance for both development and decentralization, in the sense of greater spatial equity of productions and standards of living. Small-scale enterprises and artisans cater to local demands, use a higher proportion of local inputs, and are more labor-intensive than those in primary cities. This is crucial, as a bulge of new entrants to the labor force, hitherto stored in the educational system, is emerging—just when more women desire paid work and the agricultural sector continues to contract. Moreover, production costs per unit are lower in intermediate cities, or would be if the subsidies benefiting primary cities were removed. The infrastructure of intermediate cities is cheaper and their entrepreneurs seek smaller grants that would allow a greater spread of benefit from a given sum.

The Role of Elites

A city's internal sociopolitical structure and its links with production in the environs is crucial to its ability to attract resources. Major provincial capitals have professionals, entrepreneurs, and proprietors who identify with and take pride in their city. Their social and economic status fits them to intercede with central government, and their personal interests are furthered by gaining concessions for it. The conditions within new towns do not induce the owners of enterprises in their environs to reside there; ranches and large-scale plantations can be managed much more comfortably from an air-conditioned office in Guayaquil, or at least from a major city possessing a good school. Such businessmen are more interested in pressurizing the state over matters affecting the profitability of production than over the water supply of the nearest town. Local spokesmen there are likely to be poorly educated, small-scale migrant entrepreneurs with little clout in the corridors of government. Moreover, not only does the social composition influence the organization of production, but the impact of changes instigated by either the public or private sector will be affected by the particular society's values and control mechanisms.

THE STORY OF FIVE CITIES

The interactions between the changes in production and the population redistribution that ensues with state allocation systems, tempered by the nature of the elites concerned, shape the economic fortune of peripheral cities and their respective regions in varied ways. Whether immigration to a city, for instance, is a consequence of either urban dynamism or of rural stagnation determines the nature of the elite's reactions. Similarly, state allocation systems may advantage a city while impacting negatively on its wider region. The actions of elites may bolster the wealth and physical fabric of their base but at the expense of the greater population's interests. Thus the intermediate cities of Cuenca, Loja, Machala, Ambato, and Santo Domingo de los Colorados serve to exemplify the range of specific outcomes that arise from state allocation policies as a result of the structure of production in their vicinity, and the identity and goals of the elites in their population.

Cuenca

Cuenca is the city that has probably benefited most from government policies. The poverty and out-migration from the province after the decay of the Panama hat trade led to the government's creation of the earliest regional development agency, the Centro de Reconversión Económica de Azuay, Cañar y Morona Santiago (CREA). Good land in the region is limited and the rest is still worked by archaic systems. The hill slopes are severely eroded and yield poor crops of maize and beans on minute peasant holdings. CREA is unusual, in that it has devoted most of its energies to small-scale projects, such as building rain catchment tanks and gravel roads, bridging gullies, and encouraging afforestation and crafts so that its benefits have been felt over a wide area of small-scale production. The state also located its first industrial estate in Cuenca and directed a tire company and several vehicle components works to it. Recent industrial incentives have led to the creation of a few small plants processing tomatoes, meat, and milk. As the third largest city situated at a great distance from both Guayaquil and Quito, Cuenca benefited from a greater bureaucratic presence than other provincial capitals—through the limited deconcentration by the state in 1978 and as the first locale to which some low-level administrative decisions were devolved in 1985.

Cuenca's dealings with the state are assisted by the fact that isolation has wrought an elite defined by kinship, which controls itself and others by patron-client relationships. It is difficult for outsiders to gain admittance to Cuencano society, and the Cuencano elite are not encouraged to leave, as their privileges would be lost elsewhere. There is an unusual degree of cooperation within and between public and private institutions in the city arising from the personal relationships of their leaders. These circumstances limit initiative but allow considerable accumulation of public and private resources: Cuenca's hospital and medical facilities are unusually good. Its state university has over 10,000 students, apart from those at the branch of the National Catholic University and the theological college. High-status purchases, such as vehicles, domestic durables, and high-quality goods, accounted for two-thirds of the city's retail trade by value. Since 1970 not only have more private houses per 1,000 population been built than in any other city, but their average size is much larger.

There is no doubt that Cuenca is prosperous, as testified by the hundreds of artisans and laborers who commute daily from outlying villages. The city is a dynamic market center, whose merchant buyers supply basic needs to its regional clientele. But this prosperity rests on enhanced state investment at a time of high oil prices which, filtered through the elite, stimulated a consumption boom, particularly of real estate (Lowder 1990b). Private investment in local factory production is low and usually in the form of a minority stake in subsidized enterprises. Physical isolation from the centers of decision making and low incomes in Cuenca's hinterland confine local markets to building materials, bottled drinks, clothes, and furniture; very few goods, such as high value decorative ceramics, can withstand the cost of transport to the primary cities. Moreover, the unrestrained power of the local elite is threatening local resources and the livelihoods of peasant families: luxurious residential development are supplanting the intensively worked market gardens adjacent to the city that supply vegetables both to Cuenca and the coast.

Loja

Loja is another long-standing provincial capital of an even more poverty-stricken region displaying net emigration rates. Recurrent droughts prompted the state to establish a regional development agency, the Programa Regional para el Desarrollo del Ecuador del Sur (PREDESUR). The city also benefited from considerable state investment; almost every modern commercial building in the city is occupied by a public agency and the many new housing estates are filled with state employees. Public employees outnumbered those in the private sector in 1982. The city also has a large state university occupying new buildings in a splendid landscaped campus.

The impact of such top down investment has been limited. Although the role envisioned for PREDESUR was very broad, unlike CREA it has functioned almost entirely as an irrigation authority, concentrating its efforts on a mere 3 percent of the province's area (Pietry-Levy 1986). As Loja is adjacent to the sensitive Peruvian border, international agreement was required for any hydraulic scheme, but despite considerable investment, there has been little regional overspill, as large-scale sugar and cattle raising benefited most. Moreover, most city officials were not locals. The Lojano elite, unlike the Cuencan, retained the mentality of the hereditary landowner and preferred to invest in land. There is very little industry and not much regional trade to sustain Loja, which remains overtly dependent on state resources; the national press suspects that traffic in cocaine inflates its revenues.

Machala

Private enterprise overshadowed state investment in Machala to which migrants thronged in response to perceived opportunities. Bananas were responsible for the city's growth, the area's comparative isolation being advantageous when disease hit the original exporting zones north of Guayaquil. The estates in its vicinity were not very large and the banana crop was grown in association with ranching. The coastal mangrove swamps attracted an alternative enterprise: shrimp. Tanks could easily be excavated and the shrimp larva to stock them were found in the creeks. The distance from Guayaquil and the quality of the roads ensured that a port was developed for banana and shrimp exports, which also entailed an ice plant, a cannery, and a packaging industry. The rapid development of these enterprises in an extremely poor area resulted in explosive population growth and high wages for scarce skills that reflected the hardships of living in a very poor city with few services and a ragged and inadequately built fabric to shelter its population. Machala's isolation, however, protects its artisans and petty services from the competition of the primary cities' factories. Moreover, it is the first major port town reached from Peru and benefits from an active black market; it is associated with the smuggling of consumer goods, such as American clothing. Peruvian cocaine may also use the port.

Ambato

Ambato represents the antithesis of the above cities, being long associated with open commercial competitiveness arising from the advantages of location, rather than from state policies. Ambato is strategically placed near the main routes to the coast and Amazonia, as well as to routes linking the sierra basins. Landholdings in the wider region are intensively worked and produce a range of temperate roots, vegetables, and fruits. Ambato is the potato and onion capital of the country in that its wholesalers marshal and distribute produce from all over the north and central sierra. Ambato is also Santo Domingo's older brother; it distributes coastal and Amazonian produce and dispatches sierra commodities to its emigrant contacts there. Its industries arose out of such trade; coastal cattle provided the raw materials for its long-established leather and shoe industries. Its transport needs encouraged foundries, metal workers, coachworks, and mechanics. Their functions are mostly carried out in small-scale workshops; much of the shoe production is sent out to outlying villages. Diversification into rubber boots, the universal footware in tropical forests, betrays its links and its role: Ambato provides everyday needs to the mass market.

The city benefited, like all others, from its provincial capital status. The state made its greatest contribution to Ambato after a 1940 earthquake destroyed a good deal of the center; it laid out a new fully serviced suburb and rebuilt public buildings such as the cathedral. But small-scale private enterprise over-shadows the state's presence in Ambato. Individual wages and income are comparatively low, but the city's wealth is revealed in its main street lined with twenty-story apartment buildings and offices built with Ambateño capital, its local financial institutions, and the size of its interprovincial bus station. Ambato's wealth is invested in production and spread far more widely and thinly than in the cities described above. Thus Ambato's wholesalers are concerned with the inputs for industry and the distribution of commodities; the proportion of luxury outlets is low and its new housing mostly takes the form of row houses in small plots. The municipality makes efforts to enable the poorer members of the community to build legally by waiving fees and providing free plans and economic housing layouts. Ambato's accessibility to the capital provides a market for its hinterland's produce, but it also ensures that local activities at all levels are competitive with producers and the best-qualified professionals in the country.

Santo Domingo de los Colorados

Few cities offer greater scope for development than Santo Domingo de los Colorados. This city arose at the junction of the Guayaquil-Esmeraldas and the Manta-Quito roads, which explains its relatively recent growth, why it is not a provincial capital, and why state investment in its domestic infrastructure is slight and tardy. Its location is ideal for exchanging coastal tropical and Andean temperate products. Santo Domingo's merchants organize the transfer of the plantains, bananas, oranges and beef produced on the coast to Quito and to the north and central sierra. They also control the distribution of sierra produce, such as potatoes and onions, throughout the coast. Moreover, as the bridgehead for generations of aspiring colonists, the city occupies a strategic place between Guayaquil's influence to the south and Quito's to the east. As a coastal outlier of the capital province of Pichincha, it benefits from regional rivalry and the desire of Quiteño investors to corner development further north toward Esmeraldas. State concern for the region is guaranteed; the trans-Andean oil pipeline's main pumping station is just outside the city.

Santo Domingo is still a frontier city with few paved roads. Most of its population live in shacks and wash in the river, but the dynamism of its labor-intensive commerce (it is also a collection point for the coffee grown by smallholders in the interior and for palm fruit, some of which is processed locally) and transport systems bode well for its future economy. However, as the capital of a mere canton, Santo Domingo is also a pawn in the battle for political power by the elites of the primary cities. It is doubtful whether it will acquire the infrastructure comparable with its population or dynamism without an increase in its political status.

CONCLUSIONS

Decentralization has been promoted for a long time in Ecuador. Its aims have frequently been confused with general development and associated with investments outside the capital; only recently has the state embarked on the decentralization of some minor powers affecting localities. The country's small internal market undoubtedly encourages centralization of production. Indeed, the country is fortunate that history has bestowed on it a primary city both on the coast and in the sierra. Regional sensitivity, a major issue in a country with a poor record for democratic governments lasting their terms of office, is reflected in direct intervention by central government in order to distribute development projects spatially and in the slow adaptation of the hierarchy of provinces, cantons, and parishes to demographic change. However, bureaucratic centralization, the concentration of most tax revenues and personal savings, and the range of incentives and financial measures introduced in the 1970s exaggerate the primary cities' natural advantages. Administrative reform should at least enhance local control and responsibility for locally raised resources, which should in turn stimulate small enterprises with higher employment potential.

The structure of society, filtered through patterns of power and resource control, determines what impact any measure may have locally. Cuenca and Loja benefited from adroit dealing with, or direct intervention by, the central government. Although Cuenca is undeniably a thriving city, the same cannot be said for its province of Azuay. Wealth is concentrated in few hands from which it leaks both out of the city and its region, as the Cuencano elite have invested not only in their own houses but in the real estate markets of Guayaquil and Quito. The interest of multinational agro-exporters stimulated

Machala's growth, but its population is not really master of its own destiny. The profitability of bananas depends on the continued involvement of Standard Fruit; most of the shrimp enterprises are the speculations of Guayaquileños and a few Cuencanos, and the new factories depend on both. The recent completion of an all-weather road to Loja and the promise of the completion of a direct route to Cuenca are examples of centralized efforts to stimulate regional development. Ambato's and Santo Domingo's positions in Ecuador's urban hierarchy reflect their spontaneous evolution as hubs of intensive commerce and relatively small-scale production. These activities created effective mass demand in their areas, even if only for humble goods, and are not affected by state largess or multinationals' decisions. Furthermore, small local entrepreneurs reinvest in their own environment, something drastically needed in Santo Domingo.

It will take imagination and political will to conceive of decentralization in terms other than administrative criteria based on existing structures. In the absence of regional spokesmen of some standing, decentralization—in the sense of the devolution of power to alternative locations and subgroups— will be gained by only a few areas. Unless the activities in a region become profitable to the state, or threaten its authority, the region is unlikely to achieve many concessions from highly centralized planning and administrative systems.

NOTES

1. Only a 20 percent differential in fiscal benefits separated locations outside and within the primary cities' provinces of Pichincha and Guayas.

2. Portais and Rodriguez' (1987) index was based on seventeen weighted indicators: demography (population in 1982 and intercensal growth rate); symbols of power (political status; the number of: state executives; judges, notaries and justices of the peace; local newspapers; radio stations; banks; bank employees, and telex holders); infrastructure (public health system rank; number of hospital beds; universities; number of students enrolled in the academic secondary stream; number of asphalted roads linking the city, air service); economic dynamism (growth in employees in financial outlets between 1974 and 1982).

5

Neoconservative Policies in Argentina and the Decentralization of Industry

Arthur Morris

A relatively powerful decentralization of industry occurred in Argentina in the 1980s, partially as a result of policy but also in good measure as an accidental result of the downturn in the national economy. In recent years, Argentina has seen what amounts to a decentralization of industry from the metropolitan area to the periphery, or at least to selected points within the peripheral provinces. At the same time, there has been a deindustrialization at the national level, so that regional growth stands in stark contrast to the general trend. This whole evolution contradicts standard economic theory from both left and right wings. Dependency writers argue for the deindustrialization of the periphery, generally, as a result of the exploitation of the center. Right-wing theory envisages, if not a permanent move, at least a temporary withdrawal of industry, during recession times, from peripheral regions to central areas with a better comparative advantage for production.

The aims of this chapter are, first, to show the nature and extent of decentralization of the manufacturing industry; and, second, to evaluate decentralization's effectiveness in promoting regional development. It will be useful first to place this evaluation within the context of the neoconservative policies favored in the Southern Cone.

NEOCONSERVATIVE POLICIES IN THE SOUTHERN CONE COUNTRIES

The rise of radical conservative policies in the 1970s in South America may be seen partially as a reaction to the failure of various kinds of interventionist economic policy of earlier decades, mainly failure to proceed beyond the easier first phases of import substitution and to overcome the recurrent crises of foreign debt and internal inflation that such interventionist policies encountered. The thrust of the new policies was to increase economic efficiency through the use of market signals to allocate resources, to move toward internationally acceptable exchange rates, and to promote exports and, with them, a healthier balance of trade.

Brazil moved first toward economic orthodoxy with its military government installed in 1964, though it softened the policies from 1967. Uruguay operated these policies from 1974, and Argentina, after a moderate attempt in 1967, made more radical moves in 1976 following the Peronist years. The policies consist of several major elements (Foxley 1983, 40–41). They were radically different from previous policies; rather than modifying existing rules, they called for new legislation, structural forms, and institutions. The military governments considered themselves strong enough to impose these changes without recourse to the democratic process. Structural changes included (1) the privatization of firms and services from the public sector and overall reduction of the state presence in the economy and (2) a free trade policy at the international level, moving away from the protection of previous decades. Institutional changes included the transfer of company ownership from the state to private firms, the reduction of the welfare state, and the decentralization of government and administration, giving greater power to provinces and to their constituent units, the departments. South American neoconservatism is different from Northern Hemisphere equivalents in its association with authoritarian military governments and so constitutes a genre of its own which is an interesting test case for economic theory.

THE ARGENTINE EXPERIENCE

For Argentina, the period from the early 1970s to the present has been one of industrial recession. For 1974–1985, the National Industrial Census showed a decline in the number of establishments of 11.6 percent (126,388 to 111,767) and in the number of employees of 10.9 percent (1,525,221 to 1,359,519). The GDP (gross domestic product) declined from an index value (1970 = 100) of 116.1 in 1974 to 113.2 in 1982 (Instituto Nacional de Estadística y Censos 1984, 622). This decline is concentrated in the major industrial centers of the country (see Figures 5.1 and 5.2). In the Federal District, the number of establishments declined by 32.5 percent, personnel declined by 32.4 percent. In the Buenos Aires province, the number of establishments and personnel declined by 11.2 percent and 12.3 percent, respectively. If figures for Córdoba and Santa Fe are added to central region figures, the employment decline is 20 percent, while the rest of the country—the periphery—increases by 12 percent. Employment increases are spectacular for some isolated provinces: Catamarca, 99.8 percent; Chaco, 25.1 percent; Formosa, 24.8 percent; La Rioja, 224.6 percent; and, most notably, Tierra del Fuego, 980.7 percent.

Figure 5.1
Industrial Change, 1974–1985: Number of Persons Employed

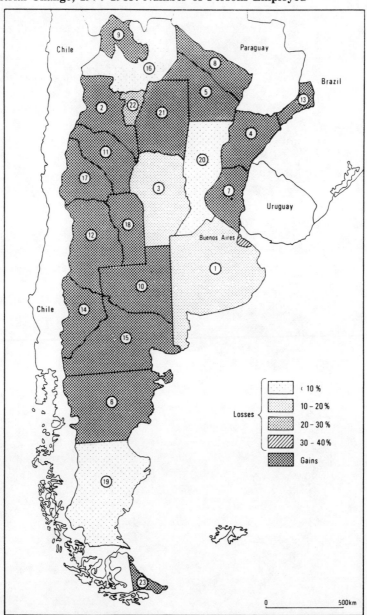

Provinces of Argentina: 1. Buenos Aires; 2. Catamarca; 3. Córdoba; 4. Corrientes; 5. Chaco;
6. Chubut; 7. Entre Rios; 8. Formosa; 9. Jujuy; 10. La Pampa; 11. La Rioja; 12. Mendoza;
13. Misiones; 14. Neuquén; 15. Rio Negro; 16. Salta; 17. San Juan; 18. San Luis; 19. Santa
Cruz; 20. Santa Fe; 21. Santiago del Estero; 22. Tucumán; 23. Tierra del Fuego.

Figure 5.2
Industrial Change, 1974–1985: Number of Establishments

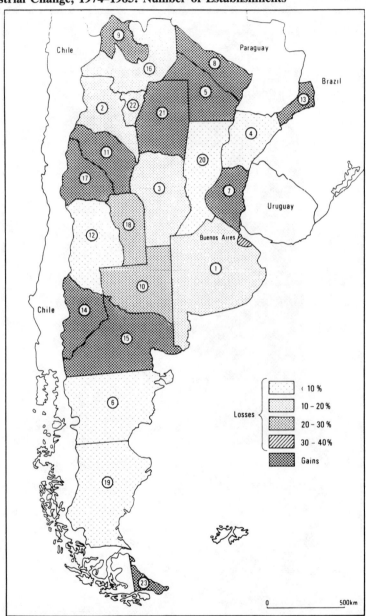

Provinces of Argentina: 1. Buenos Aires; 2. Catamarca; 3. Córdoba; 4. Corrientes; 5. Chaco; 6. Chubut; 7. Entre Rios; 8. Formosa; 9. Jujuy; 10. La Pampa; 11. La Rioja; 12. Mendoza; 13. Misiones; 14. Neuquén; 15. Rio Negro; 16. Salta; 17. San Juan; 18. San Luis; 19. Santa Cruz; 20. Santa Fe; 21. Santiago del Estero; 22. Tucumán; 23. Tierra del Fuego.

The net effect of these large relative rises is very modest in relation to overall industrial structure. The central region maintains its preeminence, even after its decline between 1979 and 1984. As Table 5.1 shows, industry is highly centralized in Argentina, where the three provinces—Buenos Aires, Córdoba, and Santa Fe—still contain over 80 percent of industrial production. Eighty-four percent of industrial workers are located in these three provinces, reflecting the greater size of their establishments compared to the average province and the acquisition of new industries. In much of the periphery, only a few cities have achieved industrial growth, so that in Patagonia's Neuquén province, virtually all growth has been at Neuquén city. Chubut has 3,500 new jobs, of which 2,200 are in the Rawson-Trelew "conurbation"; Trelew benefited especially from textile firms that moved out from the capital, and Puerto Madryn nearby received Argentina's only aluminum plant, begun in 1974. In the midwest region of Cuyo, similar concentrations are found. San Luis increased its industrial employment from 4,700 to 10,100, essentially at two towns: San Luis itself received 2,000 new jobs and General Pedernera another 3,000. San Juan's small rise of 3,400 jobs was dispersed, but Mendoza's 13,500 accrued to the suburbs of Mendoza City, where light engineering, agricultural processing, and refining and petrochemicals have all arisen since the 1960s. La Rioja gained 4,000 places, mostly at a single industrial estate at Rioja city.

AID TO INDUSTRY AND THE REGIONS

The peculiar pattern of major increases in industrial employment in remote provinces, in an era of deindustrialization, requires explanation and merits

Table 5.1
Declining Centralization

Proportion of Gross Industrial Product for Buenos Aires, Córdoba, and Santa Fe	
Date	% of GIP
1946	85.5
1954	84.6
1964	85.5
1974	86.5
1984	81.4

Source: Ferrucci (1986, ch. 4) and Schvarzer (1987a, ch. 4).

a discussion of the special regional legislation that relates to it. The role of regional aid in industrial change, the utility of the aid program, and the underlying aims of government need to be considered.

In general, the regional aid scheme was modeled after Western industrial nations and was based on financial stimuli and an increasingly sophisticated and effective regional differentiation of aid. In later stages, the "stick" of restrictions on development in the central area matched the "carrot" of credits and tax reliefs. One major difference from advanced country practice was to include remission of customs dues on imported equipment, an important element for Argentine industry with its continued reliance on imported machines and technology.

Regional policies began in 1956 with the establishment of free port status for the provinces south of 42° south—Chubut, Santa Cruz, and Tierra del Fuego—which involved the remission of any customs payment on imports and exports. This move was amplified by a new aid law in 1958 under Arturo Frondizi's liberal government. The law, however, was applied only from 1961, when it was extended to Rio Negro and Neuquén, provinces south of the Rio Colorado; its scope was widened to tax remissions and credits for new industry, whether national or foreign. This modest program had little effect and was excessively diluted by its extension to the whole northwest. It involved Catamarca, Jujuy, La Rioja, Salta, Santiago del Estero, Tucumán, western parts of Formosa and Chaco, northern Córdoba and Santa Fe, and Corrientes in the northeast. The aid was also given to existing industries, if they engaged in major expansion.

In 1964, three major regional aid areas were established under a new law:

Zone A Patagonia with Malargue in Mendoza

Zone B The northwest, Chaco, Formosa, north of Santa Fe, and San Juan

Zone C The northeast: Corrientes and Misiones provinces

The new law represented a firmer attempt by the radical government of Arturo Illia (1963–1966) to redistribute wealth and production and was accompanied by a first effort at restricting central development with the specific exclusion of benefits for the Gran Buenos Aires metropolitan area. The measures included tax exemptions and reductions and the provision of machinery and power at low prices. Sectoral industrial aid was given to the steel and petrochemicals industries. This body of legislation brought 70 percent of national territory into aided status. Published documents cited as the official reasons for aid the improvement of balance of payments, decentralization, diversification, technological advance, and the use of domestic natural resources (IIE 1976). Spatial equity was not a declared aim.

Military governments of liberal tendency followed; the government of General Roberto Lanusse (1969–1973) emphasized a growth pole approach rather than broad spectrum regional aid. This policy lasted too short a time to be implemented, but it suffered many of the deficiencies of approaches taken in Europe and elsewhere (Morris 1975).

In 1973, legislation was altered again by the second Peronist government to allow aid only to national firms and to make regional aid a more delicate tool. Manufacturing investment was prohibited in the capital city and discouraged within a 70 kilometer radius. Two regional aid zones were formed: Zone 1 had the least development and received the most support; Zone 2 had moderate development and received limited support. Zone 1 included all the old development areas, apart from a few marginal departments in Mendoza, Buenos Aires, Córdoba, and Santa Fe, which moved into Zone 2 and thus qualified for only limited support. Peronism, like Illia's radicalism, involved what has been termed a "nationalist distributionist" government, favoring domestic firms with aid and direct state intervention to build up some strategic industries.

Despite its growth in scope, regional aid had relatively small effect on industry except for the state and joint state-private industries of steel, aluminum, and petrochemicals, where it had greater effect. But special measures started earlier for specific provinces began to bite. The first was in Tucumán, where the national sugarcane industry was concentrated and where market conditions had produced a crisis. Production had increased in the 1960s while world market prices fell. Cultivation of cane was restricted from 1966 and eleven sugar mills closed, causing heavy unemployment. As a reaction, Operation Tucumán was set up by the federal government, with a program that extended over a fourteen-year period from 1966 to 1980. In 1971, special measures were adopted for San Juan, and similar measures were extended in 1974 to Catamarca, La Rioja, and San Luis, defined as the region of the "Act of Historic Reparation" in reference to the important role these provinces played in the Wars of Independence from Spain. This justification for regional aid because of events 150 years ago seems weak, and it is likely that special political influence was responsible for the pinpointing of these provinces. In effect, these provinces received all the national benefits and extra financial inducements; the provinces themselves were allowed to choose firms that would be given tax breaks and other regional aid. Further special arrangements were made in 1974 for the northwest, for Patagonia, and for Tierra del Fuego.

The change in 1976 from civilian government to military government introduced a major reaction toward radical monetarist policies combined with structural changes in the economy, such as privatization and control of the unions. Equal treatment was to be given to local and foreign capital, and the country was to be opened to world competition in manufacturing. Measures adopted by the government included the use of high interest rates and a high exchange rate for the peso (Schvarzer 1987b, Chapter 4). However, regional incentives were not abandoned though smaller amounts of money were involved, and the military government was slow to introduce a separate body of legislation for industry until 1979.

Buenos Aires

The early Argentine industrial aid had only a minor regional component. The 1958 law gave 60 percent of its approved investments to Buenos Aires province, mostly around the capital (Ferrucci 1986, 20b, Table 4.2); the same applied to the 1963 law. The 1964 law, with its three aid areas, reduced the aid apportioned to the center (consisting of Buenos Aires, Sante Fe, and Córdoba) to 50 percent; the 1973 law reduced aid to slightly over 25 percent, a proportion maintained by the military governments. The center thus received 52 percent of all national aid given over 1958–1981. The percentage of aid to the center is smaller when provincial laws, which provided a modest extra stimulus, are included in the calculations. Nevertheless, the regional aid program has been seen as highly centralist.

Only from 1973 did aid successfully push investment into the periphery. It is also true that the center received a greater proportion of "dynamic" sector investments, with 91 percent of investment in these industries, while the periphery had only 60 percent investment in such industries. Aid was used not for industrial relocation but for the initial establishment of new industries in dynamic sectors, such as steel in Buenos Aires, petrochemicals in Buenos Aires and Bahía Blanca, and vehicles in Córdoba. Governments in the 1960s were happy to see these industries come to Argentina irrespective of the chosen region.

From 1972, growing concern over metropolitan congestion caused a prohibition on new factories in the Federal District other than small units such as repair shops, and a tax was imposed on plants locating within 60 kilometers of the capital. The prohibition was extended in 1977 to Córdoba and Rosario. Restriction was intensified in 1979 by the provincial government of Buenos Aires, which listed a large number of contaminating industries and required their relocation. In 1984 this action was derogated, though urban planning controls still strictly limit industrial development. Schvarzer's view of this legislation and that in Córdoba (1987b, 83–85) is that the authorities sought social control rather than industrial decentralization at a time of increasing urban unrest; the primary aim of the legislation was to restrict the formation of large proletarian masses into organized groups. These laws did not lead to decentralization of a powerful kind; they led to a loose centralization favoring the central provinces. Although they would effectively "decentralize" in terms of human ecology and social organization, they would not do so in economic terms. The social and demographic focus of the legislation is emphasized by Schvarzer (1987b, Chapter 4). The legislation included the removal of squatter settlements, *villas miseria*, a typical reaction by authoritarian governments throughout the Third World to the threat of massive concentrations of poor people capable of radical politicization; the expulsion of Bolivians and Paraguayans for similar reasons; the building and routing of *autopistas*, to force evictions; and the transfer of service provisions to the municipalities, whose officials might be less sympathetic than the national government to organized labor.

Chubut and Patagonia

The earliest legislation brought some investment, principally to Trelew in Chubut, a town close to the 42° S limit placed by the 1956 Free Port Law. Chubut was the only peripheral province to benefit greatly by the 1958 law (Ferrucci 1986, 211) taking 12 percent of the aid funds paid out under that law. Many small textile plants were set up: thirty-four from 1956 to 1960; ninety-three in total by 1975. Because of closures, however, only forty-three remained active in 1975. By 1979 these firms were manufacturing on a medium scale, producing output of 60,000 tons of textiles, largely wool; they constituted the largest single market for Argentina's raw wool output.

Wool textiles, which took most of the investment, appears to have been a rational investment choice in terms of raw material availability, since Patagonia's main export was unwashed wool. But the operation was of dubious benefit; it cost over $10,000 for each of the 300 jobs created by 1960. Many of the firms, as elsewhere in Argentina, were attracted by financial inducements and stayed only until these expired or declined; by 1975, ninety-three firms had come but only forty-three remained (Schvarzer 1987b, 74). The industry was poorly linked to the local economy and attracted few linkages of itself. Since there was a freedom from value-added tax (VAT) payments, there was no incentive to manufacture industrial inputs locally, and a remarkable industrial geography emerged. Unwashed wool was sent to Buenos Aires for washing and spinning, was transported back to Trelew for weaving, and was transported back again on a third 1,000 kilometer trip to Buenos Aires for finishing and transformation into clothing.

A more extreme case is exemplified by Tierra del Fuego, where in addition to the general legislation enjoyed by Zone 1 (maximum aid) there was remission of VAT in 1972. This had no immediate effect, but in 1978 special circumstances arose that caused a strange new development. Color television was introduced to Argentina, and the government specification of component design for the new sets could not be met by local manufacturers. These manufacturers sought to import components; Tierra del Fuego offered at that time the best conditions for such importation, with VAT freedom on inputs and outputs, a concession then offered to no other province. The number of industrial firms increased from 60 in 1976 to 155 in 1984, and employment grew from 584 to 6,294. Apart from television set assembly from imported components, other electronic components were imported and assembled in Tierra del Fuego, which became a major port for imports to the country, growing from $0 in 1970 to $203 million in 1984. The legislation was extended in 1983 to 1993, but its stringency increased; by 1989 imported components were to comprise only 35 percent of the overall value of the product.

The 35 percent limit may still be sidestepped by "creative accounting," and the province remains a Third World export platform for the rest of Argentina. Tierra del Fuego became the leading recipient of industrial regional aid in the 1978–1981 period, taking over from Chubut, and gained over 13 percent of national aid to industry for that period.

Tucumán

At the other extreme of the country, the north received only small injections of regional aid. In the Chaco (Romero 1977) and in Formosa, the effects of regional aid were slight, despite crises in the agriculture-based economy. In the northwest there were more powerful effects, especially in recent years from the extension of VAT concessions. But Tucumán is the most notable case since it had its own special legislation dating to 1966. In 1966, the sugar industry crisis of overproduction led to closure of eleven mills and government regulation of quotas for the remainder. Tucumán has had a relatively successful aid program, although deficiencies did exist. Today, Tucumán remains a sugar economy, with over half the national cane production, but it has also diversified within agriculture and from agriculture into industry (Kurzinger et al. 1985).

As Kurzinger notes, the program, designed to diversify the economy and create new employment, was not successful in the latter aim. Nearly 18,000 workers were dismissed in 1966–1968, most of them casual labor. New jobs rose to 10,400 but only by 1980. Industry, however, did grow, its contribution to gross regional product rose from 19 percent to 29 percent over the 1970s, largely the function of a program called Operation Tucumán. The program offered aid in the form of financial inducements, tax-free profits for ten years, tax credits, tax-free inheritance of businesses, freedom from the stamp tax, freedom of import duties on machinery, preferential credit treatment for loans from state banks, special rates for power supplies, and VAT exemption from its inception in 1969. Among the peripheral provinces, Tucumán was one of the largest recipients of government aid over the 1954–1981 period (Ferrucci 1986, 211), second only to Misiones which had nearly all of its aid given to a massive paper industry to supply mechanical pulp to the nation's newspapers in Buenos Aires.

Tucumán's measures were regionally targeted within the province, with 100 percent benefits only for factories within 10 kilometers of the mills and 60 percent benefits for more distant sites. Over 1966–1974, an increasing level of credits and fiscal incentives were given to industry, and 150 firms took aid, only seventy-seven of which remained by 1981. The spread of investment was fairly wide over the 1958–1981 period: 43 percent was invested in vegetative industries (in Argentine economic jargon, food and drink, textiles, and timber are the main branches of vegetative, as opposed to "dynamic," industries; the division seems to represent one between the long-term growth industries and the others) and the remainder was invested in various dynamic industries, including the automotive sector. In the automotive sector, a heavy-truck factory was set up by Saab and a spark plug factory was set up by Bosch. One of the largest units established was the shoe factory of Alpargatas, transferred from Buenos Aires. These multinational units were set up alongside local and regional industries.

Despite a long period of industrial promotion in Tucumán, however, the industrial structure has not been transformed (Kurzinger et al. 1985, 116, Table 11). Sugar milling declined over 1970–1980 from 44 percent to 35 percent of all value added by industry; all food and drink industries from 63 percent to 53.5 percent. Other "vegetative" industries rose—shoes from 0 percent to 7 percent of the total, and textiles from 1.5 percent to 8.4 percent, while transport machinery rose only from 3.9 percent to 7.8 percent. The new industries are highly visible, but the old structure of industry is still intact. Schvarzer criticizes the concentration of aid, half of which went to some nine firms out of a total of ninety-three recipients; in a sample of fifty-one firms by Boneo (Kurzinger et al. 1985, 63), half the benefits were received by one textile spinning and weaving mill. The tax and other financial incentives received by the firms in this survey amounted to more than the actual investments in Tucumán.

Perhaps more important for long-term regional development is the relative lack of local linkages, which is studied in detail by Kurzinger (Kurzinger et al. 1985, 43). The textile firms locating in Tucumán were successful only in setting up standard mass production lines for common work-wear material. The finishing and clothing industries remained in the city of Buenos Aires. The largest clothing company, with 450 employees, closed in Tucumán in 1984. For backward linkages, the industry has good access to raw cotton from the north, as Argentine domestic production of largely short fiber cotton is adequate for the type of material made. But the important links are to Buenos Aires markets, and there are few process links between different Tucumán textile firms or between textiles and other industries, such as new engineering firms that might have supplied machinery for the mills. The shoe factory does have 40 percent of its market in northern Argentina, but its raw materials are virtually all from overseas. As for vehicle components producers, their links are firmly within international networks and relate little to the locality except through the use of labor. Given this labor link, it is curious that the local university, an old and respected one, has failed to provide technical courses linked to the new industries.

Perhaps the most hopeful sector in the 1980s relates to the development of other industries for agricultural processing. Citrus fruit, especially lemons, is processed into crystallized fruit, juice, and essential oils from the seeds; Tucumán is the main national producer and has export markets for these products. Cane alcohol is produced as a substitute for gasoline and its use is extending in northern Argentina. Paper is made from sugarcane bagasse which is suited to newspaper production and is thus an all-important import substitute.

In comparison with Chubut and Tierra del Fuego, the Tucumán industrial experience is good, with moderate levels of integration into the economy, relative stability, and localization in relation to resource and markets. The preexisting dense rural and urban population, the existing agricultural economy with processing potential, and the long period of effort over 1966–1981 have contributed to Tucumán's success, but Tucumán is scarcely representative of the periphery.

La Rioja

For most northern provinces, the national legislation (Ferrucci 1986, 206) brought only very slight investment and only after 1973. By 1973, there were only 1,848 industrial employers in La Rioja, a province with a population of 140,000. These employers were in the traditional wineries, construction companies, and minor industries, such as baking. The average firm size was 4.6 employees (Yoguel et al. 1987), and industrial employment was 1 percent of that of the nation. By 1984, there were 5,950 industrial employees, the average firm size had increased to 11 employees, and the industrial structure had broadened considerably.

Of the 219 projects (192 in industry) receiving aid over 1980–1984, 58 involving 3,645 new jobs (some were lost thereafter) were in textiles, which had been virtually nonexistent in 1973. These were large units, averaging 62.8 employees. Chemicals and plastics had forty-two projects and created 980 jobs; engineering companies had twenty-seven projects and 982 jobs. These three groups accounted for 90 percent of all jobs. Necessarily, most of the growth was by incoming companies, national and international, feeding national markets (Yoguel et al. 1987, 42–43). The incoming companies did not use local inputs other than labor.

The key law for La Rioja was a special National Law for La Rioja, No. 22021, dating to 1979, which granted remission of tax on profits and freedom from VAT on inputs and outputs, as well as remission of capital tax and customs dues on imports of materials and goods. This tax regime favored La Rioja over all other provinces, first as a result of the fifteen-year duration of concessions—a feature shared only with Tierra del Fuego—and, second, because the province was allowed to make autonomous decisions on projects up to 1,500 million pesos. As noted earlier, this interprovincial discrimination in favor of La Rioja must be attributed to political influences as it would not be justified on economic or welfare grounds. In addition, La Rioja maintained VAT remission in the critical period 1980–1982 when it was suspended for all other provinces. This regime was diluted in effect by its extension in 1982 to San Luis and Catamarca, and in 1983 to San Juan, though its effects were not totally annulled. Smaller projects and extensions to preexisting ones became more important.

Accounting for the Patterns

The individual provincial histories outlined above show that, for the peripheral provinces, regional aid was highly significant in their industrialization. There is no need for a shift-share analysis of national and regional trends since these trends are moving in opposite directions (the data are in any case inadequate). What development did take place in the periphery is thus attributable to aid; most critics believe it is attributable directly to aid since there were few multiplier effects.

For the counterbalancing decline in the center, it is necessary to mention the world recession of the mid-1970s and Argentina's peculiar susceptibility to the recession through its liberal regime's openness to capital flows. The argument so far has focused largely on the regional aid program, so a few more details on national trends are necessary.

One of the most important industrial groups in Argentina were the multinationals. Under import-substitution industrialization in the 1950s and 1960s, multinationals had built up a powerful presence in the country, in 1973 (Sourrouille et al. 1985, 144) accounting for 31.2 percent of value added in industry. By 1981, this had fallen to 28.3 percent, a fall in production level much greater than the under 1 percent decline for domestic firms. The number of establishments recorded officially as branches of foreign firms fell over 1974–1985 from fifty-three to twenty-eight.

Under liberal theory, these industries, once they had become uncompetitive in Argentina, would disappear and their owners would transfer their investments into other activities in the country. Instead, the multinationals moved away from the country altogether, causing the deindustrialization of the central region. A counterbalancing effect was fueled by the state in those industries where it was investing directly or in a partnership with private industries. The steel industry was one such example, but the effect was itself balanced by state investments in paper in Misiones and aluminum in Chubut.

There is no statistical account of the geographic distribution of the multinational industries, but it may easily be inferred that their effect was most felt in the center. The car assembly industry, located in Buenos Aires and Córdoba, declined to 70.7 percent of its 1974 value by 1985, while component manufacture, which also involved many local firms, declined to 91.3 percent. In this way, positive decentralization that occurred through regional aid was accompanied by a negative decentralization caused by the decline of industry in central areas.

INDUSTRY AND DECENTRALIZATION POLICIES

A fundamental aim of leftist and rightist governments has been to create a more even regional development process. On the left, the aim is to foster more equitable development, aiding the regions to increase their income or welfare levels; on the right, the aim is to create the conditions through which a more open choice can be made by individuals within a properly operating market. For both sides, the centralism that has been a long-term feature of development over at least 200 years must be reduced. But the two sides diverge at the policy level: the left believes that direct intervention to move physically investments and industries is necessary; the right believes that it is only necessary to create a background against which individuals can make real decisions. Administrative decentralization fits the right-wing agenda better. Left-wing decentralization can be seen as the spatial movement or transformation of economic activity.

Paradoxically, it is the economic type of decentralization that has been attempted in Argentina; Argentina's right-wing governments decentralized manufacturing, but were unable to decentralize administration in any meaningful way. The same strictures regarding administrative decentralization observed in other South American countries hold true in Argentina: what powers were transferred from the center were not paralleled by a transfer of fiscal resources, so plans could not be carried through, and local governmental officers capable of handling greater responsibilities were not available. (This situation has much in common with Colombia where the problems are described in some detail [Uribe-Echevarria 1986; Collins 1989].)

Whether the regional aid program is to be regarded as a success depends on what criteria are used to judge it. In spatial terms, its policies were only of limited value for the nation or for regions. In employment terms, a gain of 50,000 jobs in the peripheral region over 1974–1985 must be weighed against a loss of over 200,000 from the center.

Moving down the regional scale, for some individual provinces the effect of the program was powerful, notably in Patagonia and the northwest. For the first time, these provinces acquired a modern industrial structure, or at least a set of modern industries (the term *structure* implies a set of industrial linkages that does not yet exist). Whether this new industrial growth will be permanent is also uncertain, and its effects on the overall regional economy are as yet slight.

The regional aid program, however, cannot be judged purely on economic grounds, and to write it off as a poor imitation of developed country policies in an unsuitable environment would be unjust. The well-defined growth pole policy of 1968–1973 certainly could be seen as a geopolitical policy rather than an economic one (Morris 1972) since it sought to place poles in Patagonia where population and poverty levels did not justify them. The later regional policies are spatially less defined but continue to emphasize Patagonia and, notably, Tierra del Fuego; the policymakers were concerned that neighbors might covet the unpopulated areas. The central area policy also may be seen in a geopolitical light, as suggested above.

Decentralization may be seen as a measure of social control rather than of economic decongestion. As a social control measure, big industries with big labor unions were to be broken up and the threats they represented through street demonstrations against employers or government were to be extinguished by firm removal to the provinces. From this perspective (advanced by Schvarzer), one asks: Did population move or did unemployment shift?

There is also a Latin American tendency toward highly "visible" policies that demonstrate government beneficence. Sometimes this emerges as monumentalism (Brazilian new cities, Mexican power dams, Peruvian jungle roads) where great structures are built under one leader and named after him. At other times, it is a more complex gesture, such as a body of laws to favor one social or regional group (Peronism and the industrial work force, Peruvian military nationalism, and expropriation of Peruvian hierarchy oil and mines). The regional industrial aid policies allowed highly visible gestures to be made toward the interior provinces. Perhaps there was in all this a folk memory of the nineteenth-century battles among free traders, the ranchers of Buenos Aires, and the interventionists and protectionists of the interior, who would always suffer from the opening of the country to foreign trade, as they had previously supplied the national market with their craft industries in leather, metal working, and pottery.

What is the ultimate meaning of the decentralization that took place over 1975–1985? This chapter has suggested that the surface meaning—regional policy to aid poor areas of the country—was not the most important, nor was it very effective. Legitimation exercises, designed to demonstrate the democracy of government, are likely to have been one aim of government, compounded with geopolitics and a negative reaction to Fordist-type mass industries and the conflicts they generate. Neoliberal policies produced effects that might have been anticipated by government, notably the massive deindustrialization that occurred when the MNCs decided Argentina was an inappropriate platform for manufacturing and left the country, causing a powerful negative decentralization because they had located previously in the center. Compared to this effect, the governments' own decentralization program, which did not belong to neoliberal thinking, had only weak effects. A major conclusion is that neoliberal policies cannot be relied on in Latin America to produce positive economic decentralization, nor the decentralization of political and administrative mechanisms from center to periphery.

6

Decision Making in Decentralizing Companies in a City Region: The Case of Greater São Paulo

Peter Townroe

At any one point in its history, the structure of the city results from a particular portfolio of location decisions made through successive decades and centuries. These past decisions involved residence and workplace; they also involved investments by industry, commerce, and households. At the edges of an expanding city, rural land was converted to urban occupation. In each period of a city's history, within the built-up area, some location decisions involved changes in land use while others involved changes in the use made of individual buildings. Some decisions may have taken the form of a status quo in the city concerned, the decision maker able to invest or divest to fulfill his or her objectives in another city. Location decisions may be regarded, therefore, as both explicit and implicit, normally embedded within a wider decision calculus of the social actors involved.

How did decision-making actors reach their various solutions through the life of the city? Were there spatial determinants? How was the existing and the forecast geography of the city taken into account by each actor? Is there something about spatial decisions that separates them from other kinds or categories of decision? The city, as a collectivity, must live with the results of these choices. The result of each choice may be good or bad, positive or negative, for the actor concerned, for the city as a whole, and, indirectly, for the nation in terms of general welfare or narrow economic efficiency. The justification for studying decisions with a locational component lies not only with the prospective pulling of policy levers designed to influence locational outcomes but in achieving an enhanced understanding of the processes and consequences of the growth and change in the city.

The focus of this chapter is a familiar one: the decentralization of people and jobs around a major city. Specifically, the chapter focuses on the location decision making of industrial companies contemplating decentralization from a city or metropolitan core, in this case, São Paulo. The companies used to provide the empirical evidence for this study were all in the private sector, thus avoiding differences of policy pressure than can be seen in state-owned concerns. The evidence collected does not suggest any marked difference in decision-making patterns between Brazilian companies and other companies studied in Western Europe and North America.

Industrial companies may rightly be regarded as being at the cutting edge of urban economic growth, complemented by companies new to the city and by commercial firms in the export base of the service sectors of the city economy, together pulling the rest of the urban economy behind them. Many locational policies in many countries are directed at this group of firms. The geography of the decentralization (or recentralization in some cases) of these firms responds to and feeds into the changing physical and economic structure of the city. The developing patterns of industrial decentralization and growth are linked to the expansion of the city and are influenced by many elements of public policy, including locationally specific land use and urban development policies, but always against a backdrop of strong market forces.

The choice of a new site with an existing factory building or of a site for new construction is necessarily filled with uncertainties. In comparison with other economic decisions facing the typical industrial manager, the lead times are long and it is difficult to revise or to correct a decision once made. While it is true that the company will adapt to its new surroundings, just as those new surroundings will adapt to the company, the possibility of error or of a less than fully efficient choice in industrial location decisions remains high. This makes these decisions difficult to model in a way that ensures a high level of predictive capability. It also can bring into question lines of policy prescription based on too simple a view of the determinants of new industrial locations.

The market-based view of industrial location decision making rests upon the standard assumption of instrumental rationality by the actors involved. This chapter points to two further views of rationality, the procedural view and the expressive view. These views may be seen as complementary to the instrumental view and together may provide a fuller understanding of observed decision outcomes as well as of observed decision activities and sequences. The three perspectives together offer an enriched understanding.

The chapter illustrates the themes of the next section, of the special characteristics of the industrial location decision, and of the potential contribution of using three different but complementary views of rationality with evidence from the 1980 Greater São Paulo Industrial Location Study. This study used an interview survey of 581 companies recently decentralizing within and out of the Greater São Paulo Metropolitan Area to establish not only the pushes and pulls involved in the trajectory of each movement but also the pattern of decision making that took place within each of the sampled companies.

Although limited geographically, the study encompassed a wide variety of manufacturing activities and company sizes.

MANUFACTURING LOCATION DECISIONS

Explicit decisions about the location of production facilities occur very infrequently in the life of manufacturing companies. In the life cycle of a company, several relocations may take place in the early years. Thereafter the principal factory tends to remain on one site, with extensions to the initial building where necessary and possible. Major increases in floor space capacity may involve a branch unit, typically fairly local and close to the principal plant. Later, market developments and the takeover of other companies will result in new branch plants and in the acquisition of subsidiary companies at a distance. The transfer of the principal plant to a new location occurs rarely, and the establishment of a branch plant at a distance for production reasons only is not common. A "push" factor has to be involved as well as a set of "pull" factors related to the new location (Townroe 1979b). These push factors may involve cost elements (wages, access costs, the value of the land and property in alternative use, property taxes) or direct constraints (lack of adjacent space to expand into, land use planning controls, pollution controls, end of lease).

Implicit location decisions are forced upon companies much more frequently. Companies adapt to changing locational circumstances, revising internal policies as access to markets or to suppliers improves or worsens, as prices and the availability of skills in the local labor market adjust, or as property prices change. In most cases, however, this adaptation by the company will not be seen by company managers as a location decision per se.

With industrial movement and industrial location decisions, unlike other decision-making areas within the company, there is little opportunity to gain experience. The experience is not there, on file or within the acquired competence of the owner or senior managers. For these people as individuals, aside from their present company, involvement in an industrial location decision will not be common. The pool of experienced expertise available to face the task of choosing a new production site may be small or nonexistent in most companies. This may not trouble the existing managers too much if choosing a new site appears *prima facie* to be a relatively simple task. But when the common complexities and uncertainties are recognized, there are few guidelines to fall back on.

Uncertainty will be of three types: (1) uncertainty about the scope of the decision fields (for example, what areas might be considered? Is the takeover of another company an alternative?); (2) uncertainty about the trade-offs within the company between locationally related factors and nonlocational variables (for example, between wage variations and the choice of new machinery); and (3) uncertainty about how to discover and compare alternatives (for example, on the reliability of data, on sources of information, on how to assess the trade-offs). Each of these three types of uncertainty is likely to be greater for location decisions than for more routine choices. This calls into question the adequacy of the notion of rationality that is assumed in the standard "economic man" model applied to industrial location decisions.

While uncertainty may be accounted for by a model decision maker in calculating payoff probabilities against a profit-maximizing objective using subjective criteria (as suggested by Greenhut [1966]), uncertainty may induce a satisficing mode of decision making rather than a maximizing one. Simon's (1957; 1982) notion of "bounded rationality" characterized decisions as being against a target level of attainment rather than a maximum one. Given a decision dilemma, the individual proceeds through a decision sequence in which he or she learns about alternatives and then sifts and compares them against the target. Once the target or the desired minimum listing of anticipated characteristics of an outcome is discovered, the search stops and a decision is taken. Further search does not take place. There is evidence of industrial location search sequences following this pattern (Townroe 1971). It then remains an open question for the decision maker as to whether the chosen alternative is the best possible option or whether it is just the first to meet the preset target.

The satisficing mode of behavior, when modeled conceptually, requires rationality on behalf of the decision maker, just as the maximizing mode does. Without rationality, behavior can only be ascribed as random. But satisficing continues to hold the standard instrumental view of rationality at its core. Two further views of rationality, procedural and expressive, can enrich the observer's perspective not only of satisficing behavior but also of maximizing behavior (Hargreaves-Heap 1990). These further views of rationality can also be seen to have a particular relevance for the understanding of industrial location decisions. (This is discussed in detail in Townroe [1991]).

With instrumental rationality, action and the explanation of the action are intentional and purposive. The economic actor strives at means in order to achieve ends, seeking an efficient combination of inputs to achieve a target output. It is rather a utilitarian view of human behavior.

A complementary view is to see rationality as being in part procedural. This view acknowledges that the individual belongs in society, a society that has rules and norms. The behavior of the individual is influenced by these rules and norms, which are not seen as just part of the means through which ends are achieved, but as contributions to the ends, or the targets. Actions influence the observed outcomes, which may not have been the original objective of the actor.

A further perspective comes from seeing rationality as being in part expressive. The actor is capable of reflection, not just calculation. He, therefore, can be experimental. We thus "have a picture of the individual who is groping for what is worthwhile" (Hargreaves-Heap 1990, 5). Again, action is no longer simply a means toward a given end.

These further views of rationality, procedural and expressive, help to fill an explanation gap. Policy prescription, involving intervention to influence the behavior of individuals, requires explanation. Prescription based upon the partial explanation served up by the assumption of instrumental rationality alone is in danger of being partial or off-target. One example highlights this.

Studies in the United Kingdom and the United States (Townroe 1979b) suggest that industrial managers involved in a site or new building selection process typically seek to underplay their uncertainties and their lack of knowledge and skill (see also Lee 1989). They tend to fall back upon rules of thumb and to follow the example of others. The procedural rationality view of these decision makers provides a partial explanation of "herd effects" in industrial location patterns. A policy of inward investment into a region directed at a mix of industries very different from those recently established there will not benefit from an important inducement—the example of similar companies. (For a further discussion of policy alternatives, see Townroe 1979a).

Further evidence on departures from the model of instrumental rationality comes from the 1981 survey of 581 manufacturing companies decentralizing within São Paulo Metropolitan Area and out to the rest of the state of São Paulo in Brazil. The core results of this survey have been published elsewhere, including details of the background context and the push and pull location factors for various subgroups of transfers, branch plants, and births (Townroe 1983; 1984).

It should be stressed that the decentralization of economic activity in Brazil has been a major issue for several decades. It is an issue that concerns two spatial levels. At the interstate level, there are great economic inequalities between the more prosperous southeastern states, such as São Paulo, Minas Gerais, and Paraná, and the poorer states of the northeast. Very generous subsidies have been offered to companies to relocate over the 1,500 kilometers. At the intrastate level, decentralization is focused on metropolitan centers, such as Rio de Janeiro, Curitiba, Belo Horizonte, and São Paulo, and their hinterlands, with relevant policies being the responsibility of state governments.

By the end of the 1970s, the São Paulo Metropolitan Area had become the economic dynamo of the Brazilian economy. Over the thirty years to 1980 the population of the state of São Paulo (which has a land area similar to the United Kingdom or the state of Oregon in the United States) rose from 9.1 million to approximately 25 million. With 19 percent of the national population, by 1975 the state of São Paulo accounted for 49 percent of the net industrial product of the nation, employing 48 percent of the nation's industrial labor force. This activity was heavily concentrated in metropolitan São Paulo, home for half the population of the state. São Paulo experienced population growth rates of 5.4 percent per annum between 1950 and 1960, 6.0 percent per annum in the 1960s, and 4.4 percent per annum in the 1970s. The extremely rapid growth in population and industry in the so-called miracle years of 1968 to 1975 put great strains upon infrastructure and services of all kinds.

There were, therefore, considerable pressures on companies to consider the possibility of decentralization, either within the metropolitan area to the suburbs or out to the hinterland of the state. The pattern of this growth and the beginnings of a reversal of the trends of concentration are described in Townroe (1984), as a background to the large-scale survey of locational choices by recently mobile companies.

The findings on the industrial location push and pull factors in the São Paulo survey follow expectations based upon similar exercises elsewhere. The companies were asked to specify which factors they saw as being of "major importance" or of "decisive importance" in their location decisions. Among the push factors encouraging decentralization, the top four from a possible list of thirty were the need to increase production (mentioned by 81 percent of respondents), fully occupied existing premises (81 percent), a desire for internal reorganization (62 percent), and introduction of new products (44 percent). Compared with North American and European studies (Townroe 1979b), labor shortages or lack of skills as a push factor was less prominent, although the labor factor was important among the pull factors for small firms moving locally.

The 581 respondents, which included seventy multinational companies with a minimum of 25 percent foreign ownership, were presented with a list of thirty-eight potential pull factors influencing the choice of one new location over another. Here the pattern of response varied somewhat with the geographic direction and the extent of the move (See Figure 6.1.) For companies moving within the administrative city of São Paulo and within the suburbs—essentially local moves with no strong decentralizing element—the most important locational factors related to property (for 65 percent of respondents) and to labor: plentiful supply (59 percent), labor with required skills (59 percent), and public transport for workers (36 percent). These were mostly smaller companies, employing less than fifty. (All companies in the survey employed at least ten people.)

The pattern of response for the larger, longer distance decentralizing moves was somewhat different. For firms moving from inner to outer suburbs of the metropolitan area ("suburban" moves), road access was the most frequently cited factor (69 percent), followed by the land factors of the existence of a suitable plot (68 percent), and space for future expansion (66 percent). A plentiful supply of labor was referred to as an important location factor by 57 percent of the firms involved. For firms moving out of the metropolitan area altogether to locations in the rest of the state ("exurban" moves), the labor factor was mentioned by only 42 percent, and for firms moving within the rest of the state, by 38 percent. For those firms decentralizing out of the metropolitan area largely to sites within the metropolitan ring, the important locational choice influences were:

Figure 6.1
Composition of Greater São Paulo Region

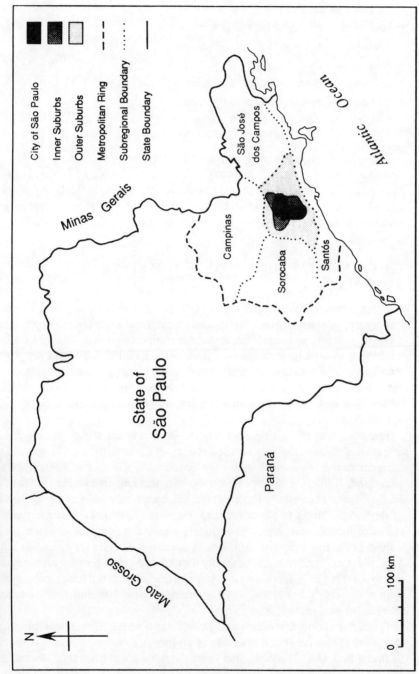

City of São Paulo
Inner Suburbs
Outer Suburbs
Metropolitan Ring
Subregional Boundary
State Boundary

Minas Gerais

State of
São Paulo

Paraná

Mato Grosso

Campinas

São José
dos Campos

Sorocaba

Santós

Atlantic Ocean

N

0   100 km

- Ease of road access (86 percent)
- Existence of suitable plot (84 percent)
- Space for future expansion (82 percent)
- Available electric power supply (79 percent)
- Price of land (69 percent)
- Available telephone and telex (66 percent)
- Proximity of main customers (55 percent)
- Proximity of main suppliers (51 percent)

The relative prominence given to infrastructure reflects the uncertainties and shortages of a rapidly growing economy. The price of land was found to be important because of the importance of speculation in the land purchase. In both these respects, there is a difference in emphasis when compared with findings from North America and Western Europe (Townroe 1984).

CHOOSING NEW LOCATIONS IN THE STATE OF SÃO PAULO

Three items of evidence from the Greater São Paulo Industrial Location Survey are presented here: the timing of the locational choice process, the range of alternatives considered, and the information sources used. The results contribute to a picture of decision-making rationality that is not simply instrumental, leading to the suggestion that policy prescription in this area cannot be based simply upon the premise that the response of economic actors to policy initiatives will follow that implied by sets of optimizing calculations alone.

The time span of the selection process for a new site varies greatly among companies, depending both on the urgency of the internal motivation and the external pressures as well as on the speed with which a suitable option is generated. Table 6.1 shows the timing distribution, in months, for the São Paulo firms. The results in this table are based upon weighted aggregates of the sample firms to allow for response bias. They present the movement status of births, branches, and transfers and the geographic distinctions involved in the movement within the city core of the original city of São Paulo ("across city"), from the city core out to the metropolitan area suburbs ("suburbanizing"), from the city core and the suburbs out to secondary cities within the city's hinterland ("exurbanizing"), and within that hinterland ("other moves outside São Paulo").

Table 6.1 shows that births and branch units required less searching time than transfer moves, but 45 percent of all moves took longer than six months to find a new site. The table also shows that the longer distance decentralizing moves ("suburban" and "exurban") involve a longer search time on

Table 6.1
The Timing of Choice by Category of Move (percentages)

	Status			Movement Categories				
	Births	Branch	Transfer	Across City	Suburban	Exurban	Outside São Paulo	Total
"How Long Did the Selection Process Take?"								
Months								
0 - 2	40	43	29	31	20	27	48	32
3 - 5	39	22	24	25	23	16	24	23
6 - 8	15	28	19	21	24	27	15	21
9 - 11	1	1	3	2	1	5	3	2
12 or more	5	6	26	17	32	25	11	21
Weighted Number of Firms (=100%)	492	314	1,808	642	369	169	279	1,945

Source: 1981 São Paulo Industrial Location Survey.

average than the two groups of shorter distance local moves. These findings are as may be expected, although the distinctions are not very clear cut. The speed and timing of the search will limit the range of alternatives considered. The search length will also reflect uncertainty about the range of possibilities and about information relevant to the decision. A "forced move" may limit the search time. The search may take longer if the company does not have the buoyancy of a full order book to take itself over a difficult period, so there will be more risk involved in a wrong or inappropriate decision.

Since smaller companies are more likely to be involved in a transfer move, their search time is longer than for larger companies, unless they can find available empty rental premises. Larger companies, it was found, were more interested in the rising land values in the suburbs and in the secondary cities and were frequently seeking to purchase more land than they required themselves. As noted earlier, this was to cover themselves for subsequent expansion, but the land was also seen as an investment and a speculation. It was found that, on average, a further twelve months must be added to the timing of the site selection process before a move-in can take place and production can start. This clearly depends on whether or not an existing building is to be used or whether construction is necessary.

The range of alternatives considered in a decision is always bounded. The criteria for deciding on the number of options to be reviewed, in overview or in detail, are normally not made explicit by the managers concerned. There are stages in the sifting process of options, where a listing moves from "possibles" toward a short list of "desirable" alternatives. In some companies the search process continues until a (normally short) list of viable alternatives is prepared. In others, the search sequence is much more akin to satisficing behavior, with the search continuing until an agreed ex-ante specification is met. In still others, the search continues until it is clear that improved options are not being generated and a return to an earlier alternative is in order: a form of maximizing behavior. Sometimes the search constitutes a learning process, as in procedural rationality, where the end is in part determined by the means, and a final choice is based upon an acceptance of both the developing criteria and the option that meets them.

Only 8 percent of the São Paulo companies considered a state other than São Paulo. This low percentage is not surprising given the distances involved. The proportion rose among large multiplant companies. Problems of market access and access to suppliers were the principal reasons for not considering other states.

Within the state of São Paulo, only 16 percent of all of the firms in the survey considered an alternative region as a possibility for their new locations. "Region" here was interpreted fairly broadly in the interview as "a municipality and the municipalities adjacent to it," so it is surprising that so few considered such alternatives overall. This is in part a reflection of the small size of many responding companies. However, the proportion rises sharply for the decentralizing group of firms; 58 percent of these looked at options within the metropolitan area as well as at regions outside. Only 41 percent of the firms considering other regions said that they did so "in depth," reflecting a preliminary sifting process of options for the majority. Infrastructure (roads, utilities, and so on) that is deemed to be inadequate after a quick overview ruled out possible options for many companies. In this respect, unevenness in infrastructure provision in a rapidly expanding economy does lead to different search patterns than those found in more fully developed nations. The "friction of distance" varies geographically.

At the scale of the individual region, one-half of all firms surveyed considered alternatives either within the municipality eventually selected or in other municipalities of the region. This is in addition to alternatives considered within the municipality of origin, where the other half of firms made their comparisons, either within the municipality or with a single external option. Table 6.2 shows how relatively more alternatives were considered for branch plant moves and for the two groups of firms decentralizing within and out of the metropolitan area.

The table also suggests a more local search for alternatives by births (which is not surprising) and by moves outside the metropolitan area. Among the reasons for rejecting alternatives, a failure to find land and buildings of a suitable specification clearly predominates. Problems related to transport (access and congestion for both deliveries and for commuting by the labor force) were more important for the moves within the metropolitan area. Surprisingly, given the general problems with communications facilities and with infrastructure of all kinds in and around the São Paulo metropolitan area in the late 1970s, these factors were cited by very few firms as reasons for rejecting one or more alternatives. "Government policy" was much more important, encompassing land use controls, lack of incentives, and local taxation levels. Only 28 percent of firms could say that they investigated alternatives "in depth" at this level, although again the proportion rose among the exurbanizing and hinterland branch and transfer moves.

As already implied in the earlier discussion, the search for a new production site may be conducted with the desirable attributes of the site for the specific project in hand listed out in advance; or the search may be less structured, the sequence being guided by locations that seem attractive at first sight but then dropped if basic requirements are not met, without systematic comparison of all attributes. The second route seems to reflect both elements of procedural and expressive rationality and was followed by 36 percent of the São Paulo firms answering the question. This compares with 50 percent of firms in a British government survey (Department of Trade and Industry 1973) and 76 percent in a smaller United Kingdom survey (Townroe 1971). One-fifth of the majority subgroup following the first route agreed that their list of requirements was revised in the course of studying various alternatives. These revisions were more common among firms choosing locations within

Table 6.2
Alternative Locations Considered within Regions of the São Paulo State by Categories of New Plant
(percentages)

	Status			Movement Categories			
	Birth	Branch	Transfer	Across City	Suburban	Exurban	Outside São Paulo
Reasons for Rejection (%)							
Land and Building	72	83	66	66	77	57	70
Labor Problems	4	8	5	3	3	18	6
Transport Problems	2	4	11	11	12	7	0
Communications	0	0	0	0	0	0	0
Infrastructure	2	1	2	0	0	2	10
Government Actions	19	24	16	20	8	16	14
Total Number (1)	247	88	418	196	175	83	53
Alternatives Considered (%)							
District in Same							
Municipality	39	34	26	37	6	16	58
Adjacent Municipality	27	47	52	53	55	52	33
Other Municipality	34	20	22	10	38	32	9
Total Number (1)	262	144	549	314	211	87	81
Number Not Responding	231	231	550	243	207	101	186

Source: 1981 São Paulo Industrial Location Survey.
(1) Weighted Number of Responses (=100%).

the metropolitan area than those outside, suggesting a greater difficulty in meeting the original requirements.

Once the search commenced for the São Paulo firms, a wide range of information sources was drawn upon. These are shown in Table 6.3. The question asked was: "In investigating the conditions offered by the location finally selected, what type of information was used?" It is, therefore, surprising that all firms did not visit their short-listed sites. The table shows the relative importance of visiting other companies for decentralizing firms and the relative unimportance of visiting local governments by short moves. The use of published material was uniformly low. Visits to local governments were important for firms moving to new areas. Seventeen percent of these firms visited either local governments or agencies of the state government (including the State Development Bank, the electricity authority, the pollution control agency, and the land use planning agency). A very small number of firms noted other sources of information they had used. These included advertising by a municipality, study of the presence or absence of other companies in the same sector, and study of the availability of raw materials. The use of special consultants was higher for branches than transfers, probably an effect of company size. But it was also higher for the births, which was unexpected. Consultants were much more important to the exurbanizing group, reflecting for this group the relatively greater step to the "unknown" location.

The companies were asked whether any financial comparisons were made between locations of the various elements of the new project: the land, the building, transport and labor costs, and the value of any incentives offered. At first sight, this may seem to be a strange question to ask. It could easily be assumed that instrumental rationality applies and so, of course, the relative costs of alternatives will be calculated as a necessary part of arriving at a choice between them. However, cautionary evidence from the United Kingdom warns against such an assumption. The uncertainties referred to earlier, the pressures for a quick answer, and the radical and sequential nature of the search all lead some companies to look for an alternative that will meet their *a priori* requirements and that is affordable in terms of their budget. They are then satisfied when this option is discovered. They do not feel the need to chase after further options to discover whether their defined needs may be satisfied elsewhere at lower cost. They may feel that, within the geographic area defined by the company as a realistic or feasible search area, locational cost variations are small, or certainly smaller than cost variations from other sources. The company therefore makes a minimum needs choice, or a satisficing choice, rather than an optimizing one.

Only 54 percent of the firms surveyed responded to the question on financial comparisons. Of these, just over one-quarter compared land costs. This percentage was lower (24 percent) for births and the across-city moves (20 percent) and noticeably higher for the suburban group of branches and transfers (39 percent) and for the exurban group (40 percent). The larger the

Table 6.3
Information Used in Site Selection (percentages)

Information Sources	Status			Movement Categories			
	Births	Branch	Transfer	Across City	Suburban	Exurban	Other moves Outside São Paulo
Visits to Sites	56	52	47	57	59	42	58
Visits to Local Government	23	19	26	14	32	42	21
Visits to Other Companies in the Region	15	16	15	3	24	34	10
Use of Published Material	4	7	4	2	3	11	8
Use of Special Consultants	15	9	4	4	4	15	1
Weighted Number of Firms Responding (1)	165	180	591	33	213	117	124

Source: 1981 São Paulo Industrial Location Survey.
(1) Percentages do not add to 100 because some companies said "yes" to more than one information source.

parent company, the more likely it was that land cost comparisons were made, a relationship that did not hold for the size of the new plant. The proportion comparing prices of buildings (or the costs of leases) was slightly smaller, 27 percent overall. Within this figure are births (44 percent), branches (27 percent), and transfers (22 percent) and a noticeably low (80 percent) proportion of branches and transfers in the hinterland group of moves. The proportion here did not seem to be linked with the size of the company, but was high for both small and large new plants and lower for intermediate sizes.

The proportion making comparisons between sites of the cost of transporting both the product and raw materials was lower again at 27 percent overall. This was higher for births (31 percent) and, as expected, higher for the decentralizing exurban group (31 percent). It was noticeably low for the across-city branches and transfers (22 percent) and for the hinterland moves (12 percent). Comparisons in the costs of labor were at the same level overall, 24 percent. This seems surprisingly low. Even among the exurban group of firms, which would be comparing sites in different labor market areas, the proportion rose only to 28 percent. It was highest among births (31 percent). Again against expectations, comparisons were more numerous among small new plants than large ones. Perhaps the explanation for these small numbers is that, within the areas being compared, variations in labor costs are small. Although there is a marked difference in average wage levels in manufacturing between the metropolitan area and the rest of the state of São Paulo, differences in wages are not strong within the metropolitan area or between principal hinterland centers for the sorts of labor skills that most of the companies in this survey were seeking (Sveikauskas et al. 1985; Hamer and Dillinger 1983). General knowledge of these facts may lead managers involved in a location decision to believe that comparative costing of labor is not really necessary. There is no evidence of strong systematic differences in the quality of labor between areas, which would be reflected in differences in labor productivity.

Very few firms compared the incentives offered by different municipalities in financial terms: one thirty-two in the whole survey. This in part reflects incentives that do not have a clear price attached to them; it really reflects more strongly how few firms received incentives or were influenced by them in their choice of new locations. On a weighted basis, branch plants (11 percent), the exurban moves (19 percent), and the hinterland moves (11 percent) were the most likely subgroups of firms to compare incentives. These are also the groups most likely to be making locational choices between the secondary cities outside the metropolitan area. The treatment of incentives within the decision-making sequence again says something about the limitations of a purely instrumental view of economic choices.

SOME CONCLUSIONS

This chapter has contributed to the theme of decentralization by bringing forward findings from a very large and detailed survey of industrial companies choosing new plant locations in Brazil. It has argued that decision making for the choice of new industrial locations might be regarded as something of a special case by virtue of the high levels of uncertainty involved and because the key decision makers typically have little opportunity to learn by doing. This brings into question issues of the appropriate perspectives for analysis, explanation, and policy prescription in the area of metropolitan employment decentralization.

Whatever level or perspective is used by the analyst, there is an explicit or implicit view of the individual decision maker involved. This individual has to be characterized, and one key attribute to be ascribed in any modeling is that of rationality. However, the standard assumption of instrumental rationality can be seen as partial or limiting. Therefore, this view of rationality can be enriched by laying alongside it the procedural and expressive views of rationality. This assertion is supported by what we know of search processes and the application of decision criteria by industrial managers making these decisions. Behavior is far from homogeneous, but the three views of rationality offer some explanation for variations in observed pathways. The results of the São Paulo survey support the need to recognize the procedural and expressive facets of the industrial location decision.

PART II

THE CASE OF MEXICO

7

Decentralization in Mexico:
The Political Context

David E. Stansfield

The spatial allocation of power and authority is a fundamental issue in the politics of most, if not all, countries.[1] However, although particular formulas of allocation, such as federalism in the nineteenth century, became virtual ends in themselves, more often the formulas are discussed as mechanisms more or less suitable for the promotion of other values (Hamilton et al. 1937; Wheare 1963). In other words, does a proposed or existing arrangement permit or restrict political participation; does it facilitate the distribution of wealth more fairly; does it encourage or hinder economic growth?

Thus political structures designed at an earlier stage of a country's history, sanctioned by contemporary political support or imposed by superior force, may be challenged by groups espousing new values or by groups promoting older values but enjoying new access to the debate. The standards by which a regime's performance is judged change over time. The current search for "efficiency" would have no equivalence in the immediate postrevolutionary situation in Mexico. This is not to say that there were no calls for the effective implementation of policy decisions, but that these calls were low on the list of contemporary political priorities. At that chaotic time, the prime demand was for nationally acceptable institutions. Their "efficiency" was measured by their acceptability.

Discussion of the spatial dimension is therefore part of a continuing and wider debate about the relationship between political institutions and political values. It is not a technical argument governed by timeless and absolute. standards. It is in this general context that the current interest in decentralization in Mexico should be placed.

Indeed, the issue of where, spatially, power is to be constitutionally located has been raised regularly over the years. The groups raising it and the detailed terms of their argument have changed, as have their methods for propagating their views. There is, however, a certain degree of continuity and familiarity about the debate. This is not to denigrate it. It is an important part of the continuing process of adjusting institutions to the continually changing society they serve.

Occasionally, the legal arrangements of a political system become atrophied and lose their effectiveness, resulting in a loss of support or legitimacy. Alternative avenues for the expression of citizens' needs may then evolve outside the official constitutional channels. The government may also insist that the existing but obsolescent arrangements be followed, offering minor modifications, perhaps, and characterizing the alternatives as the designs of those opposed to the State.

Maintaining this position is not easy. Dissent can become embarrassing and the application of force to effect compliance can become counterproductive. The USSR, for example, after decades of apparent suppression of demands for change, is involved in a major restructuring of a highly centralized State apparatus. The experience of Mexico, therefore, is not unique.

HISTORICAL BACKGROUND

It may be stretching things a little to suggest that the independence movement was an eventually successful call for the decentralization of the rule of the Spanish Crown, but demands for increased autonomy for local political institutions and the devolution of national governmental functions have surfaced regularly since the formation of the modern Mexican State. Seldom, if ever, has the constitutionally defined spatial allocation of power and authority remained universally accepted for any length of time (Meyer 1986; Falcon 1986).

Much of the conflict of the nineteenth century derived from the dissatisfaction of regional elites with the ways in which the central authority was used. The ideological division between the liberals and conservatives over the role of the State was the most obvious instance, but this was complicated by the particular demands of regional leaders defending their *patrias chicas* (Costeloe 1975; Hamill 1966; Hamnett 1986).

The *Porfiriato* (1876–1911) represented an ingenious, if temporary, solution to this period of "decentralist" conflict. It allowed for a decentralization of some governmental functions, such as the provision of local "police" forces to regional *jefes políticos*, on the understanding that other powers were at the disposal of the national Porfirian elite. In a sense, this was no more than an informal, extra-constitutional arrangement, only possible within a State with limited functions and a restricted clientele. There was no rewriting of the constitution or a formalization of administrative devolution. The *Porfiriato* did, on the other hand, provide a period of relative calm and a surge of prosperity for those sympathetic to the regime (Cosio Villegas 1965; Gonzalez 1957).

In time, of course, this spatial allocation of power, not to mention the social divisions in Mexican society, became intolerable to a variety of political groups and classes. The result was a prolonged period of political violence and administrative paralysis. In fact, the Mexican Revolution (1911–1917) fractured the centralized power of the bourgeois State. The national army disintegrated in the face of a plethora of regionally based revolutionary armies, and the national bureaucracy was bankrupted (Knight 1986). In the resulting vacuum, power fell into the hands of fractious local *caudillos*, with limited or naive views on the "national" role of the State, and bourgeois reformers whose sophisticated national aspirations were not matched by real national political support (Womack 1968; Carr 1971; Falcon 1984). Until the 1930s, despite the drawing up of a constitution in 1917 which defined the relationship between national and local government and a pattern of centralized administration, there was a considerable degree of *de facto* decentralization.

In fact, the debate about the spatial allocation of power and authority within the political classes at this juncture was largely in terms of the need for more centralization and for a diminution of the powers of local politicians. Backed by armed, personalist followers, these *caciques* were confronted by an often fragile alliance of ambitious generals and idealistic reformers. For the revolutionary generals, like Alvaro Obregon (1914–1918) and Plutarco Elías Calles (1918–1922), a more centralized State represented a means for consolidating their authority vis-à-vis their troublesome regional counterparts, whose loyalties to the Revolution were unpredictable. Regionalism was also seen as a threat to the integrity of the country, making it vulnerable to invasion and a possible loss of territory. Centralization was therefore favored for both personal and institutional reasons by the early military leaders of the Revolution (Cockcroft 1983).

For the reformers associated with the Revolution, a stronger, more centralized State represented a more effective mechanism for social change and a way of countering the conservatism of the local *caciques*. The State was portrayed as a catalyst of social and economic improvement and the regions as sources of reaction. Since local leaders were tenacious in trying to control all activity within their regions, any decentralization of government functions involved putting resources into the pockets of men whose commitment to the reformist aims of the Revolution was doubtful (Cordova 1973).

The creation of a more professional national army and the parallel elaboration of a mass-based, political party system eventually eroded the overt power of the regional bosses. The provisions for a strong centralized State, written into the constitution as an exhortation in the chaotic year of 1917, now seemed more enforceable. A group of politicians had established themselves at the apex of State power and were able to direct it along lines they thought appropriate. The challenges from the regions to national authority gradually declined. Regional bosses increasingly became agents of central government, often securing governorships of the states in which they had their power bases.

They were allowed resources to maintain their local positions, but only so long as they did not usurp national priorities.

The State in the 1930s expanded its role in society and the economy considerably. Legislation was used to push through a whole range of reforms and to create a battery of new national institutions. The commitment to educational and agrarian reform brought a massive expansion in the bureaucracies charged with their implementation. The nationalization of public utilities and oil also increased the size of the public sector in both personnel and as a proportion of the GNP (gross national product). State and *municipio* finances, always dependent upon subventions from the national government, deteriorated as the regime opted for ambitious national projects. The new reform agencies and expanded ministries were similarly dominated by centralizing tendencies. Their funds came from the national Treasury, and there were no significant attempts to divert funds from these policy areas into the States' finances. Where there were local initiatives, funds and personnel were channeled through the regional offices of the national agencies. In some cases, local politicians, both within the local government system and in the governing party, were allowed access to the resources of these local agencies, notably in the Ejidal Credit Bank. But there was little scope for these provincial offices actually to make policy or to bid for funding directly (Cockcroft 1983; Gonzalez 1987).

The steady concentration of State power was made possible only because of the burgeoning influence of the revolutionary party, the *Partido Revolucionario Mexicano* (PRM). Created by the ruling elite, and launched by the populist President Lazaro Cárdenas (1934–1940), it integrated the myriad political forces of the Revolution into four national sector organizations. It was specifically designed to reduce the regionalist tendencies of the past and to provide the basis for a truly national project. Enjoying ready access to the State's financial resources, it also benefited from the government's propaganda machine and its activities were sanctioned by the national security apparatus. In many ways it became synonymous with the State. Regional and local party activity seldom went beyond electoral mobilization and recruitment. Policies were generated at the center by the leadership.

The Postwar Era

The change of ideological style from the quasi-socialism and agrarianism of the late 1930s to the laissez-faire capitalism and industrialization of the postwar period did little to change this highly centralized pattern. The governing party changed its name to the *Partido Revolucionario Institucional* (PRI) but retained its basic structure. The national State continued to play a directing role in the economy. There may have been a switch to favoring the private sector during the Aleman *sexenio* (1946–1952), but it was a State-led process. It is true that the regime's commitment to social reform lessened and associated expenditures dropped, but this was more than compensated for by an expanded State involvement in the process of encouraging industrialization. The State expanded and improved the country's transport and energy systems and provided cheap credit for investors through the *Nacional Financiera*. Although the rhetoric of laissez-faire economics was popular, there was little in the way of liberalization of political structures. The PRI continued as a disciplined and highly centralized party (Fitzgerald 1978).

Spurred by the recovery of the international economy after World War II, this model of State-protected industrialization generated considerable economic growth, particularly for the capitalist class and the bourgeoisie. Jobs were provided in the new industries, in the service professions, and in the expanding public sector. However, working-class wages were kept low through government control of the trade unions, and conditions in the *campo* worsened as official policy moved to favor large-scale, export-directed private agriculture.

This period, known as the *milagro mexicano*, was characterized by a high level of political confidence within the political elite. There were few calls for the change of a system of economic and political management that had achieved so much. Fine-tuning of the bureaucratic procedures was mooted, but there was no large-scale rejigging of the machinery of policy-making or administration (Hansen 1971; Tuohy 1970).

Behind the complacent facade, however, there were doubts in some quarters. The government's distaste for taxation as a way of paying for its activities meant that it was now heavily in debt to foreign banks and international agencies—a burden that would reappear with even greater impact in later years. There were also those who argued the case of the urban and agrarian poor left behind by the *milagro*. Few of these complainants, however, saw a change in the spatial allocation of power as a primary mechanism for putting the economy on a safer footing or for improving the lot of those at the base of the socioeconomic system. An improvement in the performance of the regime for them would come from a shift in economic and social priorities. The "shape" of the State for leftist critics of the *milagro* was a secondary consideration (Gonzalez Casanova 1965; Aguilar and Carmona 1965).

But there were some who looked for a move away from the persistent trend toward the centralization of administrative and political structures. The bureaucracy had swelled and was a major source of employment for the middle-class products of Mexico's overcrowded university system. Lines of authority within ministries had become confused as more and more new agencies were grafted on to an already complex bureaucratic network. Calls for administrative reform began to emanate from within and without the public sector.

The private sector, particularly that based in the State of Nuevo León, voiced its concern about the cost of maintaining a large, expensive, and unresponsive public service. More strident criticisms came from the small conservative opposition party, the *Partido de Acción Nacional* (PAN), which highlighted the pervasive corruption of the bureaucrats.[2] Groups like the Nuevo León business community, however, hesitated at recommending a full program of

decentralization. Such a recommendation might have given them better access to decision makers in their own state, but they were wary of putting
resources at the disposal of local PRI politicians. Decentralization could only
really be effective, it was thought, if it was accompanied by an improvement
in the quality of the personnel involved. The experience of Yucatán in 1969
also provided a salutary lesson to the PRI's opponents. PAN's tenure of office after its victory in the mayoral elections in the state capital, Mérida, was
short-lived. The new *municipio* administration was immediately starved of
funds by the state and federal governments. Lacking an alternative fiscal base
and faced by the *priísta* governor's intimidating tactics, the mayor was quickly
forced out of office. The scope for ''independent'' local government had proved
to be limited. Henceforth PAN electoral manifestos would include references
to the need for providing a firm financial base for state and municipal administrations (Torres 1986).

Dissatisfaction within the governing party also was present. A faction, led
by the young *oaxaqueño* Carlos Madrazo, disliked the iron grip the older
machine politicians held on the party's organization. While the reform pro-
pagated by Madrazo involved giving more power to the rank and file of the
party at the state and *municipio* levels, it was not a proposal to reorganize
the party on regionalist lines. The reformers, like the *PANistas*, recognized
the dangers of giving the local *políticos* new sources of power. The Madrazo
option sought simply to bypass the local agents of the national party bosses.
Structural changes of political institutions, whether they be party organizations or governmental agencies, would only succeed if there were changes
in the informal power structures that underlay them (Bailey 1988). Madrazo's
efforts in this ambitious reformist venture were unsuccessful, and after his
death this reformist tendency within the PRI became dormant until resurrected
in recent years—with equally dubious results—by Cuauhtemoc Cárdenas.
Whether the efforts of modernizers, sponsored by President Carlos Salinas
de Gortari will finally curtail the power of the older generation of ''dinosaurs''
within the PRI is still an open question.

The most dramatic instance of political dissent in the 1960s was the student movement of 1968 that culminated in the tragic events of Tlatelolco.
The army opened fire on a large crowd of students and workers assembled
in the Plaza of Three Cultures in Mexico City, and a large number of demon-
strators were killed. The motives of the student leaders were complicated,
but there is little evidence to suggest that a desire for the decentralization
of administrative structures was a prime cause (Carrión 1970; Poniatowska
1971). The movement was fueled, among other things, by the students' resentment of the lack of responsiveness of the governing party to the growing social
problems facing Mexico. In this sense, there were echoes of the Madrazo
episode.

It is curious that the government, in its efforts to mollify its critics after
the crisis, actually introduced some decentralist measures. The government,

at least, seemed to believe that an overcentralized university system was a political liability and was partly responsible for the students' militancy. It embarked on a program of reforms designed to build up provincial universities, to break up and professionalize the higher echelons of the country's largest and most overcrowded university, the National Autonomous University of Mexico (UNAM), and to create a new metropolitan university in the Federal District (Morgan 1981).

There were, however, few *real* changes elsewhere in the administration and planning system. New jobs were created in new governmental bodies, some of which were ostensibly concerned with a devolution of central government responsibilities. But the changes were largely cosmetic. They were mainly intended to absorb the growing number of disaffected university students who had proved to be so troublesome in and around the Plaza of the Three Cultures. The main priority of the regime was the reestablishment of political order. A rearrangement of the spatial allocation of power in any fundamental sense was seen as potentially dangerous. The government fell back on traditional ways of obtaining compliance from its opponents—co-optation and coercion. It was in no mood for experiments.[3]

The early 1970s were difficult times for the political elite. The economy was slowing down and was less and less able to provide the level of prosperity that the middle classes had come to expect. The private sector, which had enjoyed a close relationship with the regime, began to experience severe economic difficulties. These difficulties were only inflamed by President Luis Echeverría's populist talk of the need for increased taxation to reduce public debt and agrarian reform to stem the flow of people into the cities. There was a perceptible increase in support for the conservative opposition party, particularly in the more prosperous and industrialized northern states (1970–1976).

Closer to home, the massed ranks of *técnicos* employed in the bureaucracy favored plan-based solutions to the country's economic problems, but few of them saw decentralization as a crucial element in their strategy. Provincial *priísta* politicians facing reinvigorated opponents, on the other hand, were hungry for resources with which to protect their position and a devolution of administration which might increase their power bases. They were not really concerned with introducing new forms of decision making or administration. They were much more concerned with having access to additional sources of patronage and wealth. The consequence was a degree of formal decentralization that provided a "political control" capability to the political machine managers without significantly altering the overall pattern of decision making. If anything, the efficiency of the system was impaired.

The "rediscovery" and eventual exploitation of Mexico's hydrocarbon reserves in the late 1970s changed the political climate almost as much as the economy. The prospect of massive oil revenues was a great fillip to the self-confidence of the political elite. To the less wary it promised the means by which the existing system of politico-administrative controls could be upgraded. The problems of the past few years were seen as little more than the products of decline in the economy's capacity to produce wealth and, more important, to distribute it to the right groups. There was nothing inherently wrong with the system that a new injection of funding could not put right. The new oil wealth was, therefore, destined for an expansion in public works, and a carefully managed decentralization of government functions would help the provincial party organizations build up their depleted patronage portfolios (Grayson 1980).

This party-led view found a degree of support from groups within the national planning community. Trained in the techniques of modern economic management, they too saw a decentralization of the administration as important. In contrast to the politicians, however, they believed it would improve the performance of the economy rather than the political system. They were particularly concerned that the new wealth be used constructively to generate economic growth beyond the hydrocarbon sector. They wanted to create a more balanced economy and to provide employment for an ever-expanding labor force (Tello and Cordero 1981).

Their influence, however, was not as pervasive as those *técnicos* who were pressing for a stronger coordinating role for the central spending ministries. They too wanted a more efficient economy and more jobs, but they were cautious about introducing too much devolution of authority. They saw the need for *coordination* of planning as the major administrative problem facing the regime. Initially, they looked for a "triangle of efficiency" of the Presidency, the Treasury, and the Ministry of National Patrimony as the unifying element in the planning process. Later, in 1977 the "triangle" was replaced by a new superministry, the Ministry of Programming and Planning (SPP).

It was no surprise, therefore, that the ambitious National Industrial Development Plan promulgated in 1979 paid only lip service to decentralization. It declared a commitment to industrial decentralization and proposed a system of incentives for firms locating in specified zones. But, as the plan admitted, "it [was] necessary to concentrate in order to decentralize" and the initiative was coordinated by a new Interministerial Commission.[4] The tax incentives and the preferential energy prices central to the scheme also were to be approved and administered at the federal level (Secretaría de Patrimonio Nacional 1979). The *Sistema Alimentario Mexicano* (SAM), another large-scale development program, was similarly characterized by a highly centralized bureaucracy.

Even the much-applauded Single Coordination Agreement (CUC) and the Integrated Rural Development Program (PIDER), which extended large multipurpose grants to state governments, were limited. State and local officials were allowed to participate in planning arrangements, but the choice of which programs were to be funded and how they were to be administered depended upon decisions made at the federal level.

A prime mover in this period was the then Minister of Planning and Programming and later president, Miguel de la Madrid (1982-1988), a highly qualified planner with a long management career in the labyrinth of the country's national bureaucracy. He was a technician and sought to create clearer lines of administrative command. He was, by temperament and political experience, very different from the politicians at the periphery of the political system. He was also unsympathetic to devolutionists within the bureaucracy.

As president of the republic at a time of severe economic crisis, however, he was forced to be more open to calls for decentralization, especially when made by influential allies and creditors or when they seemed to offer political advantages. As a consequence, decentralization, in a variety of forms, has been very much part of the political debate over the last eight years (Secretaría de Programación y Presupuesto 1985; Pardo 1984).

MEXICAN CENTRALISM

It may be useful at this point to summarize briefly the factors behind the growth of the highly centralized Mexican politico-administrative system.

1. The Constitution of 1917 was written at a time of frantic regionalism and when the authors were looking for ways of cementing the various warring factions together. The inclusion of widely popular social reform measures was accompanied by provisions for a strong executive. This legal base for the strength of the presidency has been used to good effect by its incumbents in accumulating administrative power.

2. The legal and fiscal position of state and local governments has been traditionally weak. They are ceded few opportunities for raising taxes. Indeed, until recently few of the states supported sufficient economic activity to support a truly federal system through locally generated funding.

3. Alongside the centralized State apparatus, the ruling revolutionary group has created and nurtured a tenacious political machine, which has delivered electoral victories at all levels and has been instrumental in "managing" the representation of peasants, workers, and the middle class. Although regional fiefdoms are tolerated within it, the PRI has been unambiguously directed by the political elite in the capital city. Local and regional party organizations have limited roles in the formulation of policy.

4. The pattern of economic development adopted by the regime since World War II has involved the active participation of the national government as a guarantor of capitalist development. The national government took on major financial responsibilities and created vital national institutions, setting the style of economic management and giving birth to an enormous and self-perpetuating bureaucracy. In recent years, this regime has been increasingly prone to recruit highly qualified technocrats keen to apply planning procedures that assume a high level of central coordination.

5. The spatial development of the private sector has, on the whole, followed that of the State. There are enclaves along the U.S. border, in Nuevo León, and in Jalisco, but the capital city is the hub of the country's commercial, banking, and industrial life. Even Monterrey and Guadalajara businesses deem it necessary to have offices in the *Distrito Federal* (DF). The reasons for this are obvious. The city is the political center of gravity. The capital is where political decisions are made, where regulations are drawn up, where contracts are signed, and where friends are made. Proximity to the political class and to other businesses is a powerful attraction. It improves communications and, according to many, cuts costs. It is not only expedient but also efficient. Firms will relocate if rents rise, if living conditions become intolerable, or if labor costs become uneconomic. Thus far, there is little evidence to suggest that these "natural" decentralizing pressures have had a major effect on the business sector.

In the face of this barrage of reasons for the centralized system, why have calls for a reorganization taken on a new urgency over the past few years? To answer this question, we should first identify the source of these calls.

It is popular to date these new demands for devolution from the time of the earthquake in September 1985. The devastation suffered by the capital city seemed to encourage a wide range of commentators to recommend a relocation of government offices to provincial cities, or at the very least to new sites out of the city center. In the case of ministries whose buildings had actually been destroyed, the opportunity appeared to be ideal. The widescale breakdown of telecommunications and the disruption of intracity transport systems also seemed to favor a fresh start. Apart from some temporary transfers of administrative functions and personnel, however, there was little change. New premises were acquired or constructed within the DF, and the bureaucrats waited with varying degrees of patience for their telephones to be reconnected.

Prior to the earthquake there had been a growing body of opinion in academic and journalistic circles that was concerned with the ecologic condition of the metropolitan area. It had spread inexorably since World War II, and its population had exploded dramatically. Planners spoke resignedly of the daily arrival of 1,500 in-migrants and gloomily of a total population of 30 million by the year 2000. The basic services of the city were clearly overstretched in the face of this growth, and the quality of urban life was deteriorating fast. Pollution, traffic congestion, public health worries, insufficient and inadequate housing, and rising crime rates disturbed a wide range of citizens.[5]

Those who recommended a devolution of administrative functions saw this as a contribution to the slowing down of this frightening case of *megacephalitis*. Devolution might help to create alternative poles of development that would divert the in-migrants and reduce the number of factories belching out fumes into the thin atmosphere of the Valle de Mexico. While a few *priísta* politicians took up this ecologic crusade, the political elite as a whole was not inspired.

The main thrust for administrative reform, however, particularly within the elite, stems from the economic crises of 1982 and 1985. The collapse of international oil prices in the face of a slump in demand hit government revenues, and the rise in interest rates pushed the costs of servicing Mexico's debts beyond the country's financial resources. The government's appeal to the IMF and its creditors brought a temporary respite, but the IMF insisted on a number of conditions for future support. Notably, it demanded a significant cut in public expenditure. In line with traditional IMF economic thinking, the advisors believed that this would reduce the public sector's borrowing requirements and improve the economy's efficiency.

In order to appear to be following these guidelines, the government began to look at schemes to trim the bureaucracy. Proponents of decentralization were thus given a degree of formal encouragement. Indeed, in isolated cases—such as in the provision of health care—there were real efforts to create new state bodies that would assume some of the functions previously administered by federal agencies. Efforts to decentralize the educational system were less successful and more motivated by the government's fear of the national teachers' union, the SNTE. Regional development programs, which had been in operation for many years in one form or another, were reemphasized, particularly those on the borders with Guatemala and the United States. There were also efforts to strengthen the judicial positions of the states and municipalities and to give them more financial autonomy.

The commitment to devolution on the part of the de la Madrid administration, however, was less than complete. The continuing economic trials of the country dominated the political agenda, and serious, large-scale decentralization, despite its attraction to the ecologic lobby and some international creditors, was still risky.

The government, even though frequently criticized as being dominated by technicians and as lacking in experience of the day-to-day business of politics, could not ignore the appearance of cracks in the revolutionary political consensus. There had been divisions in the party in the 1970s but they had been mended, sidelined, or suppressed. Dissidents had been accommodated within the State-Party complex or had been isolated. The oil boom had taken the wind out of the sails of many critics. But critical voices were being heard again and in more strident tones than before. They were also coming from different and potentially more dangerous quarters. As the austerity measures associated with the IMF's rescue package began to bite, politicians in and close to the official party began to complain.

For some the government was thought to be abandoning basic revolutionary principles—nationalism, State-led industrialization, and a full commitment to social development. For others, more pragmatically, government policies were causing their constituents great hardship, and by doing so were making their own jobs, as representatives or as "conflict managers," more difficult. These views were expressed in a variety of ways. There were vehement and wide-ranging denunciations from the left, but more telling, perhaps, was the cascade of carefully coded statements from senior figures within the trade unions and peasant organizations affiliated with the PRI.

These warnings were a sign that the official party, which had done so much to provide the elite with a stable political climate since its inception in 1938, was under stress. Party managers traditionally were expected to provide votes for the regime's candidates and to disseminate the government's interpretation of revolutionary principles. They were now beginning to hint that they could no longer do this effectively. The standard of living of their members was sinking and levels of unemployment were rising. They had pleaded for a "tightening of belts" too many times. Their credibility was threatened and more pugnacious "unofficial" unions looked likely to poach their members.

This raised the chilling specter of a breakdown of political order and thus made the regime cautious about any radical restructuring of the State. Consolidation rather than dispersion of State resources seemed advisable at this juncture. Indeed, the cuts in the overall size of the bureaucracy, despite promises to the IMF, were slowed down and cut back. A major transfer of resources to devolved agencies was also avoided, since there was no guarantee that these would act as generators of progovernment sympathy.

The interparty political climate, in short, was still not thought to be right for serious decentralization. The government's fears were confirmed when Cuauhtemoc Cárdenas and Porfirio Muñoz Ledo, both prominent *priístas*, defected from the party to create, in conjunction with a number of small leftist parties, the National Democratic Front (FDN) which then fought the 1988 presidential election with Cárdenas as its candidate.

The popularity of this son of the late Lázaro Cárdenas, the almost universally revered reformist president of the late 1930s, was disturbing to the regime. His public appearances drew enormous crowds and he attracted a massive vote in the presidential election in July 1988. Few people know exactly how many votes he won since it is generally agreed that the electoral returns were "manipulated" by the PRI-dominated Electoral Commission. It was, however, difficult for the government to deny his highly visible popularity completely, and the officially released figures ceded to the FDN a majority of votes cast for the presidency in the DF and in Cárdenas' home state of Michoacán. President Salinas de Gortari, therefore, took the sash of office with a smaller and less cohesive political base than any of his predecessors since World War II.

The positions of the main opposition parties on the decentralization issue are complicated, although both the Revolutionary Democratic Party (PRD)—the vehicle for Cárdenas' ambitions since the breakup of the FDN—and PAN are, on the whole, in favor. In terms of their attitude toward a planned, socialist economy, the PRD is unlikely to want any major shift of emphasis away from the State-led industrialization model evolved since 1946. The PRD wants the government to be less corrupt and more receptive to the views of the population at large. In fact, the prime concern of its leaders initially was to reform the governing party rather than the bureaucracy. Nonetheless, the strength of the PRD in certain areas encourages it to argue in favor of a devolution of powers and financial responsibilities to the states and municipalities. The PRD believes that this would allow it to build up its local base and demonstrate its capacity to effect change in municipal and state administrations. The government is equally concerned not to allow this political advantage to its opponent.

The PAN shares the interest in decentralization. It too has regionally concentrated electoral strengths, particularly in the northern states of Nuevo León, Baja California, Chihuahua, Sonora, and Tamaulipas. Although only occasionally allowed actually to take control of state and municipal governments, as in the governorship of Baja California in 1989, it looks for a reallocation of powers away from the center. Decentralization fits easier into *PANista* ideology than it does into FDN ideology. Since its foundation in 1939, the PAN has attacked the concept of a powerful State apparatus. Inspired by the laissez-faire ideas of von Hayek, the PAN argues for less governmental interference in the social and economic life of the nation. It characterizes the State as overmanned and corrupt and as damaging to the "natural" operation of the economy. It suggests that the private sector is handicapped by regulations and by the concentration of decision-making power in the capital city. It does not favor a complete dismantlement of the federal planning system, but it demands a reorganization of the system that would make it more susceptible to local economic conditions. The PAN also applauds recent moves to break up and privatize the plethora of parastatal agencies and presses for a similar operation on the great public utility monopolies (Mabry 1973).

The PAN espouses a message similar to the IMF's in the economic sphere at least. It also reflects the views of a great many businessmen, frustrated by slow, convoluted decision making and, they complain, high taxes. Many businessmen are loath to call for the complete decentralization of the State. They have little faith in the capacity of regional, state, or municipal authorities to manage affairs better than their *capitalino* counterparts. Nor do they imagine that it would be easy to transfer the administrators and technicians currently employed in the DF to decentralized offices. What they seek is a slimmed-down, more responsive public service. Decentralization could, carefully managed, help to achieve this.

CONCLUSIONS

The government is confronted by a number of forces pressing for decentralization. Their motives reflect the spread of values within society. Most, if not all, claim that a spatial reallocation of power is necessary in the name of efficiency—an understandable hope in a period of economic decline. The government has tried to go some way to mollify this demand by introducing well-publicized programs that cede a semblance of power to the periphery of the State system. The moves, however, are largely symbolic. The government's distinction between decentralization and deconcentration, and its preference for the latter, indicates its hesitancy to lose control of resources at the center.

The government can defend the status quo by reference to an "efficiency" argument. Good planning requires national mechanisms for coordination and should avoid expensive duplication of functions at subnational levels. The government also points to the shortage of technically competent people beyond the capital city. It is interesting that "efficiency," however defined, has become a prime measure of the State system and that "distributionist" measures are secondary or dependent measures.

But the government is acutely aware, or suspicious, that decentralization represents a political threat. There are reformers, like the late Jesus Reyes Heroles, who see it as a necessary way of modernizing the State and, incidentally, the governing party, but most are concerned about giving too many resources to state and local government. Patronage has been a main ingredient in the cement that holds the Mexican political system together. A reduction in the number of jobs and financial resources available to the national elite is a dangerous step to take at a time of political unease. Moreover, it runs the risk of putting those resources at the disposal of opposing political groups. The national elite is conscious of the emergence of regionalist resentments but fears that devolution may exacerbate rather than allay those complaints.

A reallocation of power, whether it is spatial or social, is an important decision. Historically, few authoritarian governments have chosen willingly to reduce or transfer their capacity to make legally binding decisions. Usually, they do so only when their authority is already severely compromised. Mexico has not yet reached this stage. The reports of the death of the centralized state in Mexico are somewhat premature.

NOTES

1. The demands for independence from the USSR by an increasing number of its constituent republics is perhaps the most dramatic contemporary example of this phenomenon. A less spectacular instance is the issue of the "devolution" of powers to a Scottish Assembly within the United Kingdom. See J. Kellas, "Prospects for a new Scottish political system," *Parliamentary Affairs* 42 (4): 519–32 (1989). For a rather technical overview of the debate about decentralization in the Third World, see D. A. Rondinelli et al., "Decentralization in developing countries: A review of recent experience," World Bank Staff Working Papers 581 (Washington, D.C., 1983).

2. The *PANista* magazine, *La Nacion*, was a constant, if sensationalist, source of stories on corruption in the PRI and the federal and state bureaucracies.

3. For an official detailed survey of the initiatives taken by the Echeverría government, 1970–1976, see Coordinanción General de Estudios Administrativos, *Bases para el programa de la reforma administrativa del poder ejecutivo federal* (Mexico DF: Presidencia de la República, 1976).

4. Ministry of National Resources, *Mexico: National Industrialization Plan: Volume 1* (London: Graham and Trotman, 1979), p. 20.

5. For a definitive description and interpretation of the growth of the capital city, see P. Ward, *Mexico City* (London: Belhaven Press, 1990).

8

Mexico's Decentralization in the 1980s: Promises, Promises, Promises . . .

Victoria E. Rodríguez

Analysts of the Mexican political system may debate about the degree of authoritarianism or democracy that prevails in the country, but on one point there appears to be little disagreement: Mexico has a highly centralized system, with political, economic, and administrative powers concentrated in the country's capital. Contemporary Mexico City, unquestionably, is the political, financial, and cultural center of the country. In an area of 1,200 square kilometers, it concentrates one-fourth of the country's total population and roughly half of the entire industrial production, commerce, services, and communications (Ward 1990, 19–20).

The increasing centralization of power caused by the massive concentration of goods and services, of industry and population, has concerned everyone in and out of the government for the past twenty years. The four most recent presidential administrations of Luis Echeverría (1970–1976), José López Portillo (1976–1982), Miguel de la Madrid (1982–1988), and Carlos Salinas de Gortari (1988–1994) have all expressed a major concern with the overwhelming centralization and have attempted to counteract it by developing a host of programs and policies. So far their success appears limited, but the decentralization policy of the de la Madrid administration must be regarded as the most forceful effort of the past twenty years. The content and an evaluation of his *sexenio*'s policies constitute the subject of this chapter.

To a large extent, de la Madrid's decentralization policy can be summarized in the municipal reform of 1984, which was aimed primarily at diffusing power. The importance of the municipal reform is much more political than administrative in nature. Elsewhere the more fundamental political aspects of the reform are discussed (Rodríguez 1987; forthcoming). From a political viewpoint it can be argued that, during de la Madrid's administration, the

Figure 8.1
Mexican States

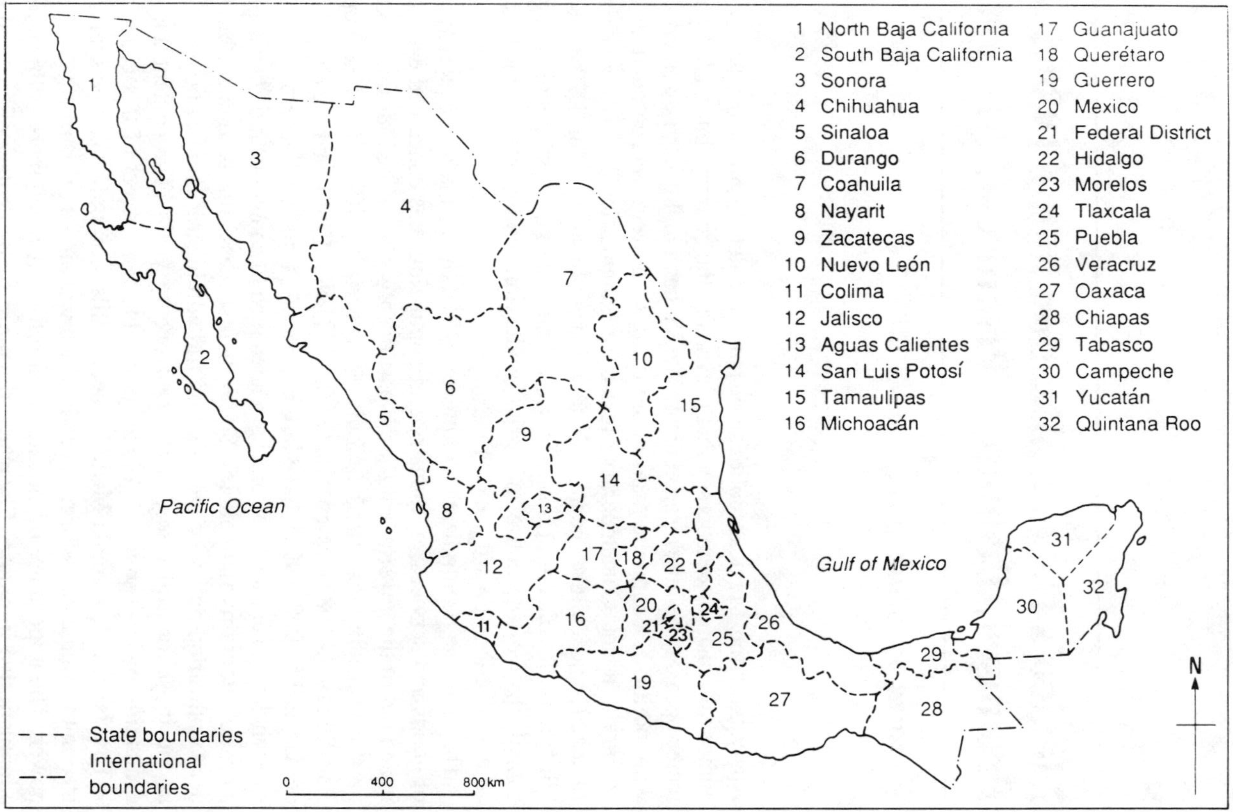

1 North Baja California	17 Guanajuato
2 South Baja California	18 Querétaro
3 Sonora	19 Guerrero
4 Chihuahua	20 Mexico
5 Sinaloa	21 Federal District
6 Durango	22 Hidalgo
7 Coahuila	23 Morelos
8 Nayarit	24 Tlaxcala
9 Zacatecas	25 Puebla
10 Nuevo León	26 Veracruz
11 Colima	27 Oaxaca
12 Jalisco	28 Chiapas
13 Aguas Calientes	29 Tabasco
14 San Luis Potosí	30 Campeche
15 Tamaulipas	31 Yucatán
16 Michoacán	32 Quintana Roo

Pacific Ocean

Gulf of Mexico

0   400   800 km

- - - State boundaries
- · - International
      boundaries

Mexican government embarked on an extensive program of decentralization to hold on to power, to bolster its faltering legitimacy, and to retain central political control while decentralizing administrative matters. The underlying purpose of Mexico's decentralization policy was to centralize by decentralizing. But the main subject of this chapter deals with the administrative aspects of the reform.

The reform claimed as its main purposes to grant *municipios* fixed sources of revenue and to strengthen their political independence. Political autonomy was expected as a consequence of financial autonomy. As a basic premise, the municipal reform set specific mechanisms through which *municipios* could obtain some autonomy in managing their own finances: hence, they could dispose of their economic resources without subordination or restrictions set forth by the federal and/or state governments. In essence, according to the reform, local governments would no longer be limited in their decision making and could attend to their communities' priorities and needs by using their own judgment.

The main theoretical concept used in this analysis is the one of devolution: by devolution we understand the creation of an autonomous entity or the transfer of important decision-making powers to autonomous regional and local organizations. In its broadest sense, to devolve means to strengthen the federal character of the relations among the federal, state, and municipal governments. This meaning implies autonomy for the states and municipalities —an overriding consideration of a true federal system. When there is devolution, important aspects of the center's control are transferred to the lower levels of government. The de la Madrid administration viewed the process of devolution as (a) functional, when specific faculties were transferred to a decentralized organization; and (b) territorial, when programs and resources were transferred to the state and municipal levels. When the federal government decentralized through devolution, it transferred faculties, functions, programs, and resources thereby granting to the decentralized organization a comprehensive autonomy; consequently, all hierarchical lines were broken (Secretaría de Salud 1984b, 160).

In general, the problem with devolution, from the central government's perspective, resides in the fact that it implies granting autonomy; in most cases, if not all, the center is reluctant to lessen its control over the subordinate units. This is particularly true when speaking of political autonomy; Mexico is no exception and has, indeed, made larger efforts to decentralize by means of administrative deconcentration.

The greater difficulty of devolution as compared to other modes of decentralization is well documented in the literature but seems particularly applicable to the Mexican case because during the 1980s the regime confronted its most serious crisis of legitimacy in modern times. Analysts have characterized this crisis as one of "public confidence" and of "public disillusionment" (Middlebrook 1985), as a "crisis of representation" (Foweraker 1987), and as an "institutional crisis" (Cornelius and Craig 1984). In essence, it is a crisis of democratization that has challenged the legitimacy of the political system, in general, and of the dominant party, the PRI (Partido Revolucionario Institucional), in particular. Both the PRI and the government, well aware of the potential outcome of the crisis, have had to engineer some response to popular pressures for democratization. In searching for solutions to the political crisis, the government has experimented carefully with political liberalization. This political "opening," or *apertura*, has been reflected in three specific issues: the political reforms of the late 1970s, the attempts at internal democratization within the party, and the recognition of opposition victories. In the context of the political crisis, decentralization can be regarded as another response of the regime.

As part of the effort to regain its lost legitimacy, the Mexican government experimented with, among other things, administrative deconcentration and political devolution. Administrative deconcentration was relatively easier to implement and, at the same time, it offered the most effective way for the regime to improve its governance (administration). Political devolution proved far more complex, in the case of the municipal reform, it was compounded further because Mexico has not only a long tradition of centralism but also a political regime that for well over fifty years has been ruled by a system of decision making dominated by a single political party. Moreover, a fundamental characteristic of the Mexican political system is the centralization of power in the figure of the president and a few of his closest followers. A key question, therefore, is whether decentralization could ever be made to work in a system where all important policy decisions are made by a handful of officeholders. Moreover, would they ever allow decentralization to succeed, if it presented a threat to their very own hold on power?

In this context, one can appreciate the difficulties inherent in attempting to implement decentralization in Mexico. President de la Madrid's programs and policies may have been well intentioned and promised a great deal, but during his administration the redistribution of political power expected as a result of his decentralization program did not occur. The financial independence promised to the lower levels of government also did not materialize. The devolution—that is, the transfer of control from the center to the localities— that was supposed to result from the municipal reform of 1984 has not materialized. If there have been any changes as a result of decentralization, they consist of a reconfiguration of power structures. This chapter suggests that the focus of control over *municipios* has shifted from the federal government to the state capitals—but *municipios* remain subordinate (see also Rodríguez 1987; forthcoming).

THE PROGRAMS AND POLICIES: PROMISES ON PAPER

One of the highlights of the presidential campaign of Miguel de la Madrid consisted of a series of public meetings throughout the country where a variety of national and local issues were discussed. At these *consultas populares*—popular consultations, as they came to be known—demands for decentralization, particularly in the form of pleas for municipal autonomy, came up repeatedly. The goal of decentralization immediately became a major, and widely trumpeted, plank in de la Madrid's campaign.

In his inaugural address, de la Madrid renewed his support for decentralization and indicated that he would promote it by transferring the health and education sectors to the states. He intended to amend Article 115 of the constitution, in order to strengthen municipal government, and to oppose strongly the further growth of Mexico City (de la Madrid 1984, 30–31). The first major decentralization statement of his administration was the *Plan Nacional de Desarrollo, 1983–1988* (National Development Plan, hereinafter PND).[1] In essence, de la Madrid proposed three broad lines of action to resolve the problems of centralization: to strengthen federalism, to promote regional development, and to invigorate municipal life (de la Madrid 1982, 96). A series of formal programs and policies were designed to achieve each one of these goals.

Decentralization of the Federal Public Administration

In June 1984 President de la Madrid issued a decree directing all agencies of the federal government to develop a program for decentralization. These programs were formally embodied in the *Programa de Descentralización de la Administración Pública Federal* (Decentralization Program of the Federal Public Administration), implemented in January 1985.[2] In formulating programs each federal agency was to consider the states' development proposals, in order to share with the state governments the responsibilities for implementing these programs. These decentralization measures contemplated more than a simple transfer of offices and personnel from Mexico City to the states, but they did propose to relocate a large group of central agencies outside Mexico City and to create field agencies to ease the burden of the center. Secretaría de Programación y Presupuesto (Ministry of Programming and Budget, or SPP) took responsibility for the coordination of this program, particularly for overseeing the three specific ways in which it would be carried out: transferring federally administered parastatal organizations to the state governments; transferring to the state governments the responsibility for coordinating the execution of development plans; and deconcentrating administrative functions. In essence, the program sought to support regional development by enlarging and improving regional infrastructures.

In early 1985 the federal government announced the transfer of various programs to the states.[3] As a result of the relocation of these programs, a total of 15,995 employees of the federal government left Mexico City. The September earthquakes accelerated the relocation program, and other reorganization plans were enlarged to include additional institutions and organizations. The relocation of federal employees, for example, was speeded up after the earthquakes; the *Comisión Nacional de Reconstrucción* (National Reconstruction Commission) reported that, in the few months following the tremors, 70,000 federal public employees (15 percent of all federal employees in Mexico City) would be relocated (Secretaría de Programación y Presupuesto [SPP] 1986a, 374). By the end of de la Madrid's administration, 62,000 public employees had been actually relocated, which represented 67 percent of the goal proposed for 1988 (SPP 1988, 34). Therefore, some deconcentration actually did occur. But by and large, the two most important—and most widely publicized—decentralizing programs in the federal administration's plan were in the areas of education and health, both carried out through agreements with the states.[4]

Education, like almost everything else, is heavily concentrated in Mexico City and a few states. In 1984–1985 the Federal District, together with the states of Mexico, Jalisco, Puebla, Nuevo León, and Veracruz, concentrated 42 percent of the country's institutions of higher education, 63 percent of the students, and 68 percent of the teaching faculty. The Federal District alone had 68 institutions, 249,236 students, and 36,820 faculty members. In contrast, the state of Quintana Roo, for instance, had two institutions, 1,299 students, and 80 faculty members (SPP 1986a, 421–22).

The main purpose of the program to decentralize education was to transfer to the states elementary and teachers' education. A series of agreements between the federal and state governments facilitated the transfer of material and financial resources and also provided the framework for the administration of federal and state educational services. In addition to a valid administrative rationale, the decentralization of education also had some major political considerations, the most important of which was that the government's main educational institution for teachers (the Escuela Normal Superior de México) had become increasingly politicized. This politicization had taken a markedly leftist turn, and the teachers trained there were, allegedly, heavily indoctrinated to oppose the government. From the government's perspective, this political activity became far more important than the teachers' academic training; decentralization away from Mexico City seemed to offer a solution, since it would break up the primacy of the center as a locus for the teachers' training.

The program to decentralize education was not overwhelmingly well received, in particular by the large teachers' union, the *Sindicato Nacional de Trabajadores de la Educación* (SNTE). The SNTE feared that decentralization would weaken its national structure, but in the end the union's national leaders did give their support to the program. By 1987, the transfer of elementary and teachers' education to the thirty-one states was complete.

The most important step taken to facilitate decentralization in the health sector was the reorganization of the Ministry of Health. The president decreed the *Ley General de Salud* (General Law of Health) in 1983, and in 1984 issued another decree by which all health services of this ministry (*Secretaría de Salubridad y Asistencia*, or SSA) would be provided by the states. The same decree stipulated that the services provided by the IMSS-COPLAMAR community participation program of the *Instituto Mexicano del Seguro Social* (Mexican Institute of Social Security, or IMSS) would also now fall under the states' responsibility (*Diario Oficial*, 8 March 1984, 6–8).

The promulgation in early 1986 of the *Ley Sobre el Sistema Nacional de Asistencia Social* (Law on the National System of Social Assistance) transferred all the functions of social assistance from the SSA to *Desarrollo Integral de la Familia* (DIF), a social welfare agency (*Diario Oficial*, 9 January 1986, 33–39). Because the SSA no longer provided services of social assistance, its name was changed from the Ministry of Health and Assistance to the Ministry of Health (*Secretaría de Salud*).[5]

Reportedly, the health decentralization program made significant progress. By mid-1986, health services provided by the states represented 50 percent of the nation's total, employed 40,000 persons, and had 4,700 centers to provide these services. A typical example of how federal allocations were made to these programs is the important state of Jalisco, where the federal govenment provided 60 percent of the expenditures and the local government the remaining 40 percent (SPP 1986a, 392–93). By 1988, the Ministry of Health had signed agreements with approximately half the states. In the remaining half, IMSS-COPLAMAR continued operating under central directive.

Regional Development

At the beginning of de la Madrid's presidency, a new *Subsecretaría de Desarrollo Regional* was created within the Ministry of Programming and Budget as the institution responsible for overseeing the country's regional development. Chapter 9 of the PND referred to the policy for regional development as "the general basis of the decentralization policy" (SPP 1983b, 375) and stated among its objectives the achievement of decentralization, primarily, by redistributing powers and responsibilities among the three levels of government, by relocating productive activities, and by directing economic activities to medium-sized cities. The PND also included provisions for decentralization that subsequently were built into the actual daily operations of all ministries and federal agencies, and an elaborate formal mechanism for the implementation of decentralization was established. The target of the regional development policy was to foster a more comprehensive development in the states.

The primary mechanism for promoting regional development was the *Convenio Unico de Desarrollo* (Development Agreement, or CUD), signed by the president and the governor of each state. It provided the framework for a variety of programs designed for the federal government to attend more effectively to the states' needs.[6] Through the first CUDs, the state govenments received federal allocations only for the sectors of education and health, but gradually the allocations grew to encompass all other federal programs for regional development. In addition to the rather complex bureaucratic structure of the CUDs, another equally complex set of agencies was established under the *Programas de Desarrollo Regional* (Programs of Regional Development, or PDR) which, overall, enjoyed relative success. The government also targeted specific areas of the country as priority development zones.

The CUDs' primary importance lay in their being formal agreements designed for the transfer of federal resources to the states. From a decentralizing perspective, this was an important step toward a more effective fiscal federalism (on this point, see Armida Graham 1983). The CUDs were also important because through them the federal and state governments promised to strengthen municipal governments. For instance, specific provisions dealt with the process of strengthening municipal governments by transferring directly to them the resources that in the past the federal government had retained. Federal revenues were to be returned directly to the *municipios*, but not through the states (as will become apparent below, this has not happened). From 1983 to 1988 the total federal investment in the CUDs amounted to 1.8 billion pesos (SPP 1988, 379).

The Municipal Reform

The municipal reform of 1984 was the cornerstone of de la Madrid's decentralization policy. In response to the generalized public pressure to decentralize, only five days after assuming the presidency, de la Madrid sent to the Mexican Congress an initiative to modify Article 115 of the constitution, which deals with municipal governments. In this initiative, the *Iniciativa de Ley de Reformas y Adiciones al Artículo 115 Constitucional*, the president outlined the historical, ideological, and juridical justification for transforming the *municipios* politically.[7] Through this constitutional amendment, approved by the Congress on 3 February 1983, and effective from 1 January 1984, *municipios* were to become more autonomous. As the first major step toward decentralization, its major purpose was to strengthen the *municipio* and, in so doing, to strengthen Mexican federalism by making local governments more independent of the state and federal governments.

The devolution of municipal autonomy was de la Madrid's key to decentralization. His address to the Senate indicated that decentralization demanded a revision of the constitutional arrangement that divided rights and responsibilities among the federal government, the states, and municipalities. He sought to determine which rights and responsibilities could be redistributed in order to attain a better equilibrium among the three levels of government. He appeared firmly convinced that this redistribution would begin by devolving to the *municipio* its basic powers, that is, the direct government of the community (Cámara de Diputados 1983, 8). The president forcefully stated that "the changes in Article 115 are aimed at strengthening the *municipio*'s finances, its political autonomy, and all those faculties that somehow had constantly been absorbed by the states and the federal government'' (Cámara de Diputados 1983, 10).

De la Madrid's proposal for devolution also attempted to deal directly with the major problems associated with the uncontrolled growth of Mexico City and other urban areas, as well as with the disparities among various regions of the country. In changing Article 115, special attention was given to the social and economic differences among *municipios*, their stages of development, and the contrasts among them. One of the major purposes of the reform was to understand and respond better to local needs and conditions.[8] As de la Madrid indicated, the municipal reform intended

to strengthen the development of *municipios* in order to increase regional development, to increase the feeling of belonging in a community, thus avoiding the constant migration from rural to urban areas and especially to Mexico City, not only with the purpose of redistributing the national wealth, but to have government decisions made by the municipal government. (Cámara de Diputados 1983, 11)

Variations among regions were also considered in restoring municipal autonomy and making it a national rule:

In accordance with the constitutional principle regarding the internal regimes of the states, the regulation of municipal communities will be guided by the local laws and constitutions in order for these to contain the norms that will correspond to the specific geographic, ethnographic, demographic, and economic characteristics that are distinctive of each one of the states. (Cámara de Diputados 1983, 12)

But by and large, the most important provisions of the reform dealt with municipal finances and their administration. In order to understand this emphasis on finances, it is useful to look briefly at the background of intergovernmental financial management. The modern system of revenue sharing in Mexico began when the Constitutional Convention met in Querétaro in 1917; the issue of how to structure and strengthen municipal public finances in order to grant autonomy to *municipios* was hotly debated—but not resolved. A series of provisions dealing with these matters was finally included in the constitution, but the *municipios'* autonomy to manage freely their finances never went past being a well-intentioned but largely rhetorical declaration. The mechanisms through which *municipios* could attain autonomy through administering their own finances were not even mentioned. And more important, *municipios* could not achieve political autonomy if they could not be autonomous financially. Since 1917 municipal autonomy had existed only on paper. Regardless of all the constitutional provisions that clearly granted autonomy to *municipios*, the practice of decentralization and dependency produced the opposite: political and economic autonomy in Mexico's *municipios* was nonexistent. President de la Madrid meant to change this widely recognized dependency.

The initiative to reform Article 115 is divided in ten sections, seven specifically related to municipal structures, two that are common to states and *municipios*, and one (without any modifications to the earlier text) related to the states. The key provisions from the ten sections of the revised Article 115 are II, III, and IV. Section II grants *municipios* autonomy in the management of their finances and enables them to design their own rules and laws of governance. Section III deals with the provision of public services and defines precisely which services must be provided by *municipios*. Section IV provides for the management of municipal finances and specifically grants municipal governments all revenues collected from property taxes and from the provision of public services.

The implementation of the revised Article 115 has had different results in the country's 2,378 *municipios*. The reform has been successful in that at least now, *by law*, local governments have become rather more self-sufficient and can enjoy some protection against encroachment from other levels of government. However, by the end of de la Madrid's administration, all indications were that the financial and political autonomy promised to municipal governments, overwhelmingly, had not materialized.

IMPLEMENTATION: KEEPING THE PROMISES

Although it has been repeated time and again that municipal autonomy depends largely on the *municipios'* ability to manage their own finances and their economic self-sufficiency, the reality of centralization presents quite a different picture. In the average Mexican *municipio*, approximately 80 percent of its income depends on allocations of the federal and state governments, while only 20 percent comes from its own resources. Hence, in order to assess the effectiveness of de la Madrid's decentralization policies and to determine if municipal financial autonomy (and, consequently, devolution) was possible in the context of the municipal reform, the management of intergovernmental finances must be considered. According to the stipulations of the reformed Article 115, *ayuntamientos* are entitled to collect revenues from three main sources: (1) fees for the delivery of public services, (2) property taxes, and (3) federal allocations.

Public Services

Prior to the reform, considerable ambiguity existed (even in the constitution) regarding which specific services were the responsibility of municipal governments. This ambiguity, coupled with the inability of some *municipios* to provide services, resulted in the provision of services resting primarily with the federal and state governments, which were not always geared to attend to local needs. Hence, the main purpose in transferring to municipalities the responsibility for providing public services was to meet local needs more effectively. An additional (and perhaps more important) purpose of the transfer was to grant *municipios* more control over their own resources and, consequently, more autonomy. The general assumption was that the fees charged for the delivery of services would constitute an important part of municipal revenues.

The intention in the transfer may appear laudable, but there are (at least) two built-in problems in carrying it out. First, the rates charged for public services most of the time are insufficient to cover the costs of providing them. Second, *municipios* lack the adequate human, technical, financial, and administrative resources to handle the provision of services. It appears that the real intention of the transfer was to shift the responsibility from higher to lower levels of government and with it the blame for any inefficiencies in the provision of services. Thus, both responsibility and criticism were deflected away from the center.

Whether the provision of public services has become more effective now is indeed questionable. It is certain that municipal dependency has been perpetuated because *municipios* have had to rely on arrangements of administrative cooperation with the state and federal governments in order to provide services. Despite allegations of the de la Madrid administration regarding how much the technical and administrative capabilities of *municipios* had improved since the reform, Salinas made an issue during his campaign about how much still remained to be done. In general, municipal administrative apparatuses will continue to prove inadequate for meeting the *municipios'* new responsibilities and tasks, and their development will be further constrained.

Property Taxes

Property taxes represent one of the most important sources of revenue for the states.[9] Prior to the municipal reform, only some state governments distributed among their *municipios* the revenues from property taxes; the amount and character of any distribution was determined by each state's Congress and not by national law. In 1982, for instance, the first year of de la Madrid's administration, only three states distributed the entire amounts collected (that is, 100 percent among their *municipios*), seventeen states distributed between 17 percent and 95 percent, and the remaining eleven states distributed nothing. Understandably, one of the main reasons for the municipal reform was the *municipios'* insistence on the unfairness of the concentration of property tax revenues at the state level, considering that a substantial amount had been collected at the municipal level. Under the new Article 115, *municipios* became entitled to collect and keep all municipal property tax revenues.

However, not all states changed their constitutions to include the provisions of the revised Article 115 (Section IV). For instance, in 1984 one-third of the states had not modified their fiscal legislation to establish the prohibition of exemptions for property taxes, in spite of the fact that *municipios* had become protected by the law in this regard. An important contradiction of the municipal reform arises here. Section IV of Article 115 establishes that no individual or organization, public or private, is exempt from paying property taxes *except* for the public goods or real estate of the federal, state, and municipal governments; none of these must pay for the provision of municipal public services either. Thus, organizations like PEMEX (Petróleos Mexicanos, the government oil conglomerate), the Comisión Federal de Electricidad (CFE, the government electricity giant), and the Instituto Mexicano del Seguro Social (IMSS, the government's huge health organization) do *not* have to pay significantly large taxes to *municipios*. No matter how one rationalizes the fact that government organizations ought to be tax-exempt, it is difficult to explain how the reform's intention was to strengthen municipal finances when *municipios* are denied important sources of revenue.

The most serious problem in implementing the property tax provision of Article 115 resides in the fact that most *municipios* do not have the administrative infrastructure required for collecting the tax and have had to sign collaborative agreements with their state governments. As a result, the states are still responsible for "administering" property taxes, and the cost of this "administration" in some cases amounts to 75 percent of the total revenue collected. Furthermore, the majority of *municipios* (and, indeed, the state governments) lack an updated registry of real estate ownership, making collection even more complicated.

As is the case with the provision of public services, *municipios* need *training* by the federal and state governments so that municipal public employees are able to collect and administer their own property taxes—federal allocations and legislative reform are not enough. Without training, the present municipal financial structure will continue to lead, on the one hand, to a lack of control on the part of municipal public employees and, on the other hand, to evasion, unjustified collections, and uncertainty and distrust on the part of the average citizen.

Federal Allocations

The main source of revenue for municipal governments consists of the allocations made by the federal government. Budgetary data indicated that from the years 1900 to 1975 these allocations had decreased dramatically in real terms; if decentralization could ever be effective they had to increase. Otherwise, the risk of increasing economic and political centralization could not be avoided, and the distribution of national and regional income among the three levels of government would continue to be inequitable. As a response, a new system of revenue sharing, the *Ley de Coordinacion Fiscal* (Law of Fiscal Coordination, or LCF), was established.

According to the LCF, federal allocations were to be distributed among the states through three mechanisms: (1) the *Fondo General de Participaciones*

(General Fund of Participations, or FGP), (2) the *Fondo Financiero Complementario* (Complementary Financial Fund, or FFC), and (3) the *Fondo de Fomento Municipal* (Fund for Municipal Promotion, or FFM). Under the LCF, the states must distribute among their *municipios* at least 20 percent of the allocations from the FGP and FFC and 100 percent of the allocations from the FFM.

The FGP is made up of 13 percent of the total annual tax revenues of the federal government and is distributed among the states according to each state's contribution to the collection of federal taxes—that is, the states that contribute most receive the larger allocations, and vice versa. The FFC is made up of 0.5 percent of the federal government's overall income; this fund makes larger allocations to the states that make smaller contributions to the FGP. It is a compensating fund for the poorer states that contributed less to the FGP and therefore received smaller allocations through that fund. The FFM is made up of a fraction of the 1 percent additional tax collected on the export of oil and natural gas and, in principle, is very similar to the FFC, except that it is exclusively for *municipios*.

Since the LCF was first implemented, federal allocations to states and *municipios* have increased considerably. From 1982 to 1988, the FFC increased by 12,110 percent, the FGP by 3,736 percent, and the FFM by 4,047 percent (SPP 1988, 29). This may appear impressive, but in real terms the total increase from 1980 to 1984, for example, estimated at 476 percent, falls well below the 679.2 percent increase of the *Indice Nacional de Precios al Consumidor* (National Index of Consumer Prices). Thus even if the allocations grow by millions through the LCF, any positive effect vanishes and the distribution of federal funds remains grossly inequitable.

As a main stipulation in the LCF, the federal government cannot determine the amount or dates of allocations made to state governments, and a state government cannot do the same in relation to its *municipios*. Allocations are made according to specific annual formulas (rather than more subjective criteria) and to a calendar set forth in advance. In this regard, the LCF seems to coincide with the municipal reform in that Article 115 reforms were aimed precisely at granting *municipios* some sort of security in obtaining the revenues and utilizing them according to their own preferences. The allocations need not be used in a specific way or for a particular program but are made so that *ayuntamientos* have the autonomy to decide how to use them according to the items in their expenditures budget.

The state government must allocate the federal funds assigned to *municipios* in a period of five days after the state receives them (LCF, Article 6); otherwise, the state will be penalized by paying interest. Article 6 of the LCF also establishes that these allocations are to be made in cash only, rather than in goods or works, without any restrictions on how they will be spent and without any deductions. These stipulations certainly provide some protection to *municipios* given that, previously, state governments often did not distribute the funds allocated, or distributed them according to the state government's interests and preferences. If the states do not distribute the funds according to the law, not only are they penalized, but the federal government will over-pass them and allocate the funds directly to the *municipios*.

Overall, the LCF has functioned as expected in that the intergovernmental fiscal arrangement has become a little more equitable: there is a fairer distribution of resources, state governments have increased their income substantially, and *municipios* can now rely on a source of revenue that in many cases is indispensable to their treasury. Prior to the municipal reform, *ayuntamientos* were totally dependent on the funds that state legislatures decided to allocate to them. At least now, by law, *municipios* can avoid the uncertainty of where their operating funds are going to come from. On paper, all these provisions seem to grant true autonomy to *municipios*—with respect to both revenues and expenditures.

But there is a larger problem. The municipal reform clearly establishes that *municipios* are entitled to federal allocations. The LCF, however, establishes that these allocations are made through the state governments. Thus, the LCF goes against the spirit of the municipal reform, which attempts to grant autonomy to *municipios*. Moreover, Article 115 itself establishes that the amounts and dates of delivery of federal allocations to *municipios* are to be determined annually by each state's legislature *according to the stipulations of the LCF*. So even the municipal reform is a contradiction. State governments still have exactly the same control over *municipios* as they did before the municipal reform. The states continue to make key decisions about municipal revenues, and everything continues as before: state legislatures subjectively decide how much each *municipio* will receive, and certain *ayuntamientos* still receive the largest share according to political criteria.

There are many examples of uneven distributions of federal funds among *municipios*. In the state of Puebla, the monies of the FFM (which must be distributed entirely among all the state's *municipios*) were allocated in 1985 as follows: 50 percent went to the *municipio* of Puebla (the state capital), 30 percent to eight *municipios*, and the remaining 20 percent was distributed among 208 *municipios* (Tesorería Municipal del Ayuntamiento de Puebla 1985). This inequitable distribution very clearly illustrates that, for those 208 *municipios* in Puebla, the municipal reform, for all practical purposes, means little.

DECENTRALIZATION: MORE THAN JUST PROMISES?

This chapter has demonstrated that devolution has not become a reality in Mexico because the municipal reform has not yet achieved the financial autonomy promised to *municipios* when Article 115 was reformed. But the unfulfilled promise of financial autonomy does not constitute the entire picture. For the center, it was never meant to. As identified at the beginning of this chapter, the real intention was to accentuate political control against a backcloth of crisis (see also Rodríguez 1987; forthcoming). As such, de la Madrid's decentralization offers a promise to be fulfilled in the future, even if it has not fulfilled the promises of the past. What is important is that it set the blueprint for future action. Municipal underdevelopment and lack of autonomy are not caused by the system's centralization in Mexico City and the actions of the federal government alone. Rather, they are caused by the actions of the *state* governments, which not only continue to make key decisions about municipal finances but retain firm political control over their *municipios*.

This is not to say that the federal government is free of all blame. In designing the LCF and reforming Article 115, the federal government clearly intended the states to retain control of the *municipios* by giving them control over municipal finance. Subsequently, however indirectly, the federal government can continue to retain political control over all levels of government. As official documents, the LCF and the reformed Article 115 may be well intentioned, but results seem to indicate that they were formulated merely to placate municipal pleas for autonomy. The law may say that *municipios* have autonomy, but practice shows the opposite; the higher levels of government are still in control.

Ultimately, the overconcentration of resources in the center continues and has perpetuated municipal dependency and the impoverishment of Mexico's *municipios*. Municipal governments are forced to seek financial support from the federal and state governments, reducing further their autonomy and simultaneously generating a vicious circle: *municipios* have lost their autonomy because they are poor, and because they are poor they require the assistance of the federal and state governments, which produces a larger dependency that makes them even poorer.

No one doubts that some progress has been made in implementing decentralization and that the federal government has taken steps to strengthen the *municipios*. Moreover, one might argue that there have been some important accomplishments. For example, the intervention of higher levels of government in many cases allows for a more efficient use of scarce resources than would be the case were municipal autonomy a reality and were local authorities obliged to administer the collection or expenditure of these resources. Even so, the results of the municipal reform are overwhelmingly discouraging. No matter how large the federal allocations to municipalities may be, they are still insufficient to provide *municipios* with the financial resources required for their development. Moreover, the federal government may continue to enlarge its allocations, but these increases necessarily have to be limited because the federal government must attend to other commitments, the most pressing of which is the payment of interest on the country's foreign debt. In the 1986 budget, for instance, payments on the debt absorbed 45.9 percent of total expenditures, while only 6.2 percent went to states and *municipios* (SPP 1986b, 218). In this context, one may envisage federal allocations to municipalities as a burden and can appreciate why the center has shifted this responsibility to the state governments.

The shift in decision-making powers over *municipios* from the federal to the state governments, however, only involves finances. Politically, the center's grip on power is sustained. The state governments' control over municipal finances appears to be just one part of a larger strategy of the central government in an effort to retain political control for both the PRI and the government in Mexico City. By granting state governments some leeway in deciding how to allocate funds among their *municipios*, the federal government expects loyalty, political support, and commitment to maintain the PRI's electoral dominance. Governors, in turn, expect the same from each mayor in their state. All concerned fully understand that, for those who decide not to play by the rules of the political game, the costs can be very high. These may include the termination of a political career which, understandably, prevents local politicians and administrators from taking the decentralizing process into their hands.

As far as municipal governments are concerned, decentralization has only produced a reconfiguration of centralization. Instead of being totally dependent on the federal government, as they have been traditionally, they now find themselves dependent on their state governments for the allocation of operating revenues and policy implementation. The amount of funds that will be distributed to each state is still decided in Mexico City, and, more important, policies are still formulated there. As long as *municipios* remain under the control of the higher levels of government, neither financial nor political autonomy will be achieved. And as long as devolution fails to materialize, Mexico's decentralization policy will continue to be a promise waiting to be fulfilled.

NOTES

1. See SPP (1983). A more detailed discussion of the decentralization efforts can be found in SPP (1984, 89–98).

2. This program includes the widely publicized *Programa de Simplificación Administrativa* (Program for Administrative Simplification), designed to eliminate, or at least reduce, bureaucratic "red tape." The program also sought to provide the population with easier access to the services of federal agencies.

3. For example, the Comisión Nacional de Zonas Aridas was relocated in Saltillo: the Centro Nacional de Investigaciones Agrarias moved to Cuernavaca; and the Empresa Nuevo Vallarta went to Puerto Vallarta.

4. Works that discuss the decentralization of these sectors include Reyes (1986), Dávila (1986), and Street (1984, 14–29). The Ministry of Health (Secretaría de Salud 1984a) also published a series of five volumes, entitled *Cuadernos de descentralización*, which discuss in detail the sector's decentralization policies and programs.

5. The DIF embarked on a very successful decentralization program, which also provided large political payoffs. For a detailed discussion of the DIF's decentralization, see Rodríguez (1987).

6. Within each CUD five major programs are subsumed including PIDER, the Programas Estatales de Inversión (PEI), the Programa de Atención a Zonas Marginadas, the Programas Sectoriales Concertados (PROSEC), and the Programas de Desarrollo Estatal (PRODES). The implementation of the various CUD programs met with varying degrees of success.

7. See Cámara de Diputados del Congreso de la Union (1983) for the entire text of President de la Madrid's speech, the entire text of Article 115, and the texts of the interventions of the deputies. The translations here are my own.

8. The argument of promoting decentralization as a measure to increase responsiveness to local needs and conditions is well documented in the literature. Cohen et al., for instance, emphasize that "decentralization aims at making the government more responsive to the varying needs and preferences of the population" (1981, 36) and that "decentralization may improve the application of general, national plans to local areas because they can be implemented in a way that specifically reflects local conditions" (1981, 41). Similarly, Rondinelli (1980) argues that governments are able to perform more efficiently if they understand the diversity of local conditions and that such understanding can be obtained only at the local level. President de la Madrid's plan follows to the letter this line of reasoning.

9. Since the collection of municipal property taxes by local governments is a new item in Mexico's political agenda, there are few written sources on the topic. Moreover, because it is delicate both politically and financially and because it so openly demonstrates the lack of adequate municipal administrative infrastructures, it has turned into a problem no one wishes to tackle. Most of the information presented here was gathered from personal conversations with Mexican public officials.

9

Industrial Decentralization in Mexico in Global Perspective

Robert N. Gwynne

The study of Third World industrialization is characterized by an interesting continental perspective in the contrasting experiences of East Asia and Latin America. Many contrasts exist, but one of the most fundamental has been the contrast in trade orientation between an outward-oriented approach in East Asia and an inward-oriented approach in Latin America (Gwynne 1990).

This contrast is of considerable interest to economic geographers. On the one hand, there is considerable evidence that trade strategies of inward orientation and related policies of import substitution industrialization have been intimately linked to the accentuated spatial centralization of industry in the capital or primate city of each Latin American country (Gilbert 1974; Gwynne 1985). On the other hand, outward-oriented industrialization has been more successfully linked to the decentralization of industry, at least away from the primate or capital city, as in South Korea and Taiwan.

The 1970s and 1980s have witnessed a degree of trade reorientation among Latin American countries, from inward- to more outward-oriented approaches. In certain countries, such as Chile and Uruguay, trade reorientation has been wholehearted and long-term in approach. In other countries, such as Mexico and most recently Argentina, conscious and meaningful shifts toward outward orientation have come about largely as a policy response to the debt crisis. In Brazil, considerable increases in manufactured exports took place in the late 1970s and early 1980s, but Brazil's overall trading structure relies on considerable state interference that restricts the possibilities for import—such as of technologically advanced capital goods. Many countries in Latin America such as Peru, still cling to inward-oriented strategies.

In order to boost exports and create large trade surpluses, Mexico has been shifting seriously to a more outward-oriented approach to industry since the late 1980s. It is too early to make a comprehensive statistical analysis of its impact on industrial decentralization in Mexico because of the recent reorientation of trade strategy and the necessary time lag for regional industrial census material to be produced.

The aims of this chapter, therefore, must be general in scope and detail. The chapter will place Mexican industrialization in an international framework in order to envisage its locational advantages for manufacturing production at a supranational level. Reference will be made to theories that economic geographers have been too dismissive of in the past—international trade theory and the product life cycle. The chapter will also examine the prospects for decentralization of Mexican industry with particular reference to the motor vehicle industry and its recent spatial evolution.

INTERNATIONAL TRADE AND THE PRODUCT LIFE CYCLE

The international context of trade in manufactured goods in general and the product life cycle in particular can best be put into perspective by a brief reference to the Hecksher-Ohlin theory of international trade. In contrast to the classical theory of international trade, the Hecksher-Ohlin model takes into account differences in factor supplies (land, labor, and capital) throughout the world on the international specialization of production (Todaro 1978). This factor endowment theory can be said to rest on two basic propositions.

The first proposition states that different products require productive factors in different relative proportions. For example, within manufacturing, certain products or activities (clothing, shoes, assembly of electronic products) require relatively greater proportions of labor per unit of capital than other goods and activities (cars, chemicals, products derived from automated and robotized technology).

The second proposition is that countries have different endowments of factors of production. Some countries like the United States have large amounts of capital per worker and are thus designated as "capital-abundant" countries, while others like India, Egypt, or Chile have little capital and much labor. They are thus designated as "labor-abundant" nations. In general, industrialized countries are assumed to be relatively capital-abundant and developing countries labor-abundant.

The factor endowment theory argues that capital-abundant countries should specialize in such products as cars, aircraft, telecommunications, computers, and other products that utilize capital intensively in their technology of production. They should then export some of these capital-intensive products in exchange for those labor-intensive products—such as clothing, shoes, and electronic subassemblies—that can be produced best by those countries that are relatively well endowed with labor. It should be noted, of course, that such researchers as Leontief (1956) have demonstrated that the empirical reality of trade can often be far from such theoretical purity and even paradoxical in nature.

The concept of the product life cycle rests not only on the propositions of international trade theory but also on Kuznets' marketing concept of the evolution of a product. As a result, the locational shifts in production inherent in the product life cycle model are much determined by the size and location of markets as well as the global diffusion of new products. It is worth pointing out in this context that international trade theory is much more supply-oriented, dependent as it is on factor endowment.

Figure 9.1 shows in diagrammatic form the three phases of the product life cycle matched against hypothetical sales volume. As can be readily appreciated, the "new" phase represents a period of low sales and low sales growth, the "growth" phase a period of rapid sales growth, and the "mature" phase a period of high sales with little change over time. Such an idealized product history reflects the operation of numerous variables, the balance of which will be different for each product.

Generally, however, certain tendencies may be common. The new phase constitutes the period that follows the placing on the market of a new invention or innovation. During this period, numerous technical problems will have to be resolved in product design and the production process. The product is likely to be expensive with limited sales, but the sales strategy for the future will need to be determined. If the product passes through this trial period, it will enter the growth phase, a period of cost reductions and increasing sales. As a mass production system is organized and economies of scale taken advantage of, costs will decline markedly, thus causing sales to increase as larger

Figure 9.1
The Product Life Cycle

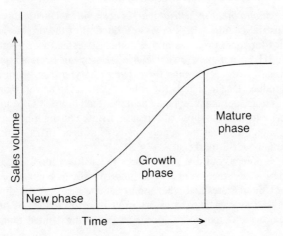

sections of the population are able to purchase the product. The mature phase arrives when the potential for further cost reductions comes to an end and annual purchasing stabilizes as markets become saturated.

THE PRODUCT LIFE CYCLE AND LOCATIONAL SHIFTS

Within the context of world trade in manufactures and of multinational manufacturing corporations, the product life cycle can also be seen as a framework for the changing location of production on a world scale (Vernon 1966). The matching of the product life cycle with global shifts in production can be formalized into four stages.

1. *Initial production.* During the 1960s and 1970s, most new inventions and innovations, even if they originated elsewhere, tended to be put on the market first in the United States (Vernon 1966), due to that country's "entrepreneurial talent, large market and large high income" (Franko 1976). During the 1970s and 1980s, this pattern changed, primarily because of the increasing strength of Japanese corporations in the world markets of new consumer goods. Japanese corporations prefer to put new products on the market first in their own country, as happened, for example, with the compact disc player and the digital audio tape (DAT) system. "The Japanese love of gadgetry has normally meant that sales in the first and most expensive year of a product's life are high enough to justify continued support from manfacturers" (Rapoport 1987, 48).

2. *Mass production in the initial production location.* If the product catches on within the high-income sectors of the United States and/or Japan, the U.S. or Japanese firm(s) involved will begin to organize the mass production of the product in the location of initial production. In terms of compact disc players, this occurred within the first year of production (1983), although mass production of DAT players was delayed longer. During this early buildup of production, U.S. and Japanese firms export the product to all other world regions.

3. *Mass production in other industrial market economies.* During this period, other leading industrial countries begin mass production of the product, including the production of Japanese products in the United States and vice versa. In Europe, for example, U.S. or Japanese subsidiaries, European firms adopting licensing agreements, and firms developing their own prototypes can begin mass production of the product. Due to slightly lower labor costs and a newer, more rationalized production system, per unit costs may be lower than those of U.S. plants although not necessarily lower than those of Japanese firms. During this phase, therefore, European plants take over the supply of the European market and perhaps encroach on other world markets.

    It should be pointed out that in Vernon's reconsideration of the product cycle in 1979, he saw this stage as of less and less significance as the technology gap between the United States and other industrial countries greatly diminished. But in some ways, this can be seen as a curiously restricted, U.S.-oriented view. Although innovations may now appear in either the United States, Japan, or

Western Europe, a subsequent stage of shifting production to the other developed regions of the world will follow. In other words, the pattern no longer automatically starts with the U.S., innovation (as already noted, Japanese innovation became much more significant in the 1980s), but the subsequent diffusion of the innovation from the initial production location in one developed country to other developed countries nevertheless occurs.

4. *Mass production in the less developed countries.* As the production process and machinery become standardized, the U.S., Japanese, or European firms may decide to locate plants in less developed countries where at least labor costs will be considerably lower. If the labor-cost component in production is large, these plants may begin to produce the product for most world markets.

It is worthwhile to note that there are two locational processes that can be seen operating within the product life cycle model (Storper and Walker 1989, 120). The first relates to the evolution of the product itself and its increasing standardization through time. Such "product maturation" allows for the "market spread" of the product as manufacturers extend their market territory. The second process identifies the standardization of the production process itself—"production process maturation." Third World countries theoretically can benefit from locational shifts caused not only by the maturation of the product but by the standardization of the process technology.

Such a formalized locational shift of world industry linked to the evolution of a product's sales and process technology provides an optimistic scenario for Third World industrialization. Certain countries in East Asia have been seen to grow rapidly based on the production of mature products manufactured with standardized technology. In particular, the example of Taiwan's industrialization has been seen to fit the model well.

Between the mid-1960s and mid-1970s, Taiwan saw a gradual increase in two main export-oriented industries, textiles and the assembly of electronic products. The assembly of electronic products fit into the product life cycle model. As worldwide electronic firms tried in the 1960s to reduce their costs of production for basic electronic products such as transistor radios and black-and-white televisions, small assembly plants were created in Taiwan; in the mid-1960s, it was estimated that Taiwanese wage rates were less than one-twentieth of those current in the United States. By 1976, the value of production of the Taiwanese electronics industry had reached $1.4 billion. However, during the late 1970s, worldwide electronics firms saw Taiwan as a cheap labor-cost location for the increasingly sophisticated products of the electronics industry—color televisions, hi-fi systems, radio cassettes. Existing plants were expanded and new plants were created by U.S., European, Japanese, and Taiwanese companies. Electronics production in Taiwan trebled in four years to $4.2 billion in 1980. Of this 1980 production figure, $3 billion (or 70 percent) were exported, causing electronic products to overtake textiles as the major export category. As much as 95 percent of these electronic exports were consumer products typical of the last stage of the product life cycle, such as radios and televisions. Further evidence of Taiwan becoming an assembly location for products drawing toward the end of their life cycles is that, in 1980, the research costs of the Taiwanese electronics industry amounted to only 0.4 percent of sales; a figure of over 10 percent of sales is recorded in the Japanese industry.

The 1980s saw another phase in the growth of the Taiwanese electronics industry as increasingly more sophisticated electronics products came to be produced in Taiwan—videotape recorders, computer terminals, mini-computers, word processors, and electric typewriters. By 1984, exports of electronic goods had reached $4.8 billion—roughly one-sixth of total exports of $30.5 billion; this proportion was broadly maintained as total Taiwanese exports reached $39.8 billion in 1986. Taiwan's export growth has been so vertiginous that by 1987 exports accounted for nearly 50 percent of GNP (gross national product).

Firms operating in and selling to the U.S. market, however, have begun to see Taiwan as an increasingly high-cost location. The two decades of rapid economic (and particularly manufacturing) growth since the mid-1960s have brought such major increases in employment that Taiwan has come to suffer from labor shortages. Labor shortages have meant higher wages; by 1987 Taiwanese wage rates were only one-third of those in the United States. It has now become imperative for some international firms to look for new locations with low labor costs in order to manufacture products coming toward the end of their life cycles.

MEXICAN INDUSTRIALIZATION AND THE PRODUCT LIFE CYCLE

Taiwan had an outward-oriented trade regime from the late 1950s; its export success in manufacturing in the three following decades is as intimately linked to outward orientation as it is to Taiwan's insertion into the global operation of the product life cycle model. In light of Taiwan's success and Mexico's shift toward an outward-oriented trade policy in the second half of the 1980s, what are the prospects for Mexican industrialization through the operation of the product life cycle model?

At the outset, one can first identify Mexico's distinctive border area and its relationship with the product life cycle model. If one compares a location in the Mexican border area (see Figure 9.2) with one in Taiwan, the former seems to offer three substantial advantages for firms operating to supply the U.S. market. First, wage rates are considerably lower, which should indicate savings in labor costs; in 1986, hourly wage rates of $0.85 were over a third lower than those of Taiwan ($2.95). Second, transport costs must be distinctly lower. Third, Mexico's border industrialization program allows for the duty-free import into Mexico of those raw materials and parts that are assembled

Figure 9.2
The Mexican Border Industrialization Program

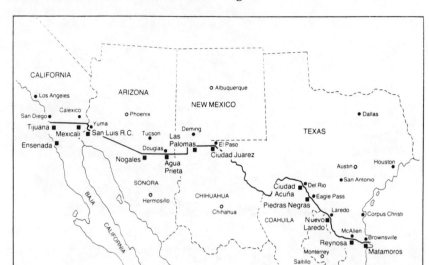

and reexported. When the finished goods enter the United States, duty is paid only on the added value. This legislation dates back to 1971. Figure 9.3 demonstrates the subsequent growth of manufacturing employment in the in-bond assembly plants (where duty-free imported raw materials and parts are assembled and re-exported), or *maquiladoras*, of the five main border towns. Employment increased fivefold between 1971 and 1979, before stagnating during the oil-boom years, when an overvalued peso proved the Mexican border to be unattractive to new investment. However, after 1982, with a policy of adopting an effectively valued exchange rate, employment in the *maquiladoras* increased rapidly once again.

In 1987, there were about 1,200 in-bond assembly plants along Mexico's border generating added value of over $1.6 billion and employing about 300,000 workers (Gardner 1987, 14). Although Mexico's border industrialization program applies to thirteen towns, over two-thirds of border manufacturing employment is generated in just five cities—Ciudad Juárez, Tijuana, Matamoros, Reynosa, and Mexicali (see Figure 9.3). Since the end of Mexico's oil-based growth in 1982 and the following debt crisis, the *maquiladoras* have come to generate Mexico's second largest flow of foreign exchange after oil. Between 1982 and 1987, the number of in-bond plants doubled, their

Figure 9.3
Mexican Border Employment, 1970–1987

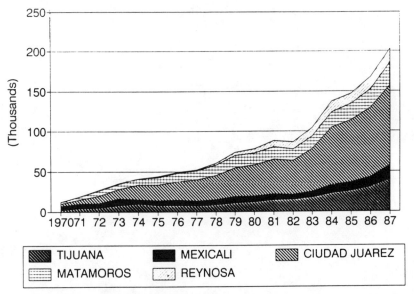

foreign earnings doubled, and the number of workers nearly trebled; in the five major border towns, employment increased from 88,000 to 205,000.

As in Taiwan, the electronic sector has been prominent in the boom with a wide variety of foreign corporations attracted to establish plants in the thirteen Mexican border towns. First of all, there are the American electrical and electronic corporations, such as General Electric, Zenith, Westinghouse, ITT, and Honeywell. In 1987, General Electric had fourteen in-bond manufacturing plants along the Mexican border, employing more than 15,000 (an average of over 1,000 employees per plant) with products ranging from electronic ceramics to motors (Gardner 1987, 14).

Even more closely following the product life cycle model, Zenith had seven television assembly and component plants along the border, employing as many as 24,000 people (an average of over 3,000 employees per plant). Zenith has concentrated its investment in the two eastern border towns of Matamoros and Reynosa, together known as the valley region. During the 1970s, U.S. corporations dominated investment in the Mexican border towns, and Zenith's investment in a large television tuner plant in Matamoros in 1970 (before the in-bond legislation had been finalized) proved highly significant for the town's subsequent development. According to Sklair, Zenith's decision put the

stamp of approval on the valley as a maquila site. Where Zenith went others followed, particularly in the electronic assembly business. In the early 1970s, a further 17 maquilas were signed up and, of rather more significance, four of these were sub-sidiaries of Fortune 500 corporations. They were all involved in one way or another with the electronic components industry. More Fortune 500 corporations followed in the mid-1970s, like Parker-Hannifin, DuPont de Nemours, ITT, Quaker Oats (Fisher Price), and the Eaton Corporation. Between 1969 and 1987, 18 Fortune 500 firms established maquilas in Matamoros. (1989, 120)

However, the effectiveness of the product life cycle model in the specific case of Mexico and its border can best be seen in terms of successful manufac-turing corporations from other world regions attempting to gain access to the North American market from a low-cost location. Indeed, the Mexican border, in particular, and the Mexican north, in general, can probably be seen as consti-tuting the growth peripheries of firms whose geographic core is non-American:

Factories therefore often move into new territory not as a way of disconnecting from, or dispensing with, the industry core area but to extend it into new growth peripheries. (Storper and Walker 1989, 88)

The Mexican border represents a geographic area, one side of a political divide (the U.S.-Mexican border), that is presently characterized by perhaps the greatest variations in factor prices (notably labor costs) in the world (par-ticularly in absolute terms). When such variations in factor prices are twinned with non-American corporations attempting to expand into the North American market, the outcome is presently a dynamic growth periphery. This is par-ticularly the case for the manufacture of standardized products or components using standardized but labor-intensive technology—that is, products (or com-ponents in products) at the end of their growth phase or in the mature phase of their life cycle.

Since the mid-1980s, Japanese corporations have been particularly evident in Mexico's *maquila* sector, seeking low labor-cost locations for consumer products oriented toward the U.S. market. Between mid-1986 and the end of 1987, eighteen new plants were established, mostly large assembly opera-tions in the electronic sector. Large assembly operations have been installed by Sony, Sanyo, Matsushita, and Hitachi in Tijuana and by Toshiba and Seiko in Ciudad Juárez, the latter location having three smaller Sony, Sanyo, and TDK plants before 1986.

Due to the less aggressive outward move of European corporations from their geographic core in the late 1980s, European electrical and electronic corporations have been less in evidence. Nevertheless, the contrasts in fac-tor pricing on either side of the border have attracted GEC, Siemens, and Philips to set up *maquiladoras* in the border towns.

With the increasing success of the newly industrializing countries of East Asia, the non-American corporate invasion of the United States is no longer restricted to Japanese and European firms. One of the most interesting re-cent developments in the economic geography of the Mexican border has been the establishment of assembly plants by the Korean conglomerates Samsung, Gold Star, and Daewoo. This development constitutes an example of corporations of a successful newly industrializing country locating in a less successful developing economy in order to gain access to the market of a large developed country.

As a result, the Mexican border has provided a key example of a product life cycle location during the last half of the 1980s. In particular, it has attracted North American, Japanese, European, and Korean corporations to set up labor-intensive assembly plants producing mature consumer products or related components with standardized technology. The products of these plants are then principally destined for the U.S. market.

Most of the non-American corporations are producing finished consumer products and not components linked into a wider continental or global system of corporate linkages. However, the U.S. corporations in the Mexican border area are producing both finished consumer goods and components, the latter linking into complex corporate supply networks at a continental and global scale. Many of these component plants are related to the electronic assembly sector, but some are linked to the motor vehicle sector. By 1987, General Motors had set up twenty-three in-bond manufacturing plants to produce components and planned to have a total of fifty components plants by the end of 1990 (Gardner 1987, 14). Rockwell International, Ford, and Chrysler have also established plants in the border zone.

Apart from being close to the United States, these component *maquiladoras* have the advantage of being located near the new export-oriented plants of Mexico's motor vehicle industry. Although these latter plants are not in-bond, they are nevertheless growing rapidly due to certain international vehicle corporations using north Mexican assembly locations to supply the U.S. market with both finished cars and engines. This is creating very close productive links between the operations of certain vehicle multinationals north and south of the U.S.-Mexican border. In particular, U.S. corporations (General Motors, Ford, and Chrysler) are developing increasingly closer links between Mexican and U.S. operations, but one Japanese corporation, Nissan, has already organized similar linkages and another Japanese corporation, Toyota, is planning to. In contrast, the two European corporations with a productive presence in Mexico, Renault and Volkswagen, have closed down their U.S. operations in the face of declining markets and increasing U.S. losses (Gwynne 1990); they have abandoned the idea of closer interaction between U.S. and Mexican operations.

There are three distinctive stages in the postwar development of the Mexican motor vehicle industry, each with its own characteristic geographic pattern. The first stage concerned the establishment of simple motor vehicle assembly plants in Mexico, basically assembling imported "knocked-down" cars with very limited incorporation of local components. The location for these plants was Mexico City, a rational location decision given the large concentration of high-income Mexican population in and around the primate city.

The second stage coincided with the perceived need within an inward-oriented, import-substituting industrial strategy of increasing by government decree (1962) the local production of components within the assembled vehicles destined for the Mexican market. The 1960s, therefore, saw the creation of a new wave of assembly plants. The combined factors of the need for a large site and the fact that land prices in Mexico City were beginning to rise gave impetus to what can best be described as short-distance decentralization—to neighboring cities within Mexico's central region, most notably Toluca, Puebla, and Cuernavaca. Again the locational decisions were broadly rational. The location of Mexican vehicle demand is heavily concentrated within Mexico's central region, and there was now an additional need to be located near the center of government regulation and lobbying and proximate to the great variety of national and international component corporations, spatially concentrated within the central region.

The third stage is linked to a more recent export-oriented phase in the development of the Mexican motor vehicle industry, within which the product life cycle model comes to have some relevance. Although government incentives for international corporations in Mexico to export go back to the early 1970s, it was not until the aftermath of the debt crisis of 1982 that serious attempts to boost vehicle exports took place. In 1981, for example, vehicle and component exports from Mexico totaled $344.9 million against imports of $2070.8 million, leaving the enormous trade deficit in vehicles of $1725.9 million (see Figure 9.4). Between 1981 and 1985, vehicle and component exports increased more than threefold to reach $1129.2 million in 1985 (see Figure 9.5).

However, of the 1985 figure, 75 percent of exports corresponded to engines, a product that can be seen as standardized in terms of technology and one in which labor costs figure prominently in overall costs. Hence, when the Mexican government insisted on the international vehicle corporations exporting more than they imported during the late 1970s and early 1980s, the decision of *all* major vehicle corporations was to locate large-capacity engine plants (annual capacity greater than 250,000) in Mexico. In general, the locations of these export-oriented engine plants were mainly in small- to medium-sized towns in northern Mexico—Chihuahua (Ford); Gomez Palacio, near Torreón (Renault); Ramos Arizpe, near Monterrey (General Motors and Chrysler); Aguascalientes (Nissan). The only major exception was the Volkswagen engine plant established in Puebla.

The vital aspect of the locational decision from the point of view of the international vehicle corporations was the proximity of these locations to U.S. assembly plants, to which most of the exported engines were directed. All six international corporations mentioned above had vehicle assembly operations in the United States in the mid-1980s—apart from the concentration of

Figure 9.4
Mexican Vehicle Trade, 1978–1987 (U.S. Dollars)

the three U.S. producers around Detroit, Nissan had a plant in Smyrna, Tennessee; Renault in Kenosha, Wisconsin (joint with American Motors); and Volkswagen in Westmoreland, Pennsylvania. Subsequently, Renault (1986) and Volkswagen (1988) closed their U.S. assembly facilities in the face of declining markets and increasing losses. However, engine production from their Mexican plants has been reoriented to supplying assembly plants in other parts of the world, such as Europe and Brazil.

Furthermore, decentralized locations in northern Mexico offered cheap land prices and various local and national incentives to locate there. Chihuahua, Gomez Palacio, and Aguascalientes were three of the twenty-two northern intermediate cities designated as industrial centers under the five-year Strategy of Intermediate Cities of the National Program for Urban Development and Housing announced in 1984.

Since the mid-1980s, the product life cycle can be seen operating in terms of U.S. vehicle corporations beginning to concentrate production of standardized subcompact cars in either new or modernized plants in Mexico for export to the North American market (see Figure 9.6). Chrysler has modernized its plant in Toluca and GM and Ford have created new plants in Ramos Arizpe and Hermosillo, respectively. Ford used its Japanese link, Mazda (in which Ford has a 25 percent interest), to install standardized Japanese process technology in order to produce a version of a European-designed model

Figure 9.5
Mexican Vehicle Exports, 1978–1987 (U.S. Dollars)

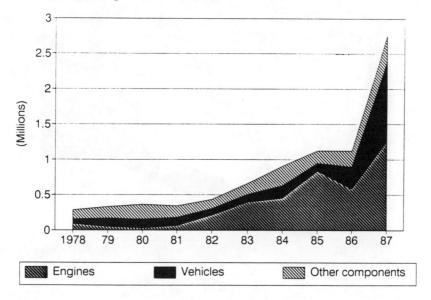

for its North American market. With U.S. corporations investing heavily in export-oriented assembly plants and facilities in Mexico during the mid-1980s, total vehicle exports more than doubled between 1985 and 1987. By 1987, finished vehicle exports corresponded to over 40 percent of the total.

The recent export-oriented phase of development in Mexico's motor vehicle industry, therefore, can be seen to have had a direct impact on industrial decentralization. The principal reasons for this must be found in international processes.

DISCUSSION

The product life cycle model provides an optimistic framework for global shifts in industrial production. However, it should be emphasized that its application depends on the nature of the product in question. It would appear that, for the manufacturing location of a product to be readily shifted from developed to less developed countries, four conditions should be fulfilled. First, there must be buoyant demand for the product in order to justify new plant investment. Second, there must be a well-defined and significant labor-intensive stage in the manufacture of the product. Third, the technology of the production process and product design must be more or less standardized. Fourth, there should be a low incidence of transport costs relative to total costs in order to make long-distance trade feasible. In Mexico, the fourth

Figure 9.6
U.S. Vehicle Corporations (Vehicle Exports), 1983–1988

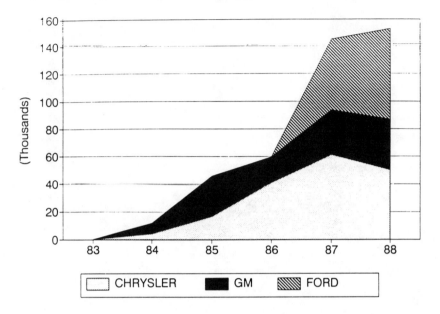

condition need not be fulfilled; as a result, the automobile and engine (characterized by high transport costs) can be seen as product life cycle products
in Mexico.

The product life cycle model explains only part of the recent boom in industrial plant creation in the north of Mexico.

The general principle of which the product cycle theory captures only a portion, is
that spatial expansion depends upon growth—regardless of whether it derives from
product innovation, process change, high exploitation of labour, or industry reorganization. (Storper and Walker 1989, 88)

The Mexican border at present not only constitutes a location that offers the
advantages of major factor price differentials (the product life cycle argument) but also coincides temporally with the expansion of East Asian and
European corporations into the North American market and their search for
new regions within which to produce for that market. Rather like the sudden
surges and kinked development in catastrophe theory, the Mexican border
during the late 1980s, registered, and is likely to continue registering, ver-
tiginous growth—such growth occurring after periods of relative slow growth
and tranquility (particularly in Mexico's years of oil-based growth).

The border region of Mexico presently constitutes a superb location for expanding corporations from the three regions of the developed world (Western Europe, the United States, and Japan) and the successful newly industrializing countries of East Asia (especially South Korea) to establish plants producing labor-intensive products that have a certain degree of standardization in terms of product design and process technology. Will there be the same impact as in Taiwan, where industrial growth linked to the product life cycle created massive increases in labor demand which eventually led to labor shortages and shifts to more up-market and technologically sophisticated production?

At present, this would seem unlikely. First, in the border region the assembly industry is characterized by a high female labor component (Fernandez 1981); thus low female unemployment can exist alongside high male unemployment. Second, employment in manufacturing in the border region has been fueled by migration from the Mexican heartland; this is likely to continue apace in the long term, acting to keep wages down. In contrast to Taiwan, such conditions should mean that the border industrialization program will constitute a long-term example of the product life cycle model in operation—with considerable implications for long-term employment growth and associated urban expansion in the border towns. The program should come to represent a powerful motor of industrial decentralization.

It should be emphasized that the considerable present potential for industrial decentralization in Mexico through the conjuncture of factors linked to the product life cycle model and the growth strategies of American and non-American firms cannot be extrapolated to other Latin American countries. At present, the U.S.-Mexican border offers perhaps the greatest "border" disparity in factor prices and economic development in the world. Not only does the average U.S. inhabitant enjoy an income ten times that of the average Mexican, but the average manufacturing worker receives an hourly wage approximately ten times that of his or her Mexican equivalent.

The locational characteristics of north Mexico, in general, and the north Mexican border, in particular, within a global economy are specific to the region and have less relevance to countries that are not adjacent to a dynamic and powerful developed country. Nevertheless, the shift toward outward orientation in Mexico may have a favorable impact on other Latin American countries in terms of expanding trade links. The traditional pattern of inward orientation in Mexico left a legacy of very meager trade links with other Latin American states.

10

International Integration and Locational Change in Mexico's Car Industry: Regional Concentration and Deconcentration

Pablo Wong-Gonzalez

It is generally acknowledged that within Mexico there is a high degree of spatial concentration of industrial activity. This concentration has been strongly linked to the enormous regional disparities and the associated effects on the unequal distribution of income, employment, infrastructure, and services, among others (López Malo 1960; Lamartine 1965; Unikel 1978; Garza 1985). Already in the 1950s and 1960s, the bulk of industrial output was known to be concentrated in Mexico's central region (the Federal District and the states of Mexico, Hidalgo, Morelos, Puebla, Querétaro, and Tlaxcala). In 1980, only two administrative regions (the Federal District and the State of Mexico) accounted for some 50 percent of the country's total manufacturing production.

The high level of industrial concentration in the central region and, in particular, in the Metropolitan Area of Mexico City (MAMC) can be seen as the spatial outcome of a pattern of accumulation based on an import substitution strategy.[1] This strategy was implemented principally in the period following World War II. There exists a close relationship between industrial growth (led by an import-substitution model within a highly protected market) and its geographic concentration. This experience has been noted in several developing countries (Gilbert and Gugler 1983; Kirkpatrick et al. 1984; Gwynne 1985). Market concentration, the existence of external economies, the level of industrial infrastructure and services, and the proximity to the centers of political and administrative decision making have all been considered as major factors for companies choosing to locate in Mexico's central region.

In the past few years, however, there has been an important degree of geographic dispersion in some manufacturing sectors. The automotive industry represents the best example of this trend. Traditionally, all of the manufacturing facilities of this sector have been located in the southern-central region. Recently, however, the trend has been to locate new operations that have a strong export orientation in medium-sized cities close to the southern border of the United States. The territorial redistribution of the Mexican automotive industry, the second in its history, is directly linked to the new and increasing process of international integration. This integration is not only a trading or capital-investment integration but a technical-manufacturing one. In this sense, the new pattern of location observed in Mexico must be understood within the context of change of the global motor industry.

As a result of the process described above, the Mexican automotive industry has entered a new phase of development. In contrast with previous patterns, the automotive industry now forms an integral part of a global network of production. The expression of this process has caused changes in the composition of output and has given Mexico a more specialized role in the global motor industry. At the present time, from an analytical point of view, the automotive sector can be divided into two segments. One segment produces for the domestic market, is in recession, and is primarily located in the southern-central region of Mexico. The other segment produces for the external market, is booming, and is located in the northern region.

It is important to point out the relevance of the process of international integration as one of the key elements in the present Mexican deconcentration/concentration of regional manufacturing. Because the process is a relatively new phenomenon, it has not been considered, or researched, in the scarce literature concerned with industrial location in Mexico. By and large, in explaining the relative redistribution of industrial capacity away from the traditional central manufacturing area, existing studies have emphasized factors such as the existence of disadvantages in the MAMC, the relative improvement of infrastructure in peripheral regions, and the effects of governmental programs designed to assist the territorial deconcentration of industry (industrial estates, new towns, and so on). Furthermore, in many cases the spatial effects of sectorial policies are more important than those that result from deliberate regional development policies including physical planning and human settlements (Harris 1983b).

The Mexican economy is going through an extraordinary process of transformation that is far from over. The situation tends to reinforce the interconnections with the world economy, and the present government policy has accelerated the process of change and international integration of the economy. As a result of the 1982 economic crisis, the Mexican government was forced to adopt a new model of development. The new model rests on the production and export of manufacturing goods, linking the industrial base with external trade. The impact on the territorial distribution of economic activity resulting from this type of relationship requires new forms of planning of the spatial economy and a restructuring of the present centralized system of political and administrative functions.

THE INTERNATIONAL INTEGRATION OF MEXICO'S MOTOR INDUSTRY

The motor industry, which already had reached high levels of internationalization of capital in the postwar period, has acquired a greater global nature in recent times (Jenkins 1987; Dicken 1986). Mexico has been increasingly integrated into a worldwide system of operations through the globalization process. Mexico's geographic proximity to the United States—sharing a border of more than 3,200 kilometers—the relatively low cost and high skill level of the labor force, the adequate industrial infrastructure and systems of transport and communications, and incentives offered by the government all make Mexico an attractive place for locating operations in the search for lowering costs of production. Furthermore, Mexico already has a high level of multinational production facilities, particularly those owned by U.S. capital (which controls over half of the market and production), which facilitates further integration within Mexican and U.S. plants (see Table 10.1).

The key element in the new stage in the Mexican automotive industry is its technical-manufacturing integration at the international level. With this the industry forms part of a global system of production that involves a progressively more specialized international division of labor. The tendency is toward the formation of a unique North American production block (Canada, the United States, and Mexico), allocating more specialized roles to each country. In reality, what is generally considered as the integration of countries in the global production process is, from the point of view of the companies, only the integration of their own plants and markets.

Stages of Development of Mexico's Motor Industry

Generally, the stages of development of the Mexican automotive industry can be explained by the following periodization.[2]

1. *The Preindustrial Stage* (1908–1962). This stage was characterized by the import of complete vehicles (1908–1924). Subsequently, assembly based on imported parts or complete knockdown kits (CKD) took place through license agreements or subsidiaries of foreign companies (1925–1961).

2. *The Import-Substitution Stage* (1962–1969). Government intervened to achieve a higher proportion of domestic content in the manufacture of the vehicle (regulation specified that Mexican-made parts must comprise at least 60 percent of the total value). Technically, vertical integration was reversed in this period, and there was a proliferation of "independent" Mexican-owned companies producing parts. At the same time, Mexican-owned companies, which

Table 10.1
Structure of Motor Vehicle Assembly Industry in Mexico, 1989

Company	Foreign Equity Participation	Shares (%) of:		
		Domestic Market	Total Exports	Total Production
Chrysler	100%	21.0	34.7	25.2
Ford	100%	19.6	20.2	19.7
General Motors	100%	16.3	20.6	17.6
Nissan	100%	21.5	12.8	18.8
Volkswagen	100%	19.3	11.6	16.8
Subtotal		97.7	99.9	97.5
Other Companies		2.3	0.1	2.5
Total		100.0	100.0	100.0

Source: Elaborated according to AMIA statistics.

had previously assembled cars under license agreements, were gradually displaced by foreign-owned subsidiaries.

3. *The Export Promotion Stage* (1969–present). This stage begins with the export of vehicles and components, in a direct and indirect way, through the final assembly section.

This periodization is a useful classification in functional terms, but it does not reflect properly the present stage of development. It is largely based on the sequence of governmental auto decrees (of 1962, 1969, 1977, 1983, and 1989). In reality, governmental decrees were only part of the influences that affected the industry's evolution, and the stages of development did not coincide with the periods defined by these decrees. For example, despite the Mexican government's decree in 1969 to expand automotive exports, it was not until the 1980s that substantial exports were achieved. In addition, the dividing line between the import-substitution and export-promotion periods is not a useful one, because import-substitution and export-promotion policies are not in contradiction to each other and, indeed, were adopted concurrently. Finally, the promotion of exports is not necessarily the same as the practice of global technical-manufacturing integration (since the exported goods could register 100 percent of domestic content), which, in itself, is an important and distinctive stage of development.

To understand more precisely the present stage of development of Mexico's motor industry, it is necessary to periodize on the basis of the different modalities of international integration, as indicated by Harris (1983a), and the internationalization of Marx's three circuits of capital, developed later by Palloix (1978) and Jenkins (1976).

1. *Trading Integration* (1908–1924). This stage was characterized by the import to Mexico of completely built vehicles and replacement parts. The vehicles distributed in the domestic market were fully assembled outside Mexico. This stage represents the beginning of interchange relationships and the international circulation of commodities—that is, the internationalization of the circuit of commodity capital.

2. *Capital-Investment Integration* (1925–1980). This stage comprised at least two functional phases of the automotive sector's development. In the first phase (1925–1965), assembly operations were established by foreign companies. Vehicles were assembled with components primarily imported from the industrialized countries which played host to the firms' manufacturing and management cores. The percentage of domestic-supplied components did not exceed 30 percent. In the second phase (1966–1980), vehicles were assembled with a growing domestic content intended to reach, as close as possible, 100 percent (with a compulsory minimum of 60 percent).

   In the period from 1925 to 1980, the nature of Mexico's role in the international integration of the automotive industry was almost exclusively as a market for foreign-produced replacement parts, components, and capital equipment imported from the firms' host countries. The links between plants located inside and outside Mexico were the result of the firms' horizontal expansion. Toward the end of this period, low-volume exports were initiated to other developing countries. In summary, this stage represents the export of capital toward Mexico and the internationalization of the circuit of money capital.

3. *Technical-Manufacturing Integration* (1981–present). This stage is characterized by a new wave of investment designed mainly to use Mexico as an export platform to developed countries. This produced a complex pattern of interconnections between plants located in Mexico and abroad. Mexico's motor industry forms part of a global system of production, and the new plants were designed to operate on an internationally competitive basis. Output tends to be more specialized and the degree of domestic content decreases. This stage represents the international integration of the production process which is expressed in an increasing international circulation of intermediate products among plants and companies—that is, the internationalization of the circuit of productive capital.

It is important to note that these three stages of international integration are distinct but not mutually exclusive. For example, trade integration has grown stronger through all stages, but the flows and nature of what is traded differ. Additionally, governmental policy could have been determinant for the first two stages; however, in the present stage of development, government policy has less influence than factors of a more global nature on the performance of the automotive sector in Mexico.

A DIVIDED INDUSTRY

In conceptual terms, Mexico's automotive industry can be divided into two distinct sectors. The first sector produces for the domestic market, is in recession, has a high proportion of idle productive capacity, and has low investment and productivity. The second sector produces for the international market, is expanding, has a high proportion of utilized productive capacity, and has high investment and productivity.

The first sector is composed of the car assembly segment, oriented to the domestic market, and domestic auto-parts manufacturers. The second sector is made up of vehicle and engine manufacturing for the export market, in-bond assembly activities (*maquiladoras*),[3] and some auto-parts manufacturing for export.

From the end of the 1970s, large multinational corporations programmed important investment for plants to produce nearly exclusively for the export market (see Table 10.2). In contrast to traditional plants, the new plants were designed to operate with the latest technology globally available with the aim of making them globally competitive. For example, the Ford car assembly plant at Hermosillo, Sonora, produces the Tracer—based on the Mazda 323— and the Escort, utilizing 128 robots, and incorporating the latest advances in flexible systems of production. This plant applies at the same time both international sourcing of components and an internationally based "just-in-time" system of inventory and delivery. In a first stage, when only the Tracer was produced, 60 percent of the components came from Japan (including the engine), 30 percent from Mexico, and 10 percent from the United States. With changes in the models produced for the year 1990, the supply composition changed in the following way: from Japan, 25 percent; Mexico, 15 percent; the United States, 60 percent. The principal cause for the dramatic change in the country of origin of the components is the appreciation of the yen against the U.S. dollar.

The performance of segments producing for the national market (the "national-traditional" sector) and the performance of segments producing for export (the "international" sector) are totally divergent with regard to key indicators such as growth (see Figure 10.1). While the national-traditional sector registered a negative growth of 4.2 percent in the 1980–1988 period in annual average terms, the international sector grew 34.8 percent for the production of automobiles, 55 percent for the production of engines, and 14.8 percent for the number of in-bond plants. Some analysts of the Mexican

Table 10.2
Major Export-Oriented Investments in Mexico's Automotive Sector in the 1980s

Company	Location City (State)	Product	Installed Capacity [a]	% of Export	Date of Start-up
General Motors	Saltillo-Ramos Arizpe (Coahuila)	Engines (6 cylinders)	451,200	80	1982
General Motors	Saltillo-Ramos Arizpe (Coahuila)	Car Assembly (4 cylinders)	130,000	65	1981
Chrysler	Saltillo-Ramos Arizpe (Coahuila)	Engines (4 cylinders)	270,000	80	1981
Chrysler	Toluca (State of Mexico) [b]	Car and Truck Assembly	n.a.	n.a.	1985
Ford	Chihuahua (Chihuahua)	Engines (4 cylinders)	450,000	80-90	1983
Ford	Hermosillo (Sonora)	Car Assembly	170,000 [c]	100	1986
Nissan	Aguascalientes (Aguascalientes)	Engines (4 cylinders)	350,000	80	1983
Nissan	Aguascalientes (Aguascalientes)	Car Assembly	150,000	30 [d]	1992
Renault	Gomez Palacio (Durango)	Engines (4 cylinders)	250,000	80	1984
Volkswagen	Puebla (Puebla)	Engines (4 cylinders)	440,000	85	1981
Volkswagen	Puebla (Puebla)	Car Assembly	n.a.	n.a.	1991

Source: The information is based upon several sources of the automotive sector, the author's questionnaire, and visits to plants.

[a] Vehicles/Engines per year.
[b] Conversion of its old plants.
[c] Ford announced an additional investment of $300 million to reach an annual output of 170,000 by 1990. The original capacity of this plant was 140,000 units.
[d] Estimated.
n.a. = not available.

automotive industry have suggested that the crisis of the national-traditional sector is a reaction to the opening and dynamism of the new export plants. Without a doubt there is a connection between the diverging behavior of the two sectors, especially if one bears in mind that a global trend toward booming export production in a slowly growing global market must cause a contraction of production somewhere. In the specific case of Mexico, however, the negative rate of growth of the national-traditional sector can be partly

Figure 10.1
**Mexico's Automobile Production for the Domestic and Export Market Segments,
1980–1988**

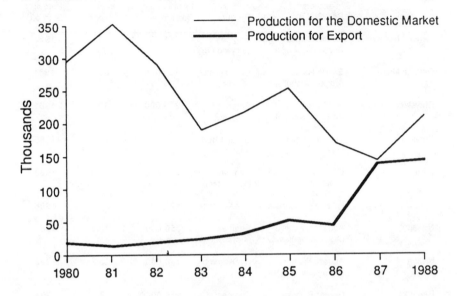

explained by the depression of the domestic market and the loss of purchasing power from 1982 onward.

Another way of looking at the growing international integration of the industry is through an analysis of the proportion of exports in relation to total output (see Table 10.3). The proportion of automobile output destined for export grew from 4.3 percent in 1980 to 48.8 percent in 1987 (dropping slightly to 41.0 percent in 1988); the proportion of engine output destined for export reached 80 percent in 1987. The export dynamism has transformed the automotive sector in Mexico from one that ran a huge trade deficit (accounting for 53.1 percent of the total balance of trade deficit in 1980) to one that now runs a substantial trade surplus (accounting for 78.4 percent of the total surplus). With these changes, Mexico's automotive industry has become the second largest export sector after oil.

The growth in the number of *maquiladoras* assembling auto parts has also been spectacular. From 1980 to 1988, the average annual growth in *maquiladora* employment was approximately 40 percent. Annual growth of added value was almost double that. The performance of this segment was rapid even in comparison to other booming areas. Although traditionally the *maquila* operations have been set up to make intensive use of labor, recent evidence suggests an increase in the technological level of the plants with resulting productivity gains (Gonzalez-Arechiga and Barajas-Escamilla 1989).

Table 10.3
The International Sector in Mexico's Motor Industry: Key Indicators, 1980–1988

Year	Export of Automobiles (Units)	Automobile Exports as a % of Total Production	Export of Engines (Units)	Engine Exports as a % of Total Production	Number of In-bond Plants
1980	13,293	4.3	43,000	12.9	53
1981	9,296	2.6	86,605	20.0	44
1982	14142	4.7	320,301	42.8	44
1983	20,768	10.0	708,234	69.2	47
1984	30,397	12.4	1,157,551	74.3	51
1985	49,856	16.8	1,317,405	74.2	63
1986	40,216	19.3	1,325,163	78.7	80
1987	135,481	48.8	1,367,380	80.0	140
1988	145,119	41.0	1,400,000	78.0	160
Average Annual rate of growth (1980-1988)		34.8%	55%		14.8%

Source: Calculated from the following statistical yearbooks: AMIA, *La industria automotriz de México en cifras*, 1972–1988; INEGI, *Estadística de la industria maquiladora de exportación*, 1980–1989.

General Motors installed its first in-bond plant in Mexico in 1978 and estimated it would run fifty in-bond plants in 1990. Chrysler and Ford followed. At the present time, there are around 160 plants producing auto parts with 92,290 workers and a growing Japanese presence. In 1987–1988 General Motors owned thirteen *maquila* ventures with a total of twenty-seven plants and 26,040 employees. In total, the U.S. "Big Three" plus Honda accounted for thirty-nine plants with 35,791 employees (see Table 10.4). The generated employment in the in-bond operations by the "Big Three" represents about two-thirds of the total employment in Mexico's final assembly section.

International Integration and Specialization: The End of the National Car

This chapter has argued that the process of international integration has produced a more specialized global role for Mexico's motor industry. This is particularly clear when analyzing the engine sector. For example, by the mid-1980s, Mexico was the source of approximately 40 percent of total internal combustion engine imports into the United States. It was estimated in

Table 10.4
Automotive-Related In-Bond Plants Installed in Mexico by Selected Multinational Corporations, 1988

Multinational Company	Number of Plants	Number of Employees
General Motors	27	26,040
Ford	7	5,991
Chrysler	4	3,636
Honda	1	124
(Subtotal)	(39)	(35,791)
Other Companies	121	56,499
Total a	160	92,290

Source: Elaborated according to data gathered from interviews and questionnaires applied to
automotive companies and complemented with the following sources: SECOFI, *Directorio de la industria maquiladora de exportación*, 1987–1989; *Expansión*, 1987–1989;
and Carrillo (1989, Appendix).

a The total figures include those plants producing auto parts that are classified under the electronics sector in the official statistics.

1985 that a quarter of Chrysler's global engine output was manufactured in
Mexico. Mexico produces for Ford 450,000 small engines for import into
the United States, which covers more than half of Ford's demand for the 2.3
liter, four-cylinder engine used in the Topaz (*Business Mexico* 1985). In addition to the specialized niche of engine manufacture, Mexico has become
the source for a growing number of subcompact vehicles for the North
American market. Among other technical factors, Mexico's geographic position offers it competitive advantages in the engine and vehicle sectors (which
involve heavy and bulky goods) due to the short distances involved and the
opportunity to use rail or truck shipment (with the subsequent savings in time,
cost, and journey time variability). In an important sense, Mexico plays in
North America a role similar to the one Spain plays in Europe. Spain has
many plants of global-scale car manufacturers, benefiting from lower costs
plus a location close to major European markets, a parallel to the Mexico–
United States relation.

Contrary to traditional theory, production segments in which Mexico
specializes are capital-intensive, and some sectors are advanced technologically
and do not make use of intensive "cheap labor." The skill content of the
labor force also has been upgraded.[4] Paradoxically—and contrary to the
classical dependency view—the new international role of Mexico's car industry has not increased Mexico's subordination to multinational corporations or the United States; it has increased the degree to which American

firms rely on Mexican facilities to remain competitive in a more and more aggressive global market.

Another indicator of the international integration process is the decreasing proportion of domestic content of final output (which is the same as an increase in the import content) in the new export plants. Vehicles produced for export register only between 15 and 30 percent of local content; engines register between 40 and 50 percent. This situation also reflects the change in the objectives and priorities of governmental policy toward the automotive sector, a change forced upon the government by the national economic crisis and by global industrial restructuring.

The original governmental plan, embodied in the 1962 automotive decree, was to achieve a total domestic integration in the manufacture of a Mexican vehicle. The objective would be supported by an import-substitution policy within which the manufacture of the engine would play a key role. However, the engine that was planned to form the basis of import substitution and the national integration of the automotive sector during the 1960s and 1970s had, by the 1980s, become the most important manufacturing export for all of Mexico. Ironically, this was achieved during a period of increasing import content and increasing, rather than decreasing, international integration.

The latest automotive decree, published in December 1989[5] explicitly shows a change in the governmental policy toward the whole sector. The globalization trend of the economy is recognized and an active and competitive insertion in the international markets is pursued.

The process described above has practically marked the end of a national dream: the manufacture of a car that in content and design is 100 percent Mexican, or the "Mex-Car." Mexico's automotive policy has shifted from the manufacturing of a "national car" to a growing participation in the "world car" strategy.

SPATIAL IMPACTS OF THE INTERNATIONAL INTEGRATION PROCESS

In conjunction with changes in (1) the composition of output, (2) the direction of trade, (3) the technological level, and (4) the organization of the labor process, the international integration process has produced changes (for the second time in its history) in the locational pattern of manufacturing capacity in Mexico's motor industry. A spatial deconcentration of capacity from the southern-central region to the northern region has been observed.

Developing economies, like Mexico's, that are on the path toward full industrialization are constantly transforming the composition of output and their labor force. In these types of economies the existing industrial capacity is not prepared to absorb an accelerated base of technological innovation or expansion. As a result, changes in product characteristics produce changes in location (Harris 1983b). In this sense, it is more efficient to invest in a new plant rather than to convert an existing one that possesses obsolete machinery, equipment, and layout.

Among the main locational factors considered in the move to the north are the following: (1) proximity to the U.S. market and production base, which reduces transport costs; (2) easy access for technical assistance; (3) low cost and incentives in plant installation; (4) a qualified and more docile work force; and (5) the possibility of imposing new and more flexible collective contracts and, in some cases, paying lower wages in relation to the old southern plants.

Another aspect related to the northward shift in the location of automotive plants is that, in the international integration process, the border region tends to be a favorite area. A certain deconcentration is also occurring within the United States and has resulted in a shift in the location of manufacturing capacity (from the traditional production area centers in Detroit to Tennessee, Pennsylvania, Kentucky, and Indiana). For the first time, some new plants are being established in the southern region.

International Integration, Technological Innovation, and Locational Change

Considering the periodization of different stages of international integration described above, it is possible to conceive corresponding changes in the technological-manufacturing nucleus[6] and changes in the pattern of location.

As Table 10.5 illustrates, the periods in which a qualitative jump in the technological-manufacturing nucleus has occurred have coincided with changes in the geographic location of facilities. The first qualitative jump occurred in the mid-1960s. This was the beginning of the manufacturing phase (as opposed to a purely assembly phase) in the development of Mexico's car industry and coincided with a geographic redistribution from the Federal District toward the adjacent states. As a result, an important southern-central region of automotive manufacture was created where the bulk of production was destined for the domestic market. The second qualitative leap occurred in the early 1980s and was characterized by the adoption of world-class production technologies. This process resulted in a new geographic redistribution of production capacity toward Mexico's northern regions where the new production was largely destined for export to the U.S. market.

Regional Concentration and Deconcentration

The change in the locational pattern of the manufacturing base toward Mexico's northern region, an outcome of the third stage of international integration, is among this chapter's major points of interest. Up to the end of the 1970s, almost the whole of automotive production was concentrated in the country's southern-central region (see Table 10.6). Because of factors previously indicated, however, there was from the early 1980s a substantial redistribution

Table 10.5
Phases of International Integration, Technological-Manufacturing Nuclei, and Locational Changes in Mexico's Motor Industry, 1908–1990

Phase of International Integration	Technical-Manufacturing Nucleus		Location of Production Capacity	
I. Trading Integration (1908-1924)	A manufacturing nucleus is non-existent; import to Mexico of completely built vehicles		____	
II. Capital-Investment Integration (1925-1980)	II. a)	Assembling of vehicles with imported parts (CKD) or domestic supplied components not greater than 30% of the total cost. Intensive level in the use of workforce (1925-1965)	II. a)	Mexico, D.F.
	II. b)	The manufacture of the engine incorporated (foundry, machining and assembly); domestic content greater than 60%; task segmentation of the workforce (1966-1980)	II. b)	State of Mexico, Puebla, Merelos and Hildalgo
III. Technical-Manufacturing Integration (1981-present)	Stamping process, robots and flexible systems of automation are incorporated; the domestic content of products decreases to levels of less than 20%		Coahuila, Chihuahua, Durango, Sonora and Aguascalientes	

of production capacity in both engines and motor vehicles. Excluding the limited production of heavy-duty trucks, Mexico's northern region, which accounted for 0 percent of the country's engine and car manufacturing capacity in 1980, accounted for almost 65 percent of installed capacity of engines and more than 40 percent of capacity for automobiles by 1988. When the growing number of in-bond automotive plants is added (around 160 in 1988 located mainly in the border fringe), it is evident that dramatic changes occurred in the geography of Mexico's motor industry during the 1980s (see Figure 10.2).

The relatively high degree of concentration of automotive-related activities in new areas of northern Mexico, such as the Saltillo-Ramos Arizpe complex, has given the area the nickname "Little Detroit." The geographic deconcentration of Mexico's car assembly and engine plants has also brought with it a certain dispersion of the auto-parts producing companies. For instance, supplies have located in Hermosillo (Sonora) in order to supply Ford's car assembly plant there. Among these companies are Carplastic, Autolin, Cima, Cisa, Goodyear Oxo, PPG Industrial, Mortell de México, and Quimica

Table 10.6
Geographic Distribution of Mexico's Motor Vehicle Production, 1970
(percentages)

Location	Automobiles	Commercial Vehicles	Total
Southern - central Region	100.0	97.1	99.2
Mexico City	16.9	29.1	20.0
Toluca	34.5	48.9	38.3
Cuernavaca	9.3	6.2	8.5
Puebla	31.3	0.2	22.9
Ciudad Sahagun	8.3	12.7	9.5
Northern Region	–	2.9	0.8
Saltillo	–	1.3	0.4
Monterrey	–	0.8	0.2
Mexicali	–	0.8	0.2

Installed Capacity 1988	Automobiles	Commercial Vehicles	Total
Southern - central Region	56.6	97.9	69.1
Northern Region	43.4	2.1	30.9

Source: Elaborated according to AMIA statistics, *La industria automotriz de México en cifras*, 1972 and 1988.

Parker, providing paint, axles, panels, electrical wiring systems, upholstery, and tires.

A New Territorial Division of Labor

The geographic redistribution of automotive production capacity is not developing evenly in terms of the segments or production lines. Although the process is still ongoing, an emerging pattern of regional specialization within Mexico is apparent.

1. In terms of the destination of output, plants located in the north produce for the external market, and plants located in the southern-central region produce for the domestic market.

2. In terms of the type of product, the northern region has specialized in the production of four- and six-cylinder engines, small and medium cars, light commercial vehicles, and export parts. The southern-central region has been specializing in six- and eight-cylinder engines, medium-sized automobiles, and heavy-duty trucks.

3. The level of integration between plants from one region to another is almost nonexistent, a fact reflected in the minimum interchange of parts and components.

Figure 10.2
Location of Mexico's Motor Vehicle Plants

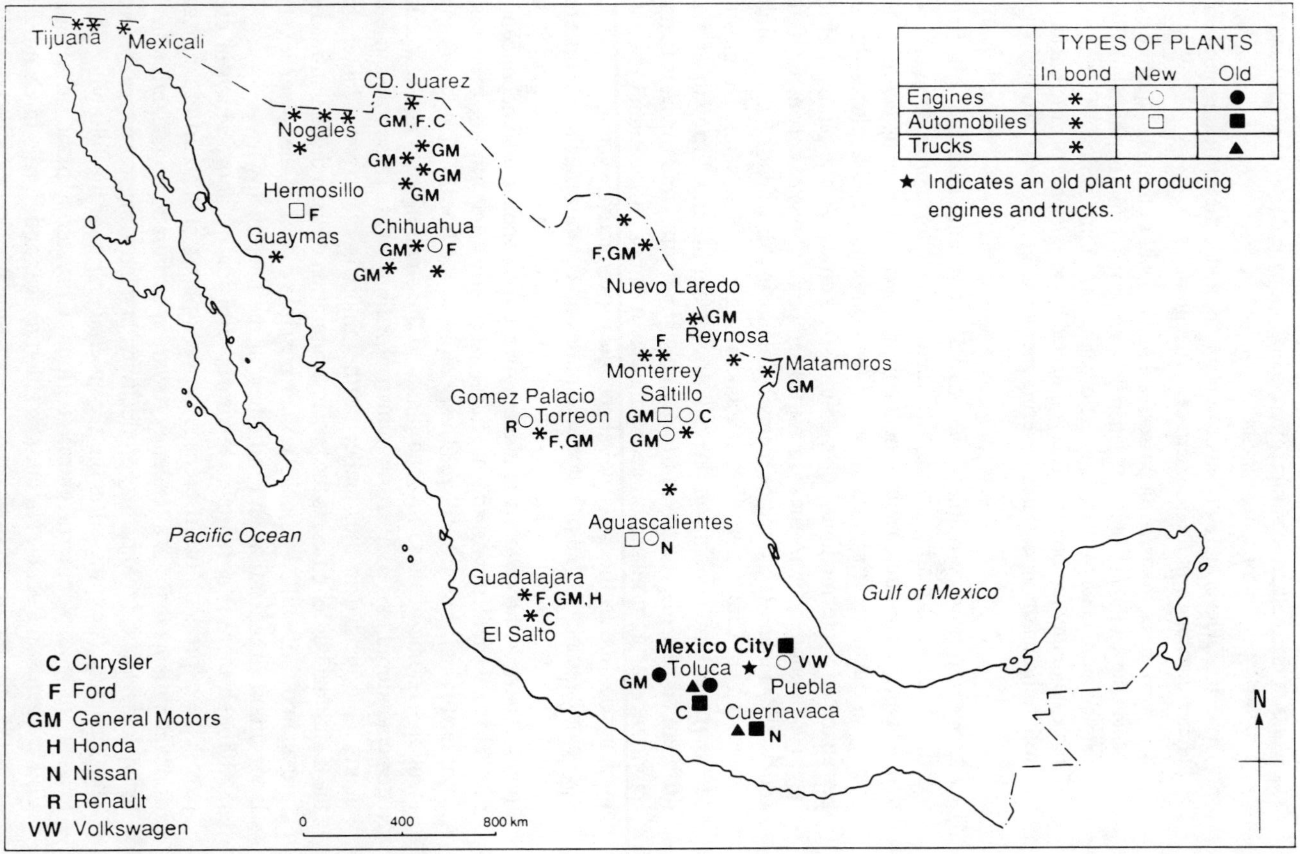

4. The plants located in the northern region are integrated to global international production and register a high level of import content in the final product. The plants in the southern-central region depend upon the domestic market and have a high proportion of local content.

5. The technical level and automation of plants located in the north are considerably higher than those in the southern-central region.

6. The work force in the north possesses a higher level of technical qualifications than in the south. The industry's management perceives the northern labor force is to be more open to changes in the organization of production which provides more flexibility for the firm. This is reflected in the existence of different clauses within the union agreements covering the work forces of the two regions.

Furthermore, it is possible to identify a geographic selectivity in firms' locational decisions within the northern region. The choice of location basically depends on the technical requirements of production. To set up car assembly or engine manufacturing activities, all the companies chose places that can be ranked as "intermediate" or medium-sized cities. At the moment of taking investment decisions, these localities had populations of between 250,000 and 500,000 inhabitants. Cities receiving plants in this category were Saltillo-Ramos Arizpe, Chihuahua, Gomez Palacio, Aguascalientes, and Hermosillo. The most striking conclusion one can draw from the rapid growth of many different centers of production in relatively small cities and towns is that the importance of agglomeration economies as a factor in locational choice is in sharp decline in the new global technical-productive system.

The in-bond plants that produce auto parts and components have a different pattern of location. They have been set up mainly in the border cities and towns. There is, however, a tendency toward a "concentrated deconcentration" to the small towns and medium-sized cities that are not necessarily "border towns" but are still relatively close to the border. The geographic location of some of these in-bond plants in the smaller cities and towns has been considered part of a "rural industrialization." One reason that in-bond plants have located in the smaller northernmost border towns, rather than the traditional border cities, is the possible saturation of the industrial infrastructure and pool of skilled labor. Another possible reason is the lower level of labor union organization and militancy in the smaller towns.

Although there is a definable territorial division of labor, which in great part is the expression of differences between plants built in different phases of development, there is a tendency toward a certain homogenization in the technological level, automation, productivity, and labor organizational systems. This tendency is expressed in the recent conversion of the following plants located in the southern-central region: Chrysler's plant in Toluca, Volkswagen's in Puebla, Nissan's in Cuernavaca, and Ford's in Cuautitlan.

Finally, the territorial division of labor within Mexico must be considered as part of a more global division of labor, in particular a regional-spatial specialization at the level of North America. Production units in northern Mexico and industrial centers in the United States produce specialized goods for a unique production base and market.[7]

CONCLUSIONS: A NEW BASIS FOR A POLICY OF DECENTRALIZATION AND REGIONAL DEVELOPMENT

The analysis of the changing locational pattern of Mexico's motor industry shows the importance of factors different from those traditionally considered in the field of industrial location—such is the case with the process of international economic integration. Frequently, nonspatial or sectorial factors have a deciding influence on the locational decisions of productive facilities. In the case of Mexico's northern region, the peso-dollar exchange rate and aspects of free trade recently have had an enormous influence. The continuing devaluation of the peso has substantially reduced the cost of labor. In addition, the existence of the U.S. 806 and 807 tariff provisions allow non-American companies to avoid trade barriers. It is possible that the expectation of a trade block (linking Mexico, the United States, and Canada) is one of the factors behind the increasing Japanese investment in northern Mexico. If a trade block is established, the Japanese companies would already be established inside an emerging North American protected market (and in an area of that market with low labor costs).

While government policy has had an impact on the geographic dispersion of the Mexican automotive sector, its role has not been vital. The Mexican government has been pursuing the deconcentration of economic activity (of industry in particular) away from Mexico's central area for more than three decades, with only minimal success. Traditionally, the existing diseconomies in the MAMC and the improvement in industrial infrastructure in peripheral regions have not influenced, by themselves, manufacturing deconcentration. Programs like industrial estates, new towns, fiscal incentives, and the determination of priority geographic zones have been available. However, in some of the automotive sector examples of northern investment, support from the three levels of government came only after the company had selected the particular location. Furthermore, some of the more peripheral towns in which companies chose to locate were outside the areas that the government thought possible to develop industrially. Governmental policy and actions have followed the process rather than directed it.

International technical-manufacturing integration has affected the spatial distribution of economic activity in Mexico favoring productive facilities closer to the U.S. manufacturing heartland rather than the geographic, population, and economic center of Mexico itself. These new economic and spatial tendencies have two interesting effects on the ability of governments to affect industrial location decisions. Central government finds itself squeezed between the growing internationalization of the companies' decision-making process, on the one hand, and the increasing deconcentration of the location of manufacturing capacity (independent of state planning or control) on the other. The deconcentration of location to the regions opens the opportunity for local and regional governments to bargain directly with multinational companies. This opportunity increases regional calls for economic and political autonomy as the regions seek to become agents of their own economic development.

From a national point of view, the geographic dispersion of the automotive sector from Mexico's southern-central region represents a relative concentration in Mexico's northern region. This trend will probably require the same, or greater, planning attention as that already expended on efforts to decentralize Mexico's central area.

The 1980s witnessed a dramatic change in the locational pattern of multinational investment, in both absolute and relative terms, from Mexico's more traditional central area to Mexico's northern region. Based on present trends, the deconcentration of industrial capacity will continue during the 1990s. Northern Mexico eventually may emulate the Catalonian region of Spain which has a standard of living closer to that of France than its own nation. Any "convergence" with the U.S. model of industrialization would place severe strains on relationships between traditional manufacturing centers and new industrial regions regarding the allocation of public resources, and new approaches to the formulation of regional development policies would become necessary.

NOTES

1. Nevertheless, it was difficult for Mexico—with its enormous 3,200 kilometer border—to follow a strict import-substitution policy, at least in the northern region.

2. See, for example, the works of Camarena (1981), Dombois (1985), and Bennett and Sharpe (1985).

3. The *maquiladora* program allows temporary duty-free entry of components and raw materials for their assembly in Mexico and reexport as final product. Correspondingly, the U.S. tariff regulations 806.30 and 807.00 permit return of the U.S. component portion duty-free, taxing only the value added in Mexico.

4. The same conclusions were pointed out by Palomares and Mertens (1987) in their analysis of Mexico's electronics, metal engineering, and secondary petrochemicals industry.

5. See *Diario Oficial de la Federacion*, Poder Ejecutivo Federal, 11 December 1989.

6. The analysis of the technological-manufacturing nuclei has been based on the work of Arteaga (1988), who describes technological changes and labor organization in Mexico's motor industry.

7. The correlation between the spatial distribution of in-bond plants in Mexico and industrial and commercial centers in the United States has been analyzed by Barajas-Escamilla (1989).

11

Decentralization in Latin America: An Evaluation of Achievements

Stella Lowder

The literature of decentralization employs so many interpretations of the concept that one can justifiably question whether such a chameleon is of any analytic use. The contributions to this book illustrate the wide range of forms decentralization can take, whether planned or spontaneous. Indeed, decentralization can be evaluated more easily as a reaction to processes promoting centralization, over which there is far greater consensus in the literature and which are much easier to define in Latin America.

CENTRALIZATION PROCESSES

The political and economic forces that have supported and reinforced the concentration of resources in one city or region have been wielded both by the state and entrepreneurs. The colonial period bestowed special status on selected port cities as mouthpieces of the continent. Settlements were legal entities from which the surrounding territory was organized; their status did not arise out of the services supplied to their hinterlands. In addition, centralized administrative systems incorporated counterchecks designed to discourage collusion among officials operating far afield. Independent governments faced similar problems when striving to remain in control of large territories bound by poor communications. This spatial and organizational centralization was the basis on which the region's growing contact with the global economy was grafted—first, primarily as an exporter of raw commodities, then through import-substitution industrialization, and, most recently, as a platform for export-led manufacturers. The processes associated with such integration have been dominantly centripetal and have served to reinforce the centralist tendency of the state and its administrative systems.

The repercussions of such political and economic processes can be appreciated particularly clearly within Latin America, which experienced not only the longest period of colonialism but the lordship of only two powers over much of its territory. This bestowed an unusual degree of homogeneity of language and religion over the continent. Independence for most of the region by the mid-nineteenth century meant that it has been exposed to the workings of the world economy for over a century and a half. In addition, Latin America's incorporation in the global economy is indelibly colored by its peculiar love-hate relationship with the most powerful member, the United States. Although originally the Monroe Doctrine enshrined Latin American rights to self-determination, few political or economic analysts fail to underline the degree of influence, if not interference, of the United States in Latin American internal affairs. U.S. influence is exerted through the support of American corporate capital and of national groups allied to it (Martz 1988) and through the influencing of policies of international institutions (such as the World Bank and the IMF) of which the United States has been a dominant contributor of funds (Hayter and Wilson 1985). The specific processes that tend to reinforce centralization include prebureaucratization, industrial structure, and recession.

Prebureaucratization

Latin America's high degree of population concentration in cities of a million or more is associated with highly centralized bureaucracies, even though several countries have federal structures. State administrations have created over time a vast number of directly and indirectly managed units alongside the main ministries. In 1979, for example, Mexico had 100 decentralized agencies, 400 parastatals (state companies) operating under private sector law, and 800 independent commissions and councils apart from the dependencies of the core ministerial system. The situation in Brazil was equally complex, as was that elsewhere, albeit on a smaller scale.

One explanation for such phenomena is that the colonial legal and administrative inheritance, in association with the great imbalance in the distribution of resources within the population, particularly of education, has given rise to "prebureaucratization"; the administrative apparatus developed before the institutions of political representation. As a consequence, elites use their power to "capture" the agency most relevant to their interests, rather than to provide a check on the unbounded expansion of the state (Harris 1983). There is litte coordinated pressure to decentralize territorially while decision making remains centralized within the government apparatus.

The proliferation of state agencies is explained by the legions of well-documented cases of the inability of dependencies of sectoral ministries to coordinate their activities, let alone work together, to achieve development project goals. Usually, progress was only achieved through directives from a presidential top committee, or by the creation of a new agency directly answerable to one. Paradoxically, programs designed to foster decentralization in the form of regional development have often been implemented through a greater degree of administrative centralization. However, these units exert considerable pressure on the organizational capacity of the apex and there is a limit to how much haphazard growth can take place before the system threatens to collapse in chaos. Many countries recognized this in the 1980s, when the overloaded apexes began to instigate top-down reforms in sheer self-defense. Most of these involved deconcentration rather than decentralization.

Industrial Structure

Import-substitution industry in countries with grossly skewed income distribution resulted in modern large-scale industry catering for the wealthier segment of the population which was concentrated in dominant regions. Given the size of these markets, both multinational corporations (MNCs) and national modern industry operated under near monopoly conditions with the aid of legislation designed to protect fledgling enterprise. However, the advantages of agglomeration and the greater profit margins granted by the absence of competition did not spawn the innovations and multiplier effects envisioned by liberal economists, as much of this industry was heavily dependent on imported technology and inputs. Thus much of this industry started out centralized and stayed centralized (Weaver 1987).

Subsequently, various countries became export platforms for manufacturers destined for the mass markets of the global core economy. Entry into this arena called for close contacts with the market, usually sustained by branch plants of MNCs and with government legislative and financial support. These conditions ensured that decision making was centralized in the headquarters of the MNC outside Latin America and in the upper echelons of the relevant ministry, although production may be decentralized territorially; beyond the exigencies of basic infrastructure and communications, such production usually seeks cheap and docile labor not "tainted" by politics or unions.

A major portion of the domestic market has limited significance for modern industry owing to its low purchasing power. By far the larger segment of the manufacturing sector is composed of small workshop, if not artisanal, units producing simple consumer goods for local markets both restricted and protected by isolation. These decentralized units are capable of responding to local tastes and needs and through their high absorption of labor, can make substantial contributions to local economies, despite their comparatively low productivity. Much analysis of the 1960s assumed that this sector would be absorbed by modern industry over time and so dismissed its potential for development as a relic of the periphery. When the International Labor Organization (ILO) recommended government support, analysts stressed its role as an urban labor reserve trapped by the logic of capitalism (Bromley 1979; Bromley and Birkbeck 1988). Although the assumption of the 1960s is rejected, the latter diagnosis does not seem entirely appropriate; the small workshop sector persists at a scale that requires serious attention to its internal dynamics (de Soto 1989).

Recession

Latin America's early independence, higher level of development, and closer integration with the global economy also accounted for the attention it received from multinational banks awash with petrodollars in the 1970s and for the magnitude of its international indebtedness. The greatest debts are owed by the most developed economies. However, the repercussions of escalating interest rates have been greatly exacerbated by the world recession which curbs the market and returns for commodities and manufactured exports. This increases global competition for the most efficient and cheapest production sites; easily mounted export assembly industries are also easily withdrawn, unless greater concessions are provided by states to maintain them. Within Latin America there have been winners (Mexico and Brazil) and losers (Peru and Argentina) in this competition (Wilson 1987). More generally, within countries, local economies closely tied to such production, such as found in capital cities, are likely to grow less quickly than those conserving a greater degree of independence at the periphery; this gives rise to a form of decentralization by default.

THE PURPOSE OF DECENTRALIZATION

Given the high degree of centralization and the advantages it bestows on decision making, decentralization policies require strong motivation. The most common motivators arise out of self-interest, in the sense of the abatement of political challenges to a government, the promotion of development, and geopolitics.

Political Challenges

Political challenges may come from individuals or organized groups. The most common methods used to diffuse the potential danger accruing from capable leaders are co-option, patronage, and oppression. Urban grassroots leaders frequently have been won over by personalist means, such as through the offer of a home or the provision of schooling for their children. District activists similarly may be bought off by providing a water supply or a school. Such deals abound prior to Latin American elections. They involve resources, however, and are not an appropriate response to mass demands.

While military regimes often have been tempted to use repression in such cases, civilian ones are more likely to consider other means of diffusing discontent.

Most governments have at some time conceptualized the problem as one of the presence of certain populations—migrants, students, unions—in the core that are particularly prone to protest. If these could be diverted elsewhere through the decentralization of services and employment, the problem would disappear. This approach is instigated from the center in the interests of the center, although it may result in greater investment by the state and the persuasion of others to invest elsewhere in the country. The result is at least the deconcentration of discontent and hence its power to do damage.

The limitations of this approach are that most central governments have proved very unwilling to relinquish control over activities elsewhere and permit a degree of devolution of power to regions or lower levels of the political hierarchy. Sometimes it is argued that local populations need protection from tyrannical local elites, but observers suggest that they are more likely to be motivated by fear—fear that devolved units might prove so successful as to challenge the central position or that opportunities for patronage or more open corruption would be lost.

Even when local authorities are charged with some of the duties previously carried out centrally, they seldom receive either adequate training or funding with which to do them. Moreover, unless enshrined by constitutional changes, there is always the underlying fear that these services may be withdrawn on a change of policy. Furthermore, such devolution may further inequality if local budgets are limited to the revenues and user charges that can be generated locally and so mirror the wealth or poverty and the state of development of the community. Although deconcentration is justified as a means of increasing local institutions' accountability, public participation is limited to reacting to the level of service provided. This form of decentralization represents a shedding of responsibility by the state for any unevenness in the level of provision across the country; it is also a useful mechanism for deflecting the anger generated by such conditions which would otherwise be directed at the center.

The Promotion of Development

The promotion of development is related to decentralization to the extent it involves the better distribution of resources. But efficiency, in the market sense of accessibility to the maximum clientele, promotes centralization of product and service; the primate capitals house in one place an even greater share of the purchasing power than of population, which ensures their continued market supremacy. Pure market considerations would deny the majority of the rural population access to services (which often is the case). However, efficiency for the provider at one stage and over the short term may be inefficient later both for the provider and wider society, as the market is curtailed by poverty or as big city growth renders the provision of services exorbitantly expensive to both provider and user.

Thus the state is forced to intervene if key resources or sectors of the economy not considered attractive by the private entrepreneur are to be developed. This attitude usually arises because of the lumpy nature of investment and its recovery over the long term or because the viability of the project is in doubt. Questionable viability often exists with metal and oil refining, which were hitherto carried out abroad, and with iron, steel, cement, and glass, which were imported. These activities may be located at either the export point or at the source of the materials and so do not necessarily involve the decentralization of investment. The specialist skills and remit of such activities spawn single-purpose or semiautonomous agencies. Such delegation does not constitute much in the way of decentralization, as these agencies' concern is usually strictly limited to the running of the concern; their budget is determined by other central authorities which ensures only a limited degree of operational autonomy.

Geopolitical Goals

Geopolitical goals are the most common reason for countries to adopt decentralist policies (Rondinelli et al. 1989). Few can claim a strong tradition of legal succession of regimes without the intervention of the military. External threats are of concern not only to the military but to the national interest which serves to displace internal dissent. Latin America contains many smouldering border disputes with neighbors, particularly in sparsely populated Amazonia. Many countries have seen this zone as an escape valve for redundant peasants, but the region also represents a geopolitical goal to occupy the national territory effectively, especially at the periphery. Brazil's roads through Amazonia and up to its borders are perceived as a threat by its neighbors, rather than welcomed as a means of opening up the interior of the continent. There is further uneasiness generated by the spontaneous migration to border zones and the indifference to borders of those involved in interests there, such as that occurring presently between Brazil and Paraguay and between Bolivia and Brazil.

Much rhetoric surrounds the issues described above, but the decentralist element becomes far stronger when it is accompanied by the desire to ensure that all the national territory contributes to the economy, particularly if the inhabitants of peripheral regions feel alienated by their extreme poverty and the seeming indifference of central government. An extreme response, and one that the states hope will serve to reorient the spatial focus of the nation, is to relocate the capital. This has often been justified on the grounds of the congestion in the capital and the need to impose greater distance between administrators and pressure groups or political leaders so as to decrease the opportunities for corruption. However, often such an act "can be most suitably interpreted as an attempt to draw a veil over the centralizing substance of executive authority" (Slater 1989, 516).

Geopolitical concerns also color a different type of problem: the need to control irresponsible or corrupt behavior by inexperienced or self-interested provincial governments. Centralism on a smaller spatial scale may not be efficient and may not promote equity or greater participation in either local economy or polity. Local minorities are just as vulnerable to discrimination by regional or local authorities. Indeed, it has been argued that the reason redundant rural labor heads for the supposed misery of squatter settlements in primate cities, rather than to more accessible intermediate ones, is because the nature of the competition in the primate cities is more open; informal means of social control may play a much greater role in restricting opportunities to those not well connected with local power groups in intermediate cities (Smith 1985). Undoubtedly, on many occasions national level supervision has worked in the general populations' favor and ensured a modicum of equity in the type and level of services available across a state.

THE ANALYSES

Decentralization is clearly a malleable concept that can be attached to a wide range of state policies and political movements; this undoubtedly underwrites its current popularity with international institutions, states, regional authorities, local governments, and political parties alike. This forces the evaluator to consider the purpose and context in which the concept is being used and to step back from the necessary, but comparatively mechanistic, process of measurement. Has decentralization been no more than "a mirage, a myth and a mask" (Slater 1989) owing to the contradictions between goals and the means of achieving them, inadequate perception of the goals in the first place, and concealment of the true goals being pursued? Is the spatial content of decentralization no more than a drafting board on which institutions and enterprises plot their strategies for their own ends?

No meaningful analysis of such a complex process can ignore the specific context in which each country finds itself in relation to the global economy. Much of Latin America's decentralization may well be a "mirage," for growth goals may result in limited multiplier effects in the vicinity of the development, while the national impact may be felt predominantly in the capital. Some countries undoubtedly feel that decentralization at the international scale remains a great "myth" after evaluating the impact of multinational and transnational companies locating in them. Unlike wealth, recession is very transportable.

In Part I of this book, Fox examines the impact of the collapse of the lead sector on a single commodity producer. The devaluation of tin eroded the economic base of Bolivia and led to not just unplanned, but extralegal activities, generating a far greater share of national wealth. The government's loss of economic authority was made plain when it encouraged tin miners to form cooperatives and mine on their own account, or offered them a lift out of the desolated mining districts. Production in the most profitable alternative region of Amazonia was, if not illegal, certainly beyond the conrol of the state. This reflected the fact that this peripheral location was ineffectively organized, let alone policed, by the state. Free market principles set the price for alluvial gold and much was sold across the border; the Bolivian state only gained a share in the market when it offered more competitive prices. Similarly, coca production was structured by the Colombian drug barons unabated until American intervention increased the risks and increased supply lowered the prices; only then was there a modest trickle of uptakers of the government scheme to substitute other crops. This surely was a case of decentralization by default, when isolation and the reduction of power in the center grants an unprecedented degree of autonomy to the periphery.

Fox also reviews conditions on the Brazilian side of the border. Although the working conditions were similar, one cannot attribute the "free for all" ambience here to the decline of central powers. At best one might interpret the Brazilian government's deliberate channeling of population to the borderlands as a measure against population concentration and the problems that it would exacerbate in the central regions if it were not diverted elsewhere; in this snese it could be considered a "pro-center" strategy. The borderlands were a handy receptacle in which to hold population redundant to the national economy; the fact something was actually produced and the land was effectively occupied was a bonus to the state.

A long campaign of state rhetoric aimed at diverting redundant populations to Amazonia resulted in spontaneous conflict between poverty-stricken putative settlers, bandits and pseudoentrepreneurs attempting to dominate resources and manpower. The state stood aside while the "law of the jungle" sorted out the actors absorbing the risks attached to resource exploration and the establishment of claims. State authority reappeared only after the profitability of the resource was known. Genuine concern over the periphery, over the fate of its indigenous Amerindian population, over the irrevocable destruction of the natural environment, and over the hazards endured by those partaking in the production of gold was expressed by foreign observers and only grudgingly acknowledged by the state subsequently. Although Brazil gained a new resource, Rondônia is hardly an example of purposeful decentralization: it has no more powers and no greater share of state investment as a result.

Few Latin American countries share Bolivia's extreme vulnerability to world market fluctuations arising from such an historic dependence on a single commodity other than oil. However, many economies, such as Chile, Colombia, Ecuador, Peru, and Uruguay have been and continue to be based on a narrow range of primary exports in which supply is highly competitive. A number have also incurred comparatively high per capita levels of international debt in efforts to diversify economies. Outside the Southern Cone, these parameters are compounded by rapid population growth. Some countries have also undergone major swings in development policy in which North American direct or indirect intervention has been implicated. One indirect result in the case of Peru is internal political dissent in the form of vigorous guerrilla attacks. It is not surprising that it is impossible to maintain centralization in the sense of effective control over the national territory and the ability to shape the economy, under such conditions.

Radcliffe's discussion of the Peruvian case supports Slater's contention that decentralization measures are often no more than a myth. The state instigated reforms ostensibly to spread development potential more widely on both the spatial and social dimensions, but these were conceived and implemented from the top. Radcliffe asserts they contributed less to decentralization than the spontaneous reactions to circumstances not formally confronted by policy, such as the creation of employment and the uneven natural endowment of the country. Thus, efforts to decentralize the benefits of development did not seem capable of overcoming the agglomeration of resources in the most advantaged regions, and the nature and level of investment in them did little to challenge the supremacy of the capital.

Radcliffe defines decentralization in Peru in terms of spontaneous population movements that resulted in a decline in the growth rate of the metropolis. Differential growth rates of departments and cities reflect the limited impact of planned development outside the capital and the spatial consequences, undoubtedly unplanned, of the macro measures adopted. But these population shifts are better understood through the appreciation of the occupations of the majority of the population, which are usually undervalued by consignment to the "informal" sector with all its pejorative overtones. Such partial perceptions of employment structure do a particular injustice to women, a greater proportion of whom migrate to cities, particularly as the previous decade's agrarian reform programs discriminated against them.

In the 1970s, unemployment arising from recession began to bite, particularly in the capital, which was most closely integrated with world capitalist forces. This caused the urban middle classes to reevaluate the attractions of intermediate cities and reduced Lima's allure to potential migrants, other than as a temporary sanctuary from violence. The spontaneous decentralization of larger contingents of the middle class to provincial towns had unplanned multiplier effects in the form of increased effective demand for goods and services, most of which were satisfied by the labor-intensive informal economy. Women benefited particularly from the increased demand for domestic workers, either in private homes or in the growing tourist facilities located in highland secondary cities.

Changes in employment and service structure in intermediate cities have been even more noticeable in Peru's much smaller neighbor, Ecuador, although fueled by oil windfalls. Ecuadorian economic policy can be summarized as the desire for (1) increased production and (2) a more even spatial spread of development promoted through the decentralization of supporting physical (roads and energy), economic (financial outlets), and social (education and health facilities) infrastructure. The instruments of the two approaches were completely independent and gave rise to the mirage created by the concentrating tendencies of capitalism responding to the first goal, while the second called for a measure of diffusion of services to settlements lower down the urban hierarchy. Administrative systems, whether public or private, underwent a degree of timid deconcentration; effective decision-making power was retained in the two major cities.

A major undertone to all Ecuadorian policy concerned the role the state should adopt with respect to private capitalism, which went beyond the mere conciliatory gestures of a weak state to the pressure of vested interests. Successive regimes designed policies to foster the private sector, and there was a marked reluctance to implement policies that constrained its initiative. The state even underwrote the entire private sector's international debt by permitting it to make repayments to it in *sucres*. This voluntary creation of space for private initiative is a form of devolution of power, rather than a spatial form of decentralization. It shifts attention to the structure of power groups in society and their bases, which may reflect broad regional allegiances rather than specific territories.

In such a small country, the past concentration of services had forcibly drawn most high aspirers in the population to one or another of the primate cities. But like Peru, the pool of graduates expanded considerably in the 1970s; the deconcentration of state education and health services increased the standard of living in intermediate cities, besides creating opportunities by expanding the numbers of professional and technical staff employed. Here greater affluence generated employment multipliers beyond that of domestic support: the new consumer group made its mark through demands for modern housing and its fittings. In Ecuador such spontaneous creation of resources would appear important for reinforcing spatial decentralization demands, as the built environment is a significant factor in creating locality identity and loyalty. However, as yet, these tendencies would seem no more than yearnings for a greater share of the pork barrel, rather than effective political demands for decentralization.

The case of Argentina described by Morris represents a different sort of effective decentralization, although similar processes have been at work elsewhere. The state attempted to decentralize industry in order to reduce the concentration of production and its diseconomies in the metropolitan region over a long period, but the desire to stimulate production was greater and mostly benefited the core. The spatial content of the measures was mostly ineffective, with the exception of the subsidies that enabled some new industries to locate in the periphery as long as they lasted. But Argentina had also opened up its economy and attracted MNCs that favored the core region. Subsequently, many of these enterprises pulled out of the country altogether; the resulting unemployment enhanced the visibility of the jobs created elsewhere, which seemingly surpassed that envisaged by the state. However, analysis of the nature of the decentralized industries and the location of their suppliers and outlets raises doubts about how long they will survive in a competitive environment. The present spatial pattern of industry reflects locational decisions by entrepreneurs integrated to various degrees in the global economy and thus subjected to differential national and international forces.

It is appropriate then to leave aside the international and national perspective and view the decentralist horizon from the viewpoint of entrepreneurs seeking a new site in one of the most congested metropolitan cores of Brazil. Townroe underlines the influences on decision making that is constrained by many factors other than sheer economic rationality or state policy. Nevertheless, up and going industry is unlikely to contemplate severing all its existing linkages in a region. Nationwide decentralization might be an appropriate strategy for developing new resource bases or for self-contained incoming assembly operations, but it is hardly an option for those who wish to keep their existing clients and suppliers, let alone their contacts with family and friends. Decentralization in São Paulo is more a case of diffusion to the adjacent districts of the state and represents one of the few documented cases of Friedmann's "trickle-down" pressures at work.

Part II's focus on a particular country allowed the examination of underlying political and economic structures in far greater depth. Mexico is a particularly interesting case in which to evaluate decentralization because of its comparatively early industrial development and because of the part early experience with primarily North American enterprise had in the key event of Mexican history. The Mexican Revolution can be directly associated with the excessive centralization of decision making under Porfirio Díaz and the unacceptable degree of uneven development in both spatial and social terms which resulted from external investment. Subsequently, Mexico confronted the U.S. oil barons by nationalizing the industry and suffered the penalties of oligopolistic corporate wrath. Such experiences underpinned continuous state policy to protect national production, restrict and monitor foreign investment, and control access to the domestic market. Continuous political centralization is one explanation of how Mexico has been able to maintain harmonious relationships with such a powerful neighbor without losing its independent stance, as evident in its attitudes to Cuba and its criticism of U.S. interventions in Central America.

The 1917 constitution was designed to weld together a nation ravaged by civil war, its multiple factions, and the regional elites that survived. Reforms, strategic nationalizations, and the concentration of funds were all mechanisms planned and implemented by a strengthening center. The process culminated in the formation of a single party and the projection of its goals as a grand "national scheme" to promote development. But as Stansfield stresses, the objective of any system must change with time, which accounts for the changes in emphasis with successive regimes. After World War II, the bureaucracy expanded in sympathy with the growing economy's complexity, thus spawning greater support and centralization. The weakness of this process lay in Mexico's propensity to live on borrowed funds. With the recession and the introduction of floating interest rates came even greater debt, alleviated only on acceptance of the IMF's austerity prescription. Thus the state ceased to be able to increase its support through an expanding bureaucracy concentrated in Mexico City. When discontent became obvious, party leaders heard more clearly the warnings of regional party activists that they too could not guarantee support and the long-standing criticisms of the rural dwellers left out of Mexico's miracle years.

Stansfield presents us with the picture of a state having to take action, labeled in public as "decentralization" and interpreted as a greater devolution of power and the spatial deconcentration of resources. However, there was no desire to devolve power to regional elites who might well use it to mount a personal political base; minor devolution could be shifted further down to give the illusion of greater participation at the grassroots level. Both planners and technocrats foresaw the efficiency of spreading investment more widely and curtailing the Federal District's sprawl, but the grand design and the coordination of the implementation of the plans involved was retained firmly in the center.

Rodríguez is convinced that the measures activated by the de la Madrid regime were never really intended to devolve power; the banner of decentralization was skillfully waved to recover lost ground and for central decision making to be reinforced. Clearly, there had to be a tangible response to the criticism voiced both within and outside the party, but the measures adopted, despite involving the tangible relocation of resources, concealed a hidden agenda.

The first objective could be considered as a measure to diffuse criticism by the physical removal of, or discouragement of, the agglomeration of potential vocal critics in the capital. The dispersal of teacher training to the states and the building up of the provincial universities served to decrease the degree of organization and the chance of vocal demonstration by politicized students undergoing training or attracted to the massive autonomous university. In addition, a large number of state dependencies were dispersed to diverse cities; the relocation of over 62,000 state employees also reduced the pressure on a capital devastated by a massive earthquake, for state buildings suffered particularly badly.

The second objective was to shift responsibility of a range of services to states and municipalities and so divert criticism previously aimed at the central government. Large sections of the health service, social security installations, and social assistance were involved, and the states also participated in the planning and execution of regional planning objectives within their territories. Finally, municipalities were made responsible for a range of basic services delivered locally.

The hidden agenda emerged when the financial and legal underpinning did not materialize. States ratify the various federal laws at their own pace; the fiscal base of municipalities enshrined in those laws was probably never sufficient but, in any case, has seldom been distributed on an equitable basis within states. Even when implemented, municipalities did not have the equipment or staff to assume the new responsibilities. Thus municipalities are tied even closer to the goodwill or patronage of traditional political figures within the state administration. Clearly, these circumstances permit the blame for the lack of adequate provision to be shifted to new levels of government, which, however, have little real autonomy over the type or level of service they provide. This device is particularly useful when municipalities are headed by opposition political parties.

The factors underlying political centralism appear far more coherent and consistent, no matter what guise they have adopted, than those in the economic sphere analyzed in Chapters 9 and 10, even though both are concerned with modern industry and primarily with MNCs. Gwynne initiates the discussion from the perspective of those goods whose production structure renders them particularly suitable for the progressive separation of productive locations as they and their markets evolve. No single factor remains fixed in the global economy: factor endowments are a product of economic relations that may favor different countries in successive decades, depending on their respective exchange rates, comparative labor costs, and the present areas of market expansion.

Mexico's current niche in the global scheme is as a cheaper location than Taiwan, where limited labor has forced wages up. Mexican industry, Gwynne argues, has used cheap female labor while dynamic internal migration has served to keep wages low. Mexico deliberately courted this industry through favorable legislation; even so employment growth shadowed the imposition of "effectively valued" exchange rates.

Mexico also enjoys the entirely fortuitous advantage of a common border with the United States. Apart from the reduction in transport costs, this has stimulated two very different processes. The first concerns the luring of U.S. industries to locate nearer the Mexican side so as to reap the advantages of shuttle manufacturing with operations in Mexico carried out in-bond. Here Mexico provides a cheap outlier of the production process, which involves a massive "putting out" phase. The second demonstrates a new twist in the complexities of global market mechanisms: Mexico as a platform through which third parties can gain entrance to the U.S. market. A regional market composed of Canada, the United States, and Mexico seems increasingly likely in order to counter the growth forces of the European Economic Community after 1992. Japanese and Korean MNCs have also set up plants in northern Mexico.

A considerable amount of industrial employment has been created by or near the northern border as a result of these processes. Government policy clearly encouraged this decentralization process, but the Border Industrialization Program has been operating for over two decades—growth responded more to factors in the international economy than to the action of the Mexican state. Indeed, the needs of this industry forced the state to modify some of its policies, as noted by Wong-Gonzalez, who provides a detailed case study of the increasingly specialized role allocated to Mexico through his analysis of the motor vehicle industry. Initially, the industry's goal was like all import-substitution strategies, to serve Mexico's domestic market; legislation called for the progressive substitution of imported parts. As the Mexican motor vehicle market was highly centralized, the plants set up in the 1960s and 1970s were either in the Federal District or within easy access of it. During the stage of monetary capitalism which lasted to 1980, there was little motive for removal. Since 1981, however, the goal switched to the export market for parts, components, and vehicles, and the industry entered the era of productive capital. The knock-on effect was the abandonment of the substitution program for Mexican-made parts.

The significance for decentralization of the automotive industry is twofold: first the government policy followed processes instigated by the MNCs involved, rather than directing them. The internal logic of the sector dictated where companies were situated and what operations took place within them. When cars and trucks were sold predominantly in Mexico City, plants located there; when a wider range of components and parts were made for export, the spatial constraints were lifted. Newer plants tended to locate in intermediate cities and towns in the north, nearer the export points. However, these cities had not been targeted by the state to receive such development; indeed, the industry shunned the larger cities involved in the Border Industrialization Program. Settlements that had no modern industry and that had never figured in state development program were often chosen. Second, the industry did not fit the stereotype of unskilled assembly work carried out by women. It is true that a higher proportion of components are imported, but the labor is becoming more male, specialized, highly trained, and rewarded. The new location pattern raises a further issue in the decentralization debate: whether the states have the power to deal directly with MNCs over the question of sites and their infrastructure or whether these matters will be decided centrally far from the locations involved.

CONCLUSIONS

Decentralization, like any other policy, can only be implemented successfully from a position of strength by a state committed to it, prepared to devote the resources to it, and prepared to persuade others that it will be of benefit to them. Rarely is this the case; decentralization schemes are more likely to be time-buying exercises in which the cards are shuffled to make it harder for the players to appreciate the strength of individual hands. The support of national leaders is no guarantee that subordinates will either understand or agree with the proposals. Entrenched seniority hierarchies discourage initiative and experimentation; changes are seen as challenges to authority rather than to ingenuity or as a chance for personal development.

Decentralization is limited not just because central authorities do not wish to lessen their power; there is a real problem of how to create an adequate local base to attach decentralization measures. The administration of service delivery to large areas of difficult terrain, inadequate communications, and frequently very sparse populations is a major challenge even to developed countries. Nor are conditions much easier in towns that have evolved spontaneously on whatever ground is available, although one is more likely to find more educated and capable personnel. However, where the local economy operates on pure market principles, able people command a price higher than most governments cannot afford to pay.

It is unrealistic in such circumstances to expect any state to institute more than gradualistic incremental measures to enhance decentralization, as would appear to be the case in Mexico. Given the instability of many regimes, most mechanisms are devised to strengthen the state apparatus; any effective grassroots leader is likely to be co-opted by the state in an effort to neutralize his efforts. Given that there is no guarantee that decentralist efforts per se will improve conditions for the average citizen, there has not been a strong bid for decentralization from the bottom.

There is much scope for decentralization in the domestic private sector. Private banks, for example, often stand accused of passing on the myriad deposits received locally to regional offices or to the national head office, which then determines the parameters governing loans; the claim is that they are biased toward applicants based in major centers seeking large amounts (Armstrong and McGee 1985). However, there is often the same mistrust of local decision making within the private sector. In Ecuador, the mistrust was often bound up with informal business methods and the niceties of the status of the owners; when referring to regional banks, for example, informants felt that confidentiality was at risk and expressed doubt about the business practices of those involved, who were perceived as rival businessmen rather than as purveyors of a service. There is no doubt that misgivings arise from the identity of the groups seen as benefiting from the concentration of resources or manipulating the mechanisms concerned.

Demands for spatial decentralization respond to the tension arising when a capital region associated with industry—the lead sector of the economy in most of Latin America during the 1960s and 1970s—enjoys a much higher standard of living than the rest of the country. Its population often resents being classified alongside others perceived to be contributing little to the nation, let alone being heavily taxed in order to support them. Fortunately, such resentment has never reached the extreme of attempted secession, as in the case of Zaire's Katanga province or the stillborn state of Biafra in Nigeria, primarily because it is the regions identified most closely to the nation that are involved. However, in these circumstances, decentralization of some resources can be sold to the capital's defendants both as part of a grand development plan for the nation and as a means of slowing expansion and the need for them to share their wealth with tides of new migrants.

Decentralization may also arise either from the reduction of control of authority or from the greater pressures responding to global capitalism. In the case of recession, these factors may operate together and lead to the privatization of state undertakings such as ENTEL, Argentina's giant telephone company. Mexico is selling off between $20 billion and $25 billion of state assets, while Colombia, Venezuela, Chile, and Costa Rica have done the same on a smaller scale. While efficiency and equity criteria may be applied to both the economic and the administrative sphere of this and other types of decentralization, the key question is whether it is those performing or those on the receiving end of the action that should be evaluating the achievements of the process. It is unreasonable to expect the goals of the private entrepreneur motivated by profit to equal those of a state responsible for the whole of society. The application of the concept at a regional or national level, without taking the context of the actors involved into account, will yield a recipe for an abstract model rather than for a policy or an explanation based in reality.

Bibliography

CHAPTER 1

Aguilar-Barajas, I., and Spence, N. 1988. Industrial decentralization and regional policy, 1970–86: The conflicting policy response. In *The Mexican economy*, edited by G. Philip, 183–228. London: Routledge.

Castells, M. 1978. *City, class and power*. London: Macmillan.

Coll-Hurtado, A., ed. 1986. *Ciudades alternativas para la descentralización*. Mexico: Instituto de Geografía, UNAM.

Collins, C. D. 1989. Rise and fall of the national "decentralized agencies" in Colombia. *Public Administration and Development* 9:129–46.

Cooke, P. 1988. Modernity, postmodernity and the city. *Theory, Culture and Society* 5:475–92.

Dear, M. J. 1986. Postmodernism and planning. *Environment and Planning* 4:367–84.

Downs, C. 1980. Politics, design and results; regionalization and decentralization in Nicaragua and Haiti, 1982–86. *Third World Planning Review* 11 (2): 131–49.

Frampton, K. 1985. Towards a critical regionalism: Six points for an architecture of resistance. In *Postmodern culture*, edited by H. Foster. London: Pluto Press.

Friedmann, J. 1966. *Regional development policy: A case study of Venezuela*. Cambridge, Mass.: MIT Press.

Gilbert, A. 1976. The arguments for very large cities reconsidered. *Urban Studies* 13:27–34.

———. 1989. Moving the capital of Argentina: A further example of utopian planning? *Cities* 6 (3): 234–42.

Gore, C. 1984. *Regions in question: Space, development theory and regional policy*. London: Methuen.

Gwynne, R. N. 1985. *Industrialization and urbanization in Latin America*. London: Croom Helm.

Jeannetti Davila, E. 1986. Descentralización de los servicios de salud. In *Descentralización y democracia en México,* edited by B. Torres, 175–204. Mexico D.F.: El Colegio de Mexico.

Johnston, R. J. 1988. The state, the region and the division of labour. In *Production, work, territory,* edited by A. J. Scott and M. Storper. Boston: Unwin Hyman.

Morris, A. S. 1975. *Regional disparities and policy in modern Argentina.* Glasgow: Institute of Latin American Studies, Occasional Paper 16.

Oates, W. E. 1972. *The political economy of fiscal federalism.* New York: Harcourt Brace Jovanovich.

O'Connor, J. 1981. *The fiscal crisis of the state.* New York: St. Martin's Press.

Richardson, H. W. 1973. *The economics of urban size.* Farnborough, U.K.: Saxon House.

Rondinelli, D. A. 1985. *Applied methods of regional analysis: The spatial dimension of development policy.* Boulder, Colo.: Westview Press.

Rondinelli, D. A., and Ruddle, K. 1978. *Urbanization and rural development: A spatial policy for equitable growth.* New York: Praeger.

Rothenberg, I. F. 1980. Administrative decentralization and the implementation of housing policy in Colombia. In *Politics and policy in the Third World,* edited by M. S. Grindle, 145–69. Princeton, N.J.: Princeton University Press.

Scott, A. J. 1988. Flexible production systems and regional development: The rise of new industrial spaces in North America and Western Europe. *International Journal of Urban and Regional Research* 12:171–86.

Slater, D. 1989. *Territory and state power in Latin America: The Peruvian case.* London: Macmillan.

Smith, B. C. 1985. *Decentralization—The territorial dimension of the state.* Hemel Hempstead, U.K.: George Allen and Unwin.

Stöhr, W., and Tödtling, F. 1978. Spatial equity: Some antitheses to current regional development strategy. *Papers of the Regional Science Association* 38:33–54.

Torres, B., ed. 1986. *Descentralización y democracia en México.* Mexico: El Colegio de México.

Uribe-Echevarria, F. 1986. The decentralization debate in Colombia: Lessons from experience. *Planning and Administration* 6:10–21.

Urrutia, M. 1990. The state: Not small, not bigger, just better; The pivotal issue of government reform. *The IDB* (June): 4–5.

Zhukin, S. 1988. The postmodern debate over urban form. *Theory, Culture and Society* 5 (2): 431–46.

CHAPTER 2

Allen, E. 1990. Calha norte: Military development in Brazilian Amazonia. Glasgow: Institute of Latin American Studies, Occasional Paper 52.

ANMM. 1991. *Memoria 1990.* La Paz: Asociación Nacional de Mineros Medianos.

Baer, W. 1989. *The Brazilian economy: Growth and development.* 3d ed. New York: Praeger.

Boisier, S. 1987. Decentralization and regional development in Latin America. *CEPAL Review* 31:133–44.

Bunker, S. G. 1985. *Underdeveloping the Amazon: Extraction, unequal exchange and the failure of the modern state.* Urbana: University of Illinois Press.

Cleary, D. 1990. *Anatomy of the Amazon gold rush.* London: Macmillan.

Eastwood, D. A., and Pollard, H. J. 1986. Colonization and coca in the Chaparé, Bolivia. *Tijdschrift voor Economische en Sociale Geografie* 77 (4): 258–68.
Fox, D. J. 1979– . Bolivia. *Mining Annual Review*. London: Mining Journal.
——. 1985– . *Bolivia: Quarterly analysis of economic and political trends*. London: *The Economist* Intelligence Unit.
——. 1989. Mining in Latin America: Contemporary change in Andean Bolivia and Amazonian Brazil. *Euro-Latin American Papers* 1. Bradford University Research Unit on European-Latin American Relations.
——. 1990. *Bolivia: Country profile 1990–91*. London: *The Economist* Intelligence Unit.
——. 1991. Perestroika in the High Andes: Government policy and restructuring of the Bolivian mining industry since 1985. In *Towards a social history of mining*, edited by K. Tenfelde and H-J. Puhle. Munich: C. H. Beck.
Goodman, D., and Hall, A. L., eds. 1990. *The future of Amazonia*. London: Macmillan.
Hall, A. L. 1989. *Developing Amazonia: Deforestation and social conflict in Brazil's Carajas programme*. Manchester, U.K.: Manchester University Press.
Hemming, J., ed. 1985. *Change in the Amazon basin*. Vol. 2. Manchester, U.K.: Manchester University Press.
IDB. 1989a. *Economic and social progress in Latin America, 1988 report*. Washington, D.C.: Interamerican Development Bank.
——. 1989b. *Annual report 1988*. Washington, D.C.: Interamerican Development Bank.
Kleinpenning, J.M.G., and Volbeda, S. 1985. Recent changes in population size and distribution in the Amazon region of Brazil. In *Change in the Amazon basin*, edited by J. Hemming, vol. 2, 6–36. Manchester, U.K.: Manchester University Press.
Mahar, D. J. 1983. Development of the Brazilian Amazon: Prospects for the 1980s. In *The dilemma of Amazonian development*, edited by E. F. Moran, 319–24. Boulder, Colo.: Westview Press.
——. 1989. *Government policies and deforestation in Brazil's Amazon region*. Washington, D.C.: World Bank.
Moran, E. F., ed. 1983. *The dilemma of Amazonian development*. Boulder, Colo.: Westview Press.
Schmink, M. 1985. Social change in the garimpo. In *Change in the Amazon basin*, edited by J. Hemming, vol. 2, 185–99. Manchester, U.K.: Manchester University Press.
Selowsky, M. 1990. Stages in the recovery of Latin America's growth. *Finance and Development* 27:28–31.
South, R. E. 1977. Coca in Bolivia. *Geographical Review* 67:22–33.
Treece, D. 1987. *Bound in misery and iron*. London: Survival International.
UNITAS. 1987. *La crisis del sector minero y sus efectos socio-económicos*. Documento de Análisis 3. La Paz: UNITAS.

CHAPTER 3

Alarco, G., comp. 1985. *Desafíos para la economía Peruana, 1985–90*. Lima: Universidad del Pacífico.
Amat y León, C., and Monroy, C. 1988. *Los cambios en la economía de las familias de Lima 1972–1975*. Lima: Universidad del Pacífico.

Aramburu, C., et al. 1983. *Población y políticas de desarrollo en el Perú*. Lima: INANDEP.

Ballon, E., ed. 1986. *Movimientos sociales y democracia: La fundación de un nuevo orden*. Lima: DESCO.

Bourque, S., and Warren, K. 1989. Democracy without peace: The cultural politics of terror in Peru. *Latin American Research Review* 24 (1): 7–34.

Caballero, J-M., and Alvarez, E. 1980. *Aspectos cuantitativos de la reforma agraria 1969–79*. Lima: Instituto de Estudios Peruanos.

Cavassa, M., and Portugal, J. 1985. *La mujer en cifras*. Lima: CENDIPP.

Collins, J. 1988. *Unseasonal migrations: The effects of labor scarcity in Peru*. Princeton: Princeton University Press.

Deere, C., and León de Leal, M. 1982. *Women in Andean agriculture*. Geneva, Switzerland: ILO.

Escobar, M., and Beall, C. 1982. Contemporary patterns of migration in the central Andes. *Mountain Research and Development* 2 (1): 63–80.

Figueroa, A. 1985. Mercados de trabajo rural en el Perú. *HISLA* 5 (1): 3–29.

Fitzgerald, E. V. 1979. *The political economy of Peru, 1956–78: Economic development and the restructuring of capital*. Cambridge, U.K.: Cambridge University Press.

Gonzalez de Olarte, E. 1982. *Economías regionales del Perú*. Lima: Instituto de Estudios Peruanos.

Gonzalez Vigil, J. 1983. Evolución de la fuerza de trabajo, empleo y mercados de trabajo. In *Población y políticas de desarrollo en el Perú*, edited by C. Aramburu et al. Lima: INANDEP.

Gregory, D., and Urry, J., eds. 1985. *Social relations and spatial structures*. London: Macmillan.

Guillen, J. 1983. *Desarrollo regional y dinámica nacional: Cuzco 1950–82*. Cuzco: Bartolomé de las Casas.

Henríquez, J., et al. 1979. *Migraciones internas, estructura urbana y estructura productiva*. Lima: Universidad Católica, Departamento de Ciencias Sociales.

Instituto Nacional de la Estadística (INE). 1974. *Censos nacionales*. Lima: INE.

——. 1983. *Censos nacionales*. Lima: INE.

——. 1984. Perú: Participación de la mujer en la actividad económica. Análisis censal 1940–80. *Boletín de Análisis Demográfico* 27.

Jameson, K. 1979. Designed to fail: 25 years of industrial decentralization in Peru. *Journal of Developing Areas* 14 (1): 55–70.

Laite, J. 1985. Circulatory migration and social differentiation in the Andes. In *Labour circulation and the labour process*, edited by G. Standing. London: Croom Helm.

Lowenthal, A., ed. 1975. *The Peruvian experiment*. Princeton: Princeton University Press.

Maos, J. 1985. Water resource development and land settlement in southern Peru: The Majes Project. *GeoJournal* 11:111–19.

Martínez, H. 1983. Migraciones internas en la región sur. In *El sur Peruano: Realidad poblacional*, edited by J. Olarte et al. Lima: AMIDAP.

Massey, D. 1984. *Spatial divisions of labour: Social structures and the geography of production*. London: Macmillan.

Morales, E. 1986. Coca, the cocaine economy and social change in the Andes of Peru. *Economic Development and Cultural Change* 35 (1): 143–62.

Portocarrero, F. 1982. The Peruvian public investment programme 1968–78. *Journal of Latin American Studies* 14 (2): 433–54.

Quehacer. 1989. La República de Huallaga. *Quehacer* 59:54–61.

Radcliffe, S. 1986. Gender relations, peasant livelihood strategies and migration: A case study from Cuzco, Peru. *Bulletin of Latin American Research* 5 (2): 29–47.

———. 1990. Ethnicity, patriarchy and incorporation into the nation: Female migrants as domestic servants in southern Peru. *Society and Space* 8 (4): 379–93.

Scott, A. 1984. Desarrollo dependiente y la segregación occupacional por sexo. *Debates en Sociología* 10:5–60.

———. 1986. Industrialization, gender segregation and stratification theory. In *Gender and stratification*, edited by R. Crompton and M. Mann. Cambridge, U.K.: Polity Press.

———. 1988. *Peruvian employment statistics since 1940: An evaluation*. Liverpool: Institute of Latin American Studies, Working Paper 8.

Slater, D. 1985. The Peruvian state and regional crisis: The development of regional movements 1969–1980. In *New social movements and the state in Latin America*, edited by D. Slater. Dordrecht, The Netherlands: CEDLA/Foris, Latin American Studies 29.

———. 1989. *Territory and state power in Latin America: The Peruvian case*. London: Macmillan.

Stepan, A. 1978. *The state and society: Peru in contemporary perspective*. Princeton: Princeton University Press.

Sur. 1989a. La regionalización y la región Inka. *Sur* 120 (April): 2.

———. 1989b. Desaguadero: Contrabando y corrupción. *Sur* 126 (October): 4.

Tamayo, J. 1981. *Historia social del Cuzco republicano*. Lima: Universo.

Thorp, R., and Bertram, G. 1978. *Peru 1890–1977: Growth and policy in an open economy*. London: Macmillan.

Verdera, F. 1986. *La migración a Lima entre 1972 y 1981: Anotaciones desde una perspectiva económica*. Lima: Instituto de Estudios Peruanos, Documento de Trabajo 14.

Wilson, F. 1985. Women and agricultural change in Latin America: Some concepts guiding research. *World Development* 13 (9): 1017–35.

Wilson, P., and Wise, L. 1986. The regional implications of public investment in Peru, 1968–83. *Latin American Research Review* 21 (2): 93–116.

Yacher, L. 1987. Peru: The 1981 census. *Geography* 72 (1): 68–71.

Yáñez, A. M. 1985. El trabajo femenino como necesidad técnica del proceso productivo. In *Mujer, trabajo y empleo*, edited by M. Barrig. Lima: ADCL.

CHAPTER 4

Acosta, A. 1982. Rasgos dominantes del crecimiento Ecuatoriano en las últimas décadas. In *Ecuador: El mito del desarrollo*, A. Acosta et al. Quito: Editorial El Conejo.

Alarcon, A. 1985. Transition, growth and basic needs in Ecuador. ISS-PREALC Working Paper No. 31, The Hague.

Allou, S., et al. 1987. *El espacio urbano en el Ecuador*. Quito: Centro Ecuatoriano de Investigación Geográfia.

Barsky, O. 1984. *La reforma agraria Ecuatoriana*. Quito: Corporación Editora Nacional.

Barsky, O.; Diaz, E.; Furche, C.; and Mizrahi, R. 1982. *Politicas agrarias, colonización y desarrollo rural en Ecuador*. Quito: CEPLAES.

Berry, A. 1984. *Employment and the role of intermediate cities in Ecuador during the coming years*. Unpublished Manuscript.

Black, J. K. 1985. Ten paradoxes of rural development: An Ecuadorian case study. *Journal of Developing Areas* 19:527–56.

C + C Consulcentro. 1986. *Atlas de areas prioritarias*. Cuenca: C + C Consulcentro.

Carrion, F., ed. 1986. *El proceso de urbanización en el Ecuador—Antología*. Quito: Editorial El Conejo.

CEPAL. 1979. Ecuador: Desafíos y logros de la política económica en la fase de expansión petrolera. *CEPAL*. Cuaderno 25.

Commander, S., and Peek, P. 1986. Oil exports, agrarian change and the rural labour process: The Ecuadorian sierra in the 1970s. *World Development* 14:79–96.

CONADE. 1981. *Estadísticas financieras*. Quito.

Corkhill, D., and Cubitt, D. 1988. *Ecuador: Fragile democracy*. London: Latin American Bureau.

Cosse, G. 1984. *Estado y agro en el Ecuador 1960–1980*. Quito: Corporación Editora Nacional.

Delaunay, D. et al. 1985. *Poblaciones de las parroquias: Ecuador 1950–1982*. Quito: Centro Ecuatoriano de Investigaciones Geográficas.

Glasser, D. E. 1988. The growing housing crisis in Ecuador. In *Spontaneous shelter: International perspectives and prospects*, edited by C. V. Patton. Philadelphia: Temple University Press.

Hirschkind, L. 1980. On conforming in Cuenca. Ph.D. Thesis, University of Wisconsin, Madison.

Instituto Nacional de Estadística y Censos (INEC). (undated draft) *Encuesta de presupuestos familiares, area urbana, 1975/1976*. Quito: INEC.

JUNAPLA. 1977. *Potencia fiscal de los municipios del Ecuador*. Quito: JUNAPLA.

Kasza, G. J. 1981. Regional conflict in Ecuador: Quito and Guayaquil. *Inter-American Economic Affairs* 35 (2): 3–41.

Larrea, C. 1986. Crecimiento urbano y dinámica de las ciudades intermedias en el Ecuador 1950–1982. In *El proceso de la urbanización en el Ecuador del siglo XVIII al siglo XX*, edited by F. Carrion. Quito: Editorial El Conejo.

Lawson, V. A. 1984. Government policy biases and Ecuadorian agricultural change. *Annals of the Association of American Geographers* 78 (3): 433–52.

Lefeber, L., ed. 1985. *Economía política del Ecuador: Campo, region, nación*. Quito: Corporación Editora Nacional.

Lowder, S. 1989. The distributional consequences of nepotism and patron-clientalism: The case of Cuenca, Ecuador. In *Corruption, development and inequality: Soft touch or hard graft*, edited by P. M. Ward. London: Routledge.

———. 1990a. Development policy and its effect on regional inequality: The case of Ecuador. In *Regional development in the Third World*, edited by D. Simon. London: Paul Chapman.

——. 1990b. Cuenca, Ecuador: Planner's dream or speculator's delight? *Third World Planning Review* 12 (2): 109–30.

——. 1991. El papel de las ciudades intermedias en el desarrollo regional: Una comparación de cuatro ciudades en el Ecuador. *Revista Interamericana de Planificación* 24 (93): 45–60.

Middleton, A. 1981. Division and cohesion in the working class: Artisans and wage labourers. *Journal of Latin American Studies* 14:171–94.

Morris, A. S. 1981. Spatial and sectoral bias in regional development: Ecuador. *Tijdschrift voor Economische en Sociale Geografie* 72:279–87.

——. 1985. Forestry and land-use conflicts in Cuenca, Ecuador. *Mountain Research and Development* 15:183–96.

Peek, P. 1982. Agrarian change and labour migration in the sierra of Ecuador. In *State policies and migration*, edited by P. Peek and G. Standing. London: Croom Helm.

Pietry-Levy, A-L. 1986. *Loja, une province de l'équateur.* Paris: Centre Nacional de la Recherche Scientifique.

Portais, M. 1987. Flujes y areas de influencia urbana. In *El espacio urbano en el Ecuador*, S. Allou et al. Quito: Centro Ecuatoriano de Investigación Geográfia.

Portais, M., and Rodriguez, J. 1987. Jerarquía urbana y tipos de ciudades en el Ecuador. In *El espacio urbano en el Ecuador*, S. Allou et al. Quito: Centro Ecuatoriano de Investigación Geográfica.

PREALC. 1982. *Creación de empleo y efecto redistributario del gasto e inversión pública: Ecuador 1980–84.* Santiago de Chile: Oficina Internacional del Trabajo.

PREALC/ISS. 1976. *Situación y perspectivas del empleo en el Ecuador.* Santiago de Chile. PREALC.

Sepúlveda, C. 1983. *El proceso de la industrialización Ecuatoriano.* Quito: IEE-PUCE.

Tokman, V. E. 1975. Income distribution, technology and employment in developing countries: An application to Ecuador. *Journal of Development Economics* 2:49–80.

Villalobos, F. 1985. Ecuador: Industrialización, empleo y distribución del ingreso 1970–1978. In *Política económica en el Ecuador*, edited by L. Lefeber. Quito: Corporación Editora Nacional.

Vos, R. 1987. *Industrialización, empleo y necesidades básicas en el Ecuador.* Quito: Corporación Editora Nacional.

World Bank. 1979. *Ecuador: Development problems and prospects.* Washington, D.C.: World Bank.

——. 1984. *Ecuador: An agenda for recovery and sustained growth.* Washington, D.C.: World Bank.

CHAPTER 5

Collins, C. D. 1989. Rise and fall of the national "decentralized agencies" in Colombia. *Public Adminstration and Development* 9:129–46.

Ferrucci, R. 1986. *La promoción industrial en Argentina.* Buenos Aires: Editorial Universitaria de Buenos Aires.

Foxley, A. 1983. *Latin American experiments in neoconservative economics.* Berkeley: University of California.

Gwynne, R. N. 1986. *Industrialization and urbanization in Latin America*. Baltimore: Johns Hopkins University Press.

Instituto de Investigaciones Económicas (IIE). 1976. *Promoción industrial en la Argentina: Análisis y evaluación de sus resultados en el período 1958–75*. Buenos Aires: IIE, Secrataría de Planificación Republic Argentina.

Instituto Nacional de Estadística y Censos (INDEC). 1984. *Anuario estadístico 1981–82*. Buenos Aires: INDEC.

———. 1988. *Censo nacional económico, industria manufacturera: Resultados definitivos primer etapa*. Buenos Aires: INDEC.

Kurzinger, E.; Brommelmeier, M.; and Weihert, U. 1985. *Industrialización y desarrollo regional en Argentina: El caso de Tucumán*. Berlin: Instituto Aleman de Desarrollo. Mimeo.

Morris, A. S. 1972. The regional problem in Argentine economic development. *Geography* 57:289–306.

———. 1975. *Regional disparities and policy in modern Argentina*. Glasgow: Institute of Latin American Studies, Occasional Paper 16.

Romero, L. A. 1977. Los efectos de la promoción industrial en una region atrasada: Chaco y Formosa 1954–72. *Revista Interamericana de Planificación* 42:5–32.

Schvarzer, J. 1987a. *La política económica de Martinez de Hoz*. Buenos Aires: Hyspamerica.

———. 1987b. *Promoción industrial en Argentina: Características, evolución y resultados*. Buenos Aires: Documentos del CISEA 90.

Sourrouille, J. V.; Kosakoff, B. P.; and Lucangeli, J. 1985. *Transnacionalización y política económica en la Argentina*. Buenos Aires: CET, Centro Editor de America Latina.

Townroe, P. M. 1983. *Location factors in the decentralization of industry: A survey of metropolitan São Paulo, Brazil*. Washington, D.C.: World Bank Staff Working Paper 517.

Uribe-Echevarria, F. 1986. The decentralization debate in Colombia: Lessons from experience. *Planning and Administration* 6: 10–21.

World Bank. 1988. *Argentina: Social sectors in crisis*. Washington, D.C.: World Bank.

Yoguel, G.; Gatto, G.; and Gutman, G. 1987. *El impacto de la promoción industrial en la provincia de La Rioja*. Buenos Aires: Concejo Federal de Inversiones, CEPAL.

CHAPTER 6

Department of Trade and Industry. 1973. Inquiry into location attitudes and experience. Memorandum submitted to the Expenditure Committee (Trade and Industry Subcommittee) on Regional Development Incentives, HC85-1: 525–668. London: HMSO.

Greenhut, M. L. 1966. The decision process and entrepreneurial returns. *Manchester School of Economics and Social Studies* 34:247–67.

Hamer, A. M., and Dillinger, W. R. 1983. Labour market behaviour in São Paulo State. *Water supply and urban development*. Department Discussion Paper 27. Washington, D.C.: World Bank.

Hargreaves-Heap, S. 1990. *Rationality in economics*. Oxford: Basil Blackwell.

Lee, K. S. 1989. *The location of jobs in a development metropolis: Patterns of growth in Bogotá and Cali, Colombia*. Oxford: Oxford University Press for the World Bank.

Simon, H. A. 1957. *Models of man, social and rational*. New York: Wiley.

———. 1982. *Models of bounded rationality*. Cambridge, Mass.: MIT Press.

Sveikauskas, L.; Townroe, P. M.; and Hansen, E. 1985. Intra-regional productivity differences in São Paulo State manufacturing plants. *Weltwirtschaftliches Archiv* 121 (4): 722–40.

Townroe, P. M. 1971. *Industrial location decisions: A study in management behaviour*. University of Birmingham, U.K.: Centre for Urban and Regional Studies, Occasional Paper 15.

———. 1979a. Employment decentralization: Policy instruments for large cities in less developed countries. *Progress in Planning* 10 (2): 85–154.

———. 1979b. *Industrial movement: Experience in the U.S. and the U.K.* Aldershot, U.K.: Saxon House.

———. 1983. *Locational factors in the decentralization of industry: A survey of metropolitan São Paulo, Brazil*. Washington, D.C.: World Bank Staff Working Paper 517.

———. 1984. Spatial policy and metropolitan economic growth in São Paulo, Brazil. *Geoforum* 15 (2): 143–65.

———. 1991. Rationality in industrial location decisions. *Urban Studies* 28 (3): 383–92.

CHAPTER 7

Aguilar, A., and Carmona, F. 1965. *México Riqueza y agonía*. Mexico D.F.: Nuestro Tiempo.

Bailey, J. 1988. *Governing Mexico: The statecraft of crisis management*, 107–11. London: Macmillan.

Carr, B. 1971. *The peculiarities of the Mexican North: An essay in interpretation*. Glasgow: Institute of Latin American Studies, Occasional Paper 4.

Carrión, J., et al. 1970. *Tres culturas en agonía*. Mexico D.F.: Nuestro Tiempo.

Cockcroft, J. 1983. *Mexico: Class formation, capital accumulation and the state*. New York: Monthly Review Press.

Cordova, A. 1973. *La ideología de la revolución mexicana: La formación del nuevo régimen*. Mexico D.F.: ERA.

Cosio Villegas, D., ed. 1965. *El Porfiriato*. Mexico D.F.: Hermes.

Costeloe, M. P. 1975. *La primera república federal de México*. Mexico D.F.: Fondo de Cultura Económica.

Falcon, R. 1984. *Revolución y caciquismo. San Luís Potosí. 1910–38*. Mexico D.F.: El Colegio de México.

———. 1986. La revolución mexicana y la busqueda de la autonomía. In *Poder local, poder regional*, edited by J. Padua and A. Vanneph. Mexico D.F.: El Colegio de México.

Fitzgerald, E.V.K. 1978. The state and capital accumulation in Mexico. *Journal of Latin American Studies* 10:263–82.

Gonzalez, L. 1957. *La historia moderna de México. La república restaurada. La vida social*. Mexico D.F.: Hermes.

——. 1987. *La historia de la revolución mexicana, 1934–40. Los dias de Lazaro Cárdenas*. Mexico D.F.: El Colegio de México.

Gonzalez Casanova, P. 1965. *La democracia en México*. Mexico D.F.: ERA.

Grayson, G. 1980. *The politics of Mexican oil*. Pittsburgh: University of Pittsburgh Press.

Hamill, H. M. 1966. *The Hidalgo revolt*. Gainesville: University of Florida Press.

Hamilton, A., et al. 1937. *The Federalist*. New York: Random House.

Hamnett, B. 1986. *Roots of insurgency: Mexican regions 1750–1824*. Cambridge, U.K.: Cambridge University Press.

Hansen, R. 1971. *The politics of Mexican development*. Baltimore: Johns Hopkins University Press.

Knight, A. 1986. *The Mexican revolution*. 2 vols. Cambridge, U.K.: Cambridge University Press.

Mabry, D. 1973. *Mexico's acción nacional*, 99–112. Syracuse, N.Y.: Syracuse University Press.

Meyer, L. 1986. Una tema añejo siempre actual: El centro y las regiones en la historia mexicana. In *Descentralización y democracia en México*, edited by B. Torres. Mexico D.F.: El Colegio de México.

Morgan, J. 1981. The politics of higher education in Mexico. Ph.D. diss., University of Glasgow.

Pardo, M. 1984. La reforma administrativa para el desarrollo social en Mexico. *Foro Internacional* 25 (2): 107–29.

Poniatowska, E. 1971. *La noche de Tlatelolco*. Mexico D.F.: ERA.

Secretaría de Patrimonio Nacional. 1979. *El plan nacional del desarrollo industrial*. Mexico D.F.: SPP.

Secretaría de Programación y Presupuesto (SPP). 1985. *Programa de descentralización de la administración federal*. Mexico D.F.: SPP.

Tello, C., and Cordero, R. 1981. *México: La disputa por la nación*. Mexico D.F.: Siglo XXI.

Torres, B., ed. 1986. *Descentralización y democracia en México*. Mexico D.F.: El Colegio de México.

Tuohy, M. 1970. *Mexico: Centralism and political elite behaviour*. Austin: University of Texas, Papers of the Comparative Administration Group of the APSR.

Wheare, K. C. 1963. *Federal government*. London: Oxford University Press.

Womack, J. 1968. *Zapata and the Mexican revolution*. New York: Knopf.

CHAPTER 8

Acosta Romero, M. 1982. Mexican federalism: Conception and reality. *Public Administration Review* 42:399–404.

Armida Graham, P. 1983. Federalismo fiscal. El caso de México. Master's thesis, ITAM.

Beyer de Roalandini, C. E. 1985. La legislación hacendaria municipal y la coordinación fiscal. *Estudios Municipales* 1:23–36.

Cámara de Diputados del Congreso de la Unión, LII Legislatura. 1983. *Proceso legislativo de la iniciativa presidencial de reformas y adiciones al Artículo 115 de la constitución política de los estados unidos mexicanos*. Mexico: Colección Documentos.

Cantu Segovia, E., et al. 1982. The challenge of managing Mexico: The priorities of the 1982–1988 administration. *Public Administration Review* 42:405–9.

Carpizo, J. 1983. El sistema federal mexicano. *Gaceta de Administración Pública Estatal y Municipal* 3.

Centro Nacional de Estudios Municipales. 1985a. *El desafío municipal*. Mexico: Secretaría de Gobernación.

Chanes Nieto, J. 1985. La descentralización en la administración pública. *Praxis* 69.

Cohen, S., et al. 1981. *Decentralization: A framework for political analysis*. Berkeley: Project on Managing Decentralization, Institute of International Studies, University of California.

Cornelius, W. A., and Craig, A. L. 1984. *Politics in Mexico: An introduction and overview*. La Jolla, Calif.: Center for U.S.-Mexican Studies, University of California, San Diego. Report and Monographs in U.S.-Mexican Studies.

Dávila, E. J. 1986. Descentralización de los servicios de salud. In *Descentralización y democracia en México*, edited by B. Torres. Mexico: El Colegio de México.

Diario Oficial. Various years and issues.

Estudios Municipales. 1985. Cuadro comparativo del Artículo 115 constitucional. *Estudios Municipales* 5:137–48.

Foweraker, J. 1987. Transformism transformed: The nature of Mexico's political crisis. University of California, San Diego, Center for U.S.-Mexican Studies. Unpublished paper.

Hoyo D'Addona, R. 1985. La hacienda pública municipal. *Estudios Municipales* 1:13–21.

Instituto de Estudios Económicos, Políticos y Sociales del Partido Revolucionario Institucional. 1982. *Diagnóstico para el fortalecimiento municipal*. Mexico: PRI.

Lajous, A., et al. 1984–1985. *Las razones y las obras. Crónica del sexenio de Miguel de la Madrid*. 2 vols. Mexico: Fondo de la Cultura Económica.

Landau, M., and Eagle, E. 1981. *On the concept of decentralization*. Berkeley: Institute of International Studies, University of California. Project on Managing Decentralization.

Madrid, M. de la. 1982. *Manual síntesis de pensamiento político*. Mexico: Partido Revolucionario Institucional, Coordinación General de Documentación y Análisis.

———. 1984. Protesta de ley como presidente constitucional de los estados unidos mexicanos, 1ero. de Diciembre de 1982. In *Testimonio Político*. Mexico: Presidencia de la República, Dirección General de Comunicación Social.

Martínez Cabañas, G. 1985. *La administración estatal y municipal*. Mexico: INAP-CONACYT.

Middlebrook, K. 1981. Political change in Mexico. In *Mexico-United States Relations*, edited by S. K. Purcell. Philadelphia: Academy of Political Science.

———. 1985. *Political liberalization in an authoritarian regime*. Research Report Series, no. 41. La Jolla: Center for U.S.-Mexican Studies, University of California at San Diego.

Ochoa Campos, M. 1979. *La reforma municipal*. Mexico: Porrúa.

Olloqui, J. J. de. 1983. La descentralización del gobierno federal: Un punto de vista. *Trimestre Económico* 50:401–18.

Olmedo, R. 1984. *Iniciación a la economía de Mexico. Descentralización, principios teóricos y ejemplos históricos.* Mexico: Grijalbo.

Pérez García, A. 1985. El impuesto predial. *Estudios Municipales* 1:83–90.

Reyes, Y. de los. 1986. Descentralización de la Educación. In *Descentralización y democracia en México,* edited by B. Torres. Mexico: El Colegio de México.

Rodríguez, V. E. 1987. The politics of decentralization in Mexico: Divergent outcomes of policy implementation. Ph.D. diss., University of California, Berkeley.

———. Forthcoming. *Decentralization in Mexico: The facade of power.*

Romano Ibarra, J. 1975. El proceso de desconcentración de la hacienda pública. *Pensamiento Político* 20:187–94.

Rondinelli, D. A. 1978. National investment planning and equity policy in developing countries: The challenges of decentralized administration. *Policy Sciences* 10:45–74.

———. 1980. *Administrative decentralization and area development planning in East Africa: Implication for United States aid policy.* Madison: Regional Planning and Area Development Project, University of Wisconsin, Occasional Paper 1.

Salinas de Gortari, C. 1988a. *Perfiles del programa de gobierno 1988–1994.* Mexico: Instituto de Estudios Políticos, Económicos y Sociales.

———. 1988b. *Compromisos.* Mexico: Instituto de Estudios Políticos, Económicos y Sociales.

Secretaría de Gobernación. 1983. *Democratización integral. Consulta popular para la reforma municipal. Memorias.* 13 vols. Mexico: Secretaría de Gobernación.

Secretaría de Hacienda y Crédito Público. 1984. *Participaciones en ingresos estatales a los municipios.* Mexico: Departamento de Análisis y Evaluación de Sistemas Fiscales Estatales.

Secretaría de Programación y Presupuesto (SPP). 1983a. *Convenio único de desarrollo: Instrumento de desarrollo regional.* Mexico: SPP.

———. 1983b. *Plan nacional de desarrollo, 1983–1988.* Mexico: SPP.

———. 1984. *Plan nacional de desarrollo. Informe de ejecución, 1983.* Mexico: SPP.

———. 1985. *Programa de descentralización de la administración pública federal.* Mexico: SPP.

———. 1986a. *Comisión nacional de reconstrucción, comité de descentralización.* Mexico: SPP.

———. 1986b. *Presupuesto de egresos de la federación 1986.* Mexico: SPP.

———. 1988. *Mexico: Desarrollo regional y descentralización de la vida nacional. Experiencias de cambio estrutural 1983–88.* Mexico: SPP.

Secretaría de Salud. 1984a. *Cuadernos de descentralización.* 5 vols. Mexico: SS.

———. 1984b. *Programa nacional de Salud, 1984–1988.* Mexico: SS.

Sepulveda Amor, A. 1985. Reforma fiscal municipal. *Estudios Municipales* 1:57–65.

Street, S. 1984. Los distintos proyectos para la transformación del Aparato Burocrático de la SEP. *Perfiles Educativos* 7.

Tesorería Municipal del Ayuntamiento de Puebla. 1985. *Presupuesto de egresos.* Puebla: Departamento de Contabilidad.

Torres, B., ed. 1986. *Descentralización y democracia en México.* Mexico: El Colegio de México.

Velazquez Carranza, Y. 1985. La hacienda municipal. *Estudios Municipales* 1:67–82.
Ward, P. M. 1990. *Mexico City: The production and reproduction of an urban environment*. London: Belhaven Press.

CHAPTER 9

Aguilar-Barajas, I., and Spence, N. 1985. Industrial decentralization and regional policy, 1970–86: The conflicting policy response. In *The Mexican economy*, edited by G. Philip, 183–228. London: Routledge.
Asociacion Mexicana de la Industria Automotriz (AMIA). 1988. *La industria automotriz de México en cifras*. Mexico City: AMIA.
———. 1989. *La industria automotriz terminal en 1988*. Boletin 277. Mexico City: AMIA.
Fernandez, M. P. 1981. The US-Mexico border: Recent publications and the state of current research. *Latin American Research Review* 16:250–67.
Franko, L. G. 1976. *The European multinationals*. London: Harper & Row.
Fuentes-Aguilar, L., and Guerrero-Gonzalez, M. A. 1988. La concentración de la industria manufacturera en México y el GATT. *Boletin del Instituto de Geografía* 18:89–110.
Gardner, D. 1986. Mexico: Aiming for exports. *Financial Times Motor Industry Survey* 14 October: 8.
———. 1987. The rich pickings in America's backyard. *Financial Times* 31 July:14.
Gilbert, A. G. 1974. Industrial location theory: Its relevance to an industrializing nation. In *Spatial aspects of development*, edited by B. S. Hoyle. London: Wiley.
Gwynne, R. N. 1985. *Industrialization and urbanization in Latin America*. London: Croom Helm.
———. 1990. *New horizons? Third World industrialization in the international framework*. London: Longman.
Jenkins, R. O. 1987. *Transnational corporations and the Latin American automobile industry*. London: Macmillan.
Kuznets, S. 1930. *Secular movements in production and process*. Boston: Houghton Mifflin.
Leontief, W. 1956. Factor proportions and the structure of American trade: Further theoretical and empirical analysis. *Review of Economics and Statistics* 38:386–407.
Rapoport, C. 1987. Japanese industry. *Financial Times Survey*, 7 December.
Sklair, L. 1988. Mexico's "maquiladora" programme: A critical evaluation. In *The Mexican economy*, edited by G. Philip. London: Routledge.
———. 1989. *Assembling for development: The maquila industry in Mexico and the United States*. Boston: Unwin Hyman.
Storper, M., and Walker, R. 1989. *The capitalist imperative: Territory, technology and industrial growth*. London: Basil Blackwell.
Todaro, M. 1978. *Economic development in the Third World*. London: Longman.
Vernon, R. 1966. International investment and international trade in the product cycle. *Quarterly Journal of Economics* 80:190–207.
———. 1979. The product life cycle hypothesis in a new international environment. *Oxford Bulletin of Economics and Statistics* 41:255–67.

CHAPTER 10

Arteaga, A. 1988. Innovación tecnologica y clase obrera en la industria automotriz. In *Testimonios de la crisis 1. Reestructuración productiva y clase obrera*, coordinated by E. Gutierrez. Mexico: Siglo XXI.

Asociacion Mexicana de la Industria Automotriz (AMIA). Various issues, 1972–1988. *La industria automotriz de México en cifras*. Mexico City: AMIA

Banco Nacional de Comercio Exterior (Bancomext). Various issues, 1980–1989. *Comercio exterior*. Mexico: Bancomext.

Barajas-Escamilla, R. 1989. Complejos industriales en el sur de los Estados Unidos y su relación con la distribución espacial y el crecimiento de los centros maquiladores en el norte de México. In *Las maquiladoras. Ajuste estructural y desarrollo regional*, compiled by B. Gonzalez-Arechiga and R. Barajas-Escamilla. Mexico: El Colegio de la Frontera, Fundación Friedrich Ebert.

Bennett, D., and Sharpe, K. 1985. *Transnational corporations versus the state. The political economy of the Mexican auto industry*. Princeton: Princeton University Press.

Business Mexico. 1985. February issue.

Carrillo, Jorge. 1989. Calidad con consenso, ¿Asociación factible? *Frontera Norte* 1(2): 107–31.

Camarena, L. M. 1981. *La industria automotriz en México*. Mexico: Instituto de Investicaciones sociales, UNAM, Cuadernos de Investigación Social No. 6.

Dicken, P. 1986. *Global shift: Industrial change in a turbulent world*. London: Harper & Row.

Dombois, R. 1985. *La producción automotriz y el mercado de trabajo en un país en desarrollo. Un estudio sobre la industria automotriz mexicana*. Berlin: International Institute for Comparative Social Research.

Expansión. Various issues, 1987–1989. Mexico D.F.: Grupo Editorial Expansión.

Garza, G. 1985. *El proceso de industrialización en la ciudad de Mexico 1821–1970*. Mexico: El Colegio de México.

Gilbert, A. G., and Gugler, J. 1983. *Cities, poverty and development*. London: Oxford University Press.

Gonzalez-Arechiga, B., and Barajas-Escamilla, R., comps. 1989. *Las maquiladoras. Ajuste estructural y desarrollo regional*. Mexico: El Colegio de la Frontera, Fundación Friedrich Ebert.

Gwynne, R. N. 1985. *Industrialization and urbanization in Latin America*. London: Croom Helm.

Harris, N. 1983a. *Of bread and guns. The world economy in crisis*. London: Penguin.

———. 1983b. Spatial planning and economic development. *Habitat International* 7 (5/6): 67–77.

———. 1986. *The end of the Third World. The newly industrial countries and the decline of an ideology*. London: Penguin.

Instituto de Estadística, Geografía e Informática (INEGI). Various issues, 1980–1989. *Estadística de la industria maquiladora de exportación*. México: SPP.

Jenkins, R. H. 1976. The internationalization of capital in the motor industry. *Bulletin of the Conference of Socialist Economists* 2, no. 14 (October): 1–14.

———. 1987. *Transnational corporations and the Latin America automobile industry*. London: Macmillan.

Kirkpatrick, C. H., et al. 1984. *Industrial structure and policy in less developed countries*. London: George Allen and Unwin.
Lamartine, P. 1965. *El desarrollo regional en México*. Mexico: El Banco de México.
López-Malo, E. 1960. *Ensayo sobre la localización de la industria en México*. Mexico: UNAM.
Nacional Financiera, S. A. (NAFINSA). Various issues, 1980–1989. *La industria mexicana en cifras*. Mexico: NAFINSA.
Palloix, C. 1978. *La internacionalización del capital*. Madrid: H. Blume.
Palomares, L., and Mertens, L. 1987. Automatización programable y nuevos contenidos de trabajo (experiencias de la industria electrónica, metalmecánica y petroquímica secundaria en Mexico). *Análisis Económico* 6 (11): 61–78.
Poder Ejecutivo Federal. 1989. *Diario oficial de la federación*, 11 December (Mexico).
Secretaría de Comercio y Fomento Industrial (SECOFI). Various issues, 1987–1989. *Directorio de la industria maquiladora de exportación*. Mexico: SECOFI.
Unikel, L. 1978. *El desarrollo urbano en México. Diagnóstico e implicaciones futuras*. Mexico: El Colegio de México.

CHAPTER 11

Armstrong, W., and McGee, T. G. 1985. *Theatres of accumulation: Studies in Asian and Latin American urbanization*. London: Methuen.
Barat, J. 1982. The financing of urban development in Brazil: The case of São Paulo metropolitan area. *Third World Planning Review* 4:128–44.
Boisier, S. 1987. Decentralization and rural development in Latin America today. *Cepal Review* 31:133–44.
Bromley, R., ed. 1979. *The urban informal sector: Critical perspectives on employment and housing policies*. Oxford: Pergamon.
Bromley, R., and Birkbeck, C. 1988. Urban economy and employment. In *The geography of the Third World: Progress and prospect*, edited by M. Pacione. London: Routledge.
Bromley, R., and Gerry, C., eds. 1979. *Casual work and poverty in Third World cities*. Chichester, U.K.: Wiley.
Cheema, G. S., and Rondinelli, D. A. 1983. *Decentralization and development: Policy implementation in developing countries*. Beverly Hills, Calif.: Sage.
Collins, C. D. 1988. Local government and local protest in Colombia. *Public Administration and Development* 18:421–36.
Conyers, D. 1983. Decentralization—The latest fashion in development administration. *Public Administration and Development* 3:97–109.
———. 1986. Future directions in development studies: The case of decentralization. *World Development* 14:593–601.
Friedmann, J. 1972. A general theory of polarised development. In *Growth centres in regional economic development*, edited by N. M. Hansen. New York: Free Press.
———. 1986. The world city hypothesis. *Development and Change* 17 (1): 69–84.
Harris, R. L. 1983. Centralization and decentralization in Latin America. In *Decentralization and development*, edited by G. S. Cheema and D. A. Rondinelli. Beverly Hills, Calif.: Sage.

Hayter, T., and Wilson, C. 1985. *Aid: Rhetoric and reality.* London: Pluto.

Lipton, M. 1977. *Why poor people stay poor: Urban bias in world development.* Cambridge, Mass.: Harvard University Press.

Martz, J. D. 1988. *United States policy in Latin America. A quarter century of crisis and challenge, 1961–1986.* Lincoln, Nebr.: University of Nebraska Press.

Portes, A. 1985a. The informal sector and the world economy: Notes on the structure of subsidised labour. In *Urbanization in the world economy,* edited by M. Timberlake. New York: Academic Press.

——. 1985b. Latin American class structures: Their composition and change during the last decades. *Latin America Research Review* 20 (3): 7–39.

Roddick, J. 1988. *The dance of the millions: Latin America and the debt crisis.* London: Latin American Bureau.

Rondinelli, D. A.; McCullough, J. S.; and Johnson, R. W. 1989. Analysing decentralization policies in developing countries: A political-economy framework. *Development and Change* 20:57–87.

Rondinelli, D. A., and Nellis, J. R. 1986. Assessing decentralization policies in developing countries: A case for cautious optimism. *Development Policy Review* 4:3–23.

Safa, H. I. 1982. *Towards a political economy of urbanization in the Third World.* New Delhi: Oxford University Press.

——. 1987. Urbanization, the informal economy and state policy in Latin America. In *The capitalist city: Global restructuring and community politics,* edited by M. P. Smith and J. R. Feagin. Oxford: Basil Blackwell.

Samoff, J. 1990. Decentralization: The politics of interventionism. *Development and Change* 21:513–30.

Slater, D. 1989. Territorial power and the peripheral state: The issue of decentralization. *Development and Change* 20:501–31.

Smith, B. C. 1986. Spatial ambiguities: Decentralization within the state. *Public Administration and Development* 6:455–65.

Smith, C. A. 1985. Class relations and urbanization in Guatemala: Towards an alternative theory to urban primacy. In *Urbanization in the world economy,* edited by M. Timberlake, 121–67. New York: Academic Press.

Smith, N. 1984. *Uneven development: Nature, capital and the production of space.* Oxford: Blackwell.

——. 1986. On the necessity of uneven development. *International Journal of Urban and Regional Research* 10:87–104.

de Soto, H. 1989. *The other path. The invisible revolution of the Third World.* London: I. B. Tauris.

Timberlake, M. 1987. World-system theory and the study of comparative urbanization. In *The capitalist city: Global restructuring and community politics,* edited by M. P. Smith and J. R. Feagin. Oxford: Basil Blackwell.

Walton, J. 1985. *Capital and labour in the urbanized world.* London: Sage.

Weaver, F. S. 1987. *Class, state and industrial structure: The historical process of South American industrial growth.* Westport, Conn.: Greenwood.

Wilson, P. A. 1987. Lima and the new international division of labour. In *The capitalist city: Global restructuring and community politics,* edited by M. P. Smith and J. R. Feagin. Oxford: Basil Blackwell.

Index

About the Editors and Contributors

DAVID J. FOX is a Senior Lecturer in Geography at the University of Manchester. He has a long-term interest in the mining industry of Latin America and in Bolivia. He writes on a regular basis for the Economist Intelligence Unit, the Mining Annual Review, and other reference bodies and contributes to the academic literature. He is a past Chairman of the British Society for Latin American Studies, past Vice-Chairman of Oxfam's Latin America Committee, General Secretary of the International Congress of Americanists, and Honorary Consul for Chile in Manchester.

ROBERT N. GWYNNE is a lecturer in the School of Geography at the University of Birmingham, U.K. His research concentrates on Third World industrialization and regional economic development with particular reference to Latin America. His books include *Industrialization and Urbanization in Latin America* and *New Horizons? Third World Industrialization in an International Framework*. He has also published on industrialization and regional development in Chile, Chile's economic prospects under democracy in the 1990s, and Venezuela's recent attempts at economic restructuring. His present research is focused on the relationship between outward orientation and regional economic development, particularly in Chile and Mexico.

STELLA LOWDER is a Lecturer in the Department of Geography and Topographic Science at the University of Glasgow. She has lifelong interests in Latin America, where she grew up. She has done research in Peru, Ecuador, and Mexico in such diverse fields as migration, colonization of tropical forests, urban land development, and housing. Her interest in comparative urban forms and processes led to a book, *Inside Third World Cities*, and recent articles have appeared in *Third World Planning Review, Cities*, and the *Revista Interamericana de Planificación*. At present she is researching the structure of the Mexican shoe industry.

ARTHUR MORRIS is a Reader in Geography in the Department of Geography and Topographic Science at the University of Glasgow. His research interests include economic geography, regional planning, and regional development. His regional interests in Latin America have included both South America and Mexico, and he has conducted extended field studies in Argentina, Ecuador, Venezuela, and Mexico. In Ecuador, Venezuela, and Mexico, he has taught postgraduate courses to Latin American students. Outside Latin America, he has studied and published on local planning in Catalonia, Spain, and on quality of life in Britain. Recent publications on Latin America include *South America* and a chapter in David Preston's *Latin American Development*

SARAH A. RADCLIFFE is a Lecturer in Geography at Royal Holloway and Bedford New College, University of London. Her research interests include peasantries, gender and migration, and sociopolitical change, largely in the Andean countries. Her articles have appeared in journals such as *International Migration Review, Journal of Latin American Studies, Society and Space*, and the *Bulletin of Latin American Research*.

VICTORIA E. RODRÍGUEZ graduated with a Ph.D. in Political Science from the University of California, Berkeley, and at the LBJ School of Public Affairs of the University of Texas, Austin. She is currently co-director of a major research project funded by the U.S. National Science Foundation, which analyzes politics, power, and public administration among opposition governments in contemporary urban Mexico.

DAVID E. STANSFIELD is a Lecturer in Latin American Politics in the Institute of Latin American Studies at the University of Glasgow. He has edited a book, *Dependency and Latin America*, and has written articles on modern Mexican and Cuban politics. His current research interest is in the regional bases of opposition politics in Mexico.

PETER TOWNROE is a Professor and the Director of the School of Urban and Regional Studies at Sheffield City Polytechnic. Previously in the School of Economic and Social Studies at the University of East Anglia, he has written extensively in the areas of industrial location and regional economic development. He has worked in Pakistan, Brazil, Indonesia, and Swaziland and spent a year in Washington, D.C., with the World Bank in 1980–1981. He has also undertaken empirical work in the United Kingdom on industrial location decision making, on small firm support policies, and on urban labor markets.

He has an interest in technology transfer and is currently involved with a Europeanwide research network looking at the future of European cities.

PABLO WONG-GONZALEZ is the Director of the Development Section at the Center for Food and Development Research in Hermosillo, Mexico. He has a degree in Economics from the University of Sonora and a master's degree from the London School of Economics. He is a Ph.D. candidate at the Development Planning Unit at University College, London. He has contributed to several plans for the integrated rural development of Sonora, Mexico, and reports on the distribution of manufacturing industries in the Mexican border region. He has also written articles on nutrition in Mexico.